Edwards … One-Nil!

The Keith Edwards Story

Keith Edwards with Andy Pack

Vertical Editions
www.verticaleditions.com

First published in the United Kingdom in 2014 by Vertical Editions, Unit 4a, Snaygill Industrial Estate, Skipton, North Yorkshire BD23 2QR
www.verticaleditions.com

ISBN 978-1-904091-88-2

A CIP catalogue record for this book is available from the British Library

Cover design by HBA, York

Manufacturing managed by Jellyfish Solutions Ltd, Swanmore
Printed and bound by Gutenberg Press Ltd, Malta

To my father.
My life has been all about football and he was the beginning and the end for me

Contents

Acknowledgements

I would like to thank the following who, in their various ways, have contributed to the publication of this book: Andrew Kirkham and David Bond for supplying statistics and research checking, and to Martyn Harrison of Blades Photography, Sheffield Newspapers, Sheffield United FC, Hull City FC, Andrew Varley and Andy Pack for the majority of images which have been acknowledged by credit wherever possible or necessary, and to Bill Brearley. My appreciation extends to my brother, Steve, whose memory and memorabilia far exceeds my own and who was able to correct errors in my own recollections of my early years. If I have left anyone out please accept both my thanks and apologies.

I would also like to express my gratitude to Andy Pack who persuaded me to undertake this venture; it has been a refreshing, sobering but often amusing trawl through my memory bank over many hours on some long, dark nights. Thanks, mate, I'm really glad we've finally done it.

Keith Edwards

Prologue

Don't be misled by the phrase 'flawed genius'. We are all dogged by failings and shortcomings, whoever we are and whatever we do, so the problem is that few of us measure up to the genius bit. If you can't be one, there is nevertheless a great deal of pleasure in watching a genius at work, and I had plenty of that watching Keith Edwards right at the start at Sheffield United.

No-one would have known at that time how he would go on and put together such a goal-laden career, and become a huge fans' favourite at both clubs that he served twice. Goalscorers are lucky. They enjoy the thrill of putting the ball in the net and the most adulation. But at the end of the day they are human like the rest of us.

I have learnt a lot about that working with Keith on this book – he is indeed flawed. But he's loyal, honest, very funny and endearingly self-deprecating ... for a genius. There has been no Sheffield United footballer made me so confident that he would score when a chance came his way. When it did there was such anticipation and certainty about it that I was compelled to utter out loud a phrase that I had borrowed and amended from a famous piece of televised soccer commentary ...

Edwards ... One-Nil!

Andy Pack

1

Here Come the Boys

If only I had been a girl.

A few knucklehead centre backs would have been denied the opportunity of trying to kick me into orbit, but more importantly for Ruby, my Mam, her life would have been immeasurably different.

Her misfortune, if ever it could be considered that way, was to marry a man in Charles Edward Edwards who evidently was well endowed – at least with more than his fair share of the masculine gene. Large families were not uncommon in those post war days, particularly in industrial areas like Stockton in the north-east, but the arrival of Ted, then Len twelve months later and Steve four years after that must have made my impending birth a source of more intrigue than normal.

Whether my mother wanted a girl to break the male dominated household none of us ever knew, but when I appeared on 16 July 1957, four years after Steve, it was to be her last chance of any female bonding in the Edwards household. Since reaching adulthood and becoming a father I have always thought her life would have been more pleasant if I had indeed been Katy rather than Keith.

But as we grew, we lads were blissfully ignorant about anything like that for it never crossed our minds. There was no reason to because our upbringing was in every other way as happy and normal as the next working class kid. Even the fact that Mam and Dad split up in my early teens didn't seem to harm us because we had experienced love, care and attention whilst hardly noticing that our parents were not well matched. They just didn't seem to get on, didn't have much in common. Dad was from the East End of London and had the appropriate accent that was out of kilter up north. Standing at around five feet eleven inches tall and very trim, he never had a beer belly because he didn't drink until he was forty odd years old and he only smoked a pipe.

Ruby Wheatley was a classic Stockton lass from a large family which probably lost one or two of its members in the war. She smoked from about ten years of age but was slim with beautiful shoulder length hair which is how all women seemed to wear it then. Dad had come up to Knaresborough, aged sixteen, with his Mam because of the wartime evacuation programme and eventually settled in Stockton. I loved that he was a little unusual, coming from 'that London' and having a different accent to the rest of us.

My three brothers were all born in Stockton, County Durham, and although I first saw the light of day three miles away in Middlesbrough everything about me is Stockton bred. When I later played cricket at quite a high level as a youth Dad said, 'It's great that you were born in Middlesbrough because you will be classed as a Yorkshireman and be able to play for the county.' Even as a Londoner he evidently had respect for the traditions of the White Rose County, at least as far as cricket was concerned anyway.

We were all brought up at 106 Rosslare Road, a three bedroom new-build on one of those estates that was typical of the re-housing programme across the whole country. Owing to the spread in ages, sleeping arrangements altered as each brother left home. Steven and I initially shared although we both coveted the box room that we each eventually graduated to when somebody moved on, because then you had your own space.

Being energetic lads we were always scrapping, 'oggy

raiding' (scrumping apples) and going down the back of a nearby farm where there were swings across a beck. Today's health and safety brigade would have kittens at the prospect of what we did and how we never had a major accident beyond the odd broken limb is beyond me. I wasn't the bravest and stopped short of attempting anything too dangerous but there were also loads of playing fields close by that we used all the time until Dad shouted us back in.

Owning a car was still pretty rare but although we had one it didn't feel as if we were better than anyone else. We weren't well off and I just thought that Dad had done well to get one. He seemed to me very bright because he knew the answer to everything and helped me with stuff, just to make sure his lads didn't go without, and he was always in work as a cost clerk with ICI, the big chemical plant. Maybe him being relatively bright didn't quite sit right with Mam's more basic outlook and they might have been closer if he had been doing a tough man's job, taking dirty boots off after work in the northern way she was accustomed to.

Dad couldn't do DIY or decorate so Mam would have to do it herself or get someone in, but I remember him coming home once when the decorating had been done, I think by Mam's brother in law, and he was furious. Why, I could never fathom out. I know lots of lads who benefitted from their Dads being handy and passing those skills on but we had none of that. Mam basically did it all but anyway, I was out playing footy and didn't appreciate how things got done.

We kids never got involved with aunts and uncles and so on, not like they do in Sheffield where years later, my wife, Julie, had loads she was in touch with and some weren't even properly related! Up there we were totally different. I didn't want to go to Granny's for 'fadji' a sort of breadcake that was like concrete and she would always try and make me bring the coal in when I just didn't want to. Mam forced me even though I would say that I was okay and warm enough! My humour used to get me out of doing jobs like that because practical skills and chores just bored the pants off me.

Dad would potter about in the garden and we might help occasionally but even that would have been sport orientated in the end because we would dig a hole and he would go out and buy us a putter. Once again he would have gone back to what he was comfortable with, which was sport. It was never about Mam who was quite tough and couldn't show her feelings.

For example, I had weak gums which led to numerous dental problems and once Dad had to book a day off work to take me for treatment because Mam found that difficult to deal with. The gum had bled throughout the night and I must have spat out about half a bucket of blood so we got a taxi to the dentist rather than take the car. Just as we arrived back outside our house I threw up and it was Mam who had to clean the mess up. Later that day I tried to go to the upstairs toilet, fainted, and fell down the stairs from top to bottom. Being young, I just bounced and wasn't injured but I recall Dad saying that Mam couldn't cope with one of her children being ill so he had to. That resonates with me to this day because although I inherited many traits from my father, on this one I recognise my mother in me because on numerous occasions I have also struggled inside to cope with my own children's illnesses. It hurt too much to know that they were in pain and now I know where that came from.

When we gather as a family now and there are grandchildren all around, I always see danger before it happens. I am an absolute wreck all day and although invariably nothing happens, Julie will be sitting there saying, 'You still can't relax can you, Keith?' And I can't.

Our house wasn't large and with Mam's fags and Dad's pipe it must have been full of smoke. All my brothers eventually smoked but were not allowed to in the house so they had to keep it hidden. I once caught Steve smoking on the school fields and promptly grassed him up, just to get my own back for him having picked on me on far too many occasions! My parents never really swore but they were not churchgoers or music lovers and everyday entertainment was restricted just to the TV which then boasted only three channels. I absolutely loved being able to watch football on it and would never miss Match of the Day which was about all the football televised in those days. It is hard to imagine now the pride I felt in telling school friends that Dad was taking us to the pictures to see the World Cup, the first time I had ever seen colour screening of the game. To see the pitch, players and stadium in colour was just phenomenal to a young boy and the memory stayed with me. It was spectacular, a big influence and I just thought ... I really want that.

There was nothing like jigsaws in our house, it was sport all the time. On winter nights when it was too dark to play outside we would put stools at either end of the living room so we could dribble against each other, scoring a goal by hitting the stool with the ball. Or there was the miniature cricket bat which we used, playing the whole game on our knees. How we managed in such a crowded space I don't know but it still ended up with me in tears every single time. Either I'd get a leathering because they couldn't get me out and I was getting cocky, or they got me out and I said I wasn't.

Steve and I played a tremendous amount of games like that in the front room and I suppose we got shouted at for being too noisy or hitting the ball too hard. It brings it back to me now just how totally male dominated it must have been for my long suffering mother.

She worked as a school cook throughout my education at different schools and it seemed as if she followed me around so I could never get into too much trouble, although if I did she let me know about it. That job did result in a certain inevitability about our meals at home for if we had semolina at school at lunchtime I knew we would get it again for tea at night! Her work meant that she would be around when Steve and I were at home in the holidays and it must have been comforting for us to always have her around, and we probably took her for granted. All our clothes were beautifully clean and pressed, and my football kit was the same – and nobody had more kits than me.

I think Ted and Len, the eldest sons, got on really well

whereas Steve was four and six years younger than them. He was four years older than me and the instruction to him from Dad when he was going out to play a game of footy with his mates used to be, 'Take our Keith along with you and he can join in the football, he's more than capable of that.' But as soon as we got round the corner Steve would shove me to the ground, run off to his pals and never be seen again, so that was another occasion when I would go back home like a big cry baby! It was frustrating but character building and I didn't realise at the time that getting accustomed to it was to have a benefit when I became a professional footballer. My first game was against QPR, up against David Webb who was a tough so and so, and the first thing he did was boot me up in the air. I shrugged it off as if it was nothing, just part and parcel of football. To me it was just another game in that respect.

My father suffered from a weak stomach, a kind of dodgy nervousness inside, and I followed suit, but whereas Dad had it throughout his life I was more fortunate because I toughened up once I got into football and I don't have it now. I suppose my brothers behaved with me as all brothers do with their younger ones, and I don't remember them being too keen on the 'Look after little brother, Keith' idea. Can't blame them for that!

The two eldest were real grafters. Our Ted played football but didn't have the heart for it in a more serious sense. In fact he couldn't get to work quickly enough and was more interested in going out and earning. Len was the footballer who should have made it but didn't quite, going to Coventry City when Jimmy Hill was there before moving on to a few other clubs. He played reserve team football for the likes of Huddersfield and Bury, bordering on getting a contract but not doing until he was offered one at Darlington. Eventually he decided to pack it in because he was a welder and there was more money abroad doing that.

Back home though he was able to play semi-professionally as an inside forward with Billingham Synthonia and won everything with what is a famous club up there. It was the first ground that I went to that had a stand overlooking the pitch, which seemed fantastic. And as a ten year old ball boy at Ayresome Park when Billingham beat a team in some final or other, I recall trotting out with Len wearing a bright tangerine kit which was just the best ever at that time. These were perhaps the occasions of football in the raw, rather than watching games on television or in the flesh, that fired my imagination and set me on course to try and 'be a footballer', as vague as that ambition was for many youngsters.

2

Going for Goal

In many respects, I think Dad was naturally the most influential person in my life and I still think of him so much today. His team was Orient and although his relatives love London they are still fairly close to the family, coming up on occasions for christenings and weddings and so on.

As a youngster he grew up and was pals with Eddie Bailey who went on to play with Spurs and England. Dad insisted that he was a better player than Eddie – now you see where my arrogance originates from, but unfortunately he had flat feet which was serious enough to subsequently prevent him from going to war. He worked in a parachute factory and then became a telephone engineer and I am really pleased he had the foot problem because those workers were often first out towards the front line and not many survived. When we were older my brothers and I used to say things like, 'What did you do in the war then, were you just a cook, and didn't you kill any Germans?' which was humorous at first but I think Dad got a bit pissed off with it and made some story up that he had killed loads, but we still don't believe it.

In his playing days he was an inside forward and a very gifted sportsman which was apparent when we played different sports with him. We couldn't get the ball off him at football and he could get us out at cricket whenever he wanted, as well as being a beautiful thrower of the ball. Although he didn't play serious sport after becoming a young man he definitely had something and we boys, all gifted to some extent, were regularly flummoxed by his skills. That was Dad and he can't be given enough accolades for what he did for us in setting a sporting example.

I suppose most of us look back and remember our Dads being better than ourselves but I do think mine was a bit ahead of his time because he showed me skills such as spinning a cricket ball. Throwing, as I said, he was excellent at and he amazed us by also being able to throw a ball underarm so far and accurately that none of us could match it. He taught us on the school field that we were lucky to have very close to our home, and although he wouldn't join in if we were playing a game with our mates, in family situations he would play a bit of cricket and football.

To give you another instance of him doing what was basically coaching instead of just encouraging me, when I was about fifteen he introduced me to passing the football with the outside of the foot which nobody did in those days. Explaining that it was quicker and could be disguised so that it would be unexpected, he then got me to play shorter passes and learn how to curl the ball both ways. When I was still fairly new to the professional game with Sheffield United in about 1978, Danny Bergara, who was to be the best coach I ever had, started introducing that particular skill to the players. Unbelievably I had actually done that with Dad which is a great credit to him because I don't think too many other kids would have been privileged enough to learn that from their fathers.

Len had been a fabulous footballer at school and Dad put an awful lot of work into helping him. When I say work I mean such as taking him to Coventry which in the 1960s wouldn't have been as easy to do as it is now, especially as it was for a kind of extended trial which necessitated a number of visits. We were one of the first in our neighbourhood to have a car and to my recollection it was a blue Ford Popular. Although only on trial, Len was in the team photographs and I remember seeing them and thinking, 'God, our Len's made it' but he wasn't destined to progress to the first team.

As a father several times over myself I know where Dad was coming from in his efforts because Ted, who played football for a bit of fun, really wanted to become a diesel fitter and get there as quickly as he could. He still is a diesel fitter even now, and a great bloke, but that was him as far as playing was concerned. Then along comes Len who looked like he could make it and Dad thinks, this lad is going to be a professional footballer, so he put everything into him and rightly so because he could see the potential. It was common then for professional clubs to follow the progress of young potential players so you always knew the identity of scouts and when they were at the matches. Billingham Synthonia were so good, winning everything in the area, that there were always scouts there asking about Len so it must have been quite an exciting time for him and Dad.

But if Dad did have a favourite it was most likely to have been Steve. There were likenesses and in particular they were both bright, not a characteristic I particularly shared with them. Steve and Dad were more gentle, more thoughtful, and as they got older you could spot the similarities even more easily. Steve I think, was a better cricketer than a footballer although he did play football at school, and by the time I came along I think Dad was a bit fed up about having yet another protégé. He must have wondered what he was going to do with this, having already done everything with three others before me. After going from one football pitch to another for years he was going to be faced with yet another round.

His hobby was going to the greyhounds and his little habit was to go to what would then have been Cleveland Park, three miles away in Middlesbrough, often with Steve, on Saturday nights. When we got a bit older we had a bit of a betting thing going on, watching the ITV Seven at Rosslare Road, although I basically just wanted to play football and my dedication didn't allow me to become too distracted by anything else.

My father was very much a man driven by routine and self discipline. It would be the dogs on a Saturday night, and call in at the pub for a drink – but never more than two pints. He came home from work at the same time each day and always walked it. I don't know if it was to save cash because as far as I knew we were quite well off and if I ever needed football boots or kit, Dad would make sure I got them. The downside was that when he took me to the shop to buy the stuff he used to embarrass me by asking, 'Don't I get any bleedin' discount off that, then?'

His Cockney accent wasn't something I really noticed until we got older and when he was talking about his Leyton Orient days. We went to watch Middlesbrough once, when Spurs were there, because Dave Mackay was playing and the old Scottish warhorse was one of Dad's favourite players, but he didn't watch football as a fan because every Saturday he was running his sons about from one pitch to another. He didn't mention being in London much or talk about Orient, although we knew that the O's had been his team. Meanwhile, for no real reason other than we chose famous successful clubs to support, Steve took a liking to Spurs whilst I had a thing about Liverpool. I don't know why but I could still name you that team now: Lawrence, Milne, Lawler, St John, Hunt, Thompson ...

My father's weak stomach meant he couldn't deal with the nerves and pressure of big occasions very well, even when they didn't directly involve him. When Eusebio got a penalty for Portugal in the World Cup, Dad had to go and walk round the block, but I like to think that with his guidance I became stronger at dealing with big occasions and grew to love them. Why would you want to go and score at somewhere like Gigg Lane or Plainmoor? Big deal, nobody would know about it. So why would you when you could play and score at much bigger clubs and grounds? That was the way things began to pan out in my head as I moved up the ladder when nerves might have affected other players.

The three schools I attended, Roseworth Infants, Roseworth Junior and Roseworth Secondary Modern, were all close by and I hadn't been at the Juniors long before I realised that I wasn't the brightest academically. Fortunately though, we did play football there which was unusual because there weren't too many teams around. They might have been only friendly fixtures but it was nice to have proper games and a competitive edge which was important to me even at that age.

Our Junior team had a snazzy shirt featuring blue and yellow stripes with a great big badge and lapels, and they weighed a ton because they were massive on us. They had old fashioned tails at the back so when they were tucked into our shorts we looked like a team of Max Walls! Even then I played up front and had that thing about scoring goals that stayed with me, and as I had watched Steve play at the same school I had an advantage as everything in terms of kit and surroundings was familiar to me.

The succession line of the Edwards clan often meant that some teachers had taught more than one of us, especially Steve, and I was often reminded of it. My brothers' teams had done well, as did mine, so our family was well-known for sport in school circles and in that respect staff were probably glad to see us coming along. I got the feeling that it was important for the teachers to have their teams winning things because it obviously meant an awful lot to them. Ted, Len, Steve and me achieved some kind of fame through football results being read out in assembly, and I realised that in most schools the best footballers were quite a popular set of lads.

I lived for sport, not just football, and represented the school at basketball through Fred Ramshaw, a good coach who also put on table tennis sessions which I loved. Malcolm Danby taught me for football at Roseworth Juniors and it was he who invited me to play for the Intermediates, a big thing for a junior. I played quite well although that nervous stomach reared up again and there was another tears episode. Steve likes to remind me that I was also the first pupil from the juniors to be picked to play for the seniors, and Mr Danby had a big hand in that as he had a say about the first two years at the secondary level as well.

Although Mr Ken Tiffin was in overall charge of football it was Mr Danby's influence that was the key factor and I maintained contact with him for a long time after leaving. He went on to become an MBE for service to football in schools and for Middlesbrough which was a fabulous achievement and was announced in the local paper. Future England International Gary Pallister and me were also mentioned in that article as having benefitted from his work. Malcolm did a lot for us and not just football training, matches and trips, but also hostelling which was fantastic. I was away from home and it was an adventure even though I had to make my own bed which I had never had to do – 'Wheerz mi Mam?'!

But away from football I struggled to make much headway in general school work. I was a very late developer in spelling and reading although I wasn't too bad at maths. In fact, I came sixth in the class one year but unfortunately the girl who was sitting next to me coincidentally came sixth as well. Wonder how that happened ...! I got into trouble occasionally and was suspended once, not surprisingly for kicking a ball around. At playtime we weren't allowed to play on the nicer parts of the school pitch right in front of the car park but me and my pals did and were subsequently banned from the school team. Funnily enough, the ban only lasted from Monday to Friday because we played matches on Saturdays.

Steve and I had both picked up the nickname 'Eddie' and I breezed into Secondary School without the fear and trauma some kids have about the move because I had an older brother there to protect me – or so I thought. He would have been in the fourth year when I arrived but instead I got no support from him whatsoever, he just sort of kicked me to one side as if to say, 'On you go.' On the other hand, I think I was one of the lucky ones in that I didn't get my head shoved down the bog, probably because everybody liked Steve.

Whilst progressing through school and making a success of football I was probably regarded by some as big-headed, but I was rubbish academically so had to show off in some capacity. There is a trend these days to analyse behaviour and try and work out why someone is like they are, usually delving back to childhood and unearthing some incident or process that affected them in later life. Well, at the time, my own rationale was devastatingly simple. I am not the brightest but I am good at sport so I will brag about that so much that nothing else gets a look in.

But I wasn't over arrogant and it wasn't a problem, although sporting prowess would get you known at other schools. There was always the usual battle between my school and Hardwick, future Blades manager Ken Furphy's old school. Their lads regarded me as a big head and although I was better at football than Steve I wasn't as popular.

In the classroom most things seemed to be a bit of a struggle. Mr Moore, I think he taught Geography, could shout the school down and must have recognised I was a bit behind some others and put as much on my school report. My father's humour surfaced because he just put on the bottom of the report, 'Where there's muck, there's money.' That's all he put. And, as we all know, there is muck on a football field – not that I ever got any on me! He would have gone and spoken to these teachers and said, 'I am aware of this and his deficiencies, but he will be okay.' Once again he was right and I tell that story all the time to my children and grandchildren, just to encourage them.

My mates were generally all from the football team with Ernest Kilvington my best pal and we stayed in touch for years. He got a very worthwhile welding job and did well for himself, whilst Charles Pilgrim was also a lovely guy I remember having a laugh with. Our team was winning trophies, we stuck together for quite a while and by the time we reached the later school years we were popular with the girls as well because of our exploits. Then, as now probably, you scored the goals and got the girls. The best sporty one was Pat Porteous and I eventually went out with her although it didn't take long for her to dump me. I didn't know that others who would do the same would regularly emerge ...

Eventually people were talking about Jackie Stott, Anthony 'Tiger' Roberts and me going for trials at Middlesbrough in the holidays. We would go to the training ground at Hutton Park, quite a distance from Ayresome Park, and wonder where the hell we were. Jackie and 'Tiger' seemed to be really good players to me but neither made it and I suppose as a kid you don't really know what all the ingredients are to go all the way.

Our Len was always the smallest of us, a great little midfield player, but Dad spotted a couple of things in me when I must have been around ten years old. I started to run a lot faster than most and was always the quickest in the teams I played for. Secondly, he noticed that I had stronger legs than Len because I could kick the ball further than he could and I suppose Dad started to compare us. He had thought I would be a runner, an athlete, but then I showed I could strike a ball well and take corner-kicks which Len hadn't been able to at the same stage. Dad would have been quite thorough about things like that.

But as one of the smallest I would be bullied out of it when we played the tougher teams, and it is true that at the younger ages physical size differences can be massively advantageous. At fourteen, after trials at Stockton and Cleveland, I went to another at Leeds United with two other lads. One, called Thompson, was a centre-half, huge in comparison and with good strength and ability. Three of us, including him, were walking through a park in Leeds when we saw a gang of five or six youths running at us, intending to fill us in. The other lad with us saw discretion as the better part of valour and immediately said, 'We'd best run for it.' I didn't say anything but didn't run, and Thompson was so big and strong that he just drawled with complete confidence, 'Just let 'em come, I'll sort this lot out.' And, of course, he did. I soon learned that having a big mate alongside me might come in handy and in future years, big Billy Whitehurst occasionally filled that role on the field!

My stature must have bothered me in certain situations but Dad never failed to reassure me, saying, 'You haven't developed yet, son, don't worry. They will have a couple of years of standing still and you will catch them up,' and he was absolutely right. I believed everything he said, even though I was too young to realise that every kid at that stage has body issues, whether that be wearing specs, being too small or too ugly, or wanting to fit in. Mind you, being ugly was never going to be a problem! I didn't always get into my county team and sort of struggled when there was a bit of a lift in standard, owing largely to the physical levels, a bit of a confidence problem, and the stomach complaint.

But the Leeds trial ensured that I was going to have to start standing on my own two feet because it was something I did on my own. On this occasion Dad didn't come with me but put me on the train and just said, 'Go on son, do your best – I don't like goodbyes,' and just walked off. I wanted someone to wave at me as it pulled out, thinking, I hope this flippin' train is going in the right direction because I haven't got a Scooby Doo where I'm going. I just hoped it was going to Leeds but Dad always said. 'If you've got a tongue in your 'ed, son, you won't ever get bleedin' lost.'

My parents called it a day shortly after I reached my fifteenth birthday and had just started work, and presumably they had waited for that event before Dad went back to London. Although I dealt with it pretty well because we always knew they didn't get on, to see him walk to the bus and get on it was very sad. I distinctly recall one of his parting comments to me. He said 'I know you are working now but this is not what you are going to do. You have to pursue your football with the Youth Club because scouts will be watching.' Significantly, although he had moved away, he would still come up and deal with club scouts and trials. This influence from afar did help me focus on my football and I knew what he needed me to do – to keep playing to the best of my ability.

There was no way I was going to continue my education and the truth was that I couldn't wait to leave school and find a job. I went to the Careers Office and landed the chance of a position with a Timber Merchant. After the interview I was told that the other lad who had applied would probably get it because he had arrived an hour before me. I went back to the Careers Officer and told him, 'I don't mind a race and you can give him ten minutes start because I will still beat him, but don't give him an hour!' That was Dad's humour coming through again. But I did get a job more or less straightaway at Whitelocks Dairy Firm as a van lad. It paid me, I think, three quid a week – in a wage packet as well – and I handed it straight over to Mam who gave me some back for the pictures and going out with the lads.

Working on the vans at the cheese factory in Stockton centre may not have been the best job in the world but I can honestly say that I loved every minute of it. That was in no small part due to the relationship I developed with the guy who looked after me, David Johnstone, who was later best man at my wedding. I used to collect the orders, load them on the huge van which was probably a three and a half tonner, and got quite good at it even though I say it myself. That meant Dave could arrive a bit late and I would have everything done and packed before we went off to deliver to shops all over the north-east. We really got on.

He was a very tough character but lovely with me. He liked me, I liked him and I told him that when I made it in football I would buy him a car for all that he had done for me. It was a tongue-in-cheek comment and it never happened, but I appreciated him. We would nip to his house and get sandwiches from his wife Shirley, and I was very reliable although I tried once to wangle a day off. I was going to throw one in but he came round in the van, beeped loudly and I was so horrified with shame that I ran out as if I was coming anyway.

He was about twenty-seven so there was quite an age gap and he would tell me about his scrapes in life, scrapping and so on. David was a good drinker so I ended up going out with him and some of the older drivers and getting on with them. At only sixteen-years-old I was drinking but coping and dealing with these blokes who were up to around twice my age, and I was comfortable in their company.

Lads tended to start drinking at around fifteen but my father introduced me to it in a sensible way because he didn't want to keep drink away from me as something evil. In the pub he would say, 'Have a bottle of Jubilee, son,' and then eventually introduced me to Black 'n Tan which was a beer with a Mackeson. I stopped drinking it when I came to Sheffield because I got sick of explaining what one was. Nobody knew what I was on about so they used to put cider with beer which was a Snakebite. It sounds as if I should have been a publican but in all honesty I didn't know a lot about drinks. Naturally my brothers drank so I suppose I could have gone off the rails like a lot of lads do, but Dad kept insisting that, 'You are not going to be a lorry driver, son.' He was worried that I would go down the same route as his eldest, on the lorries, instead of persevering with my football. I was his last hope.

Ernie started buying nicer clothes to wear in pubs and look for girls but we must have looked well underage. Although times were more relaxed we were challenged occasionally by publicans and turned away, even though we would try and memorise fictional dates of birth which I invariably kept forgetting. One day we decided to go for a meal in a really nice pub – God knows why at that age – and we wore jean jackets with white T-shirts. The licensee was a bit abrupt, moaning that although we weren't quite smart enough he would let us stay. So, we decided that we were going to eat as much as we could and then do a runner. The restaurant section was on the far side of the pub and away from the door but we timed it perfectly to get away.

Further on we were walking down the road when Ernie looked over his shoulder and barked, 'They're 'ere.' Frightened as hell, I set off like a rocket but he was only joking. He really got me and I was gutted because I hadn't thought of it myself, but we never stopped laughing all night. We were good pals and if we went to his mother's she would set us off laughing again by putting on a popular record by an artist called Heinz, which was called 'Just like Eddie' – my nickname.

When Steve left home I was with Mam on my own because Dad had already gone by then. Although she had devoted herself to looking after five blokes and now there were just the two of us at home, I was now working and wanted to go out with my mates. Again she didn't get any attention whatsoever, no love, nothing. If ever I brought a girlfriend back home my mother would always have a warm bottle of Newcastle Brown in front of the fire – it had to be warm for her. She had work colleagues to share bingo and caravanning with later in her life but they were her only releases and it now seems totally unfair.

I was too busy finding my feet as a young man, battling with hormones and enjoying work and play in equal measure. My first kiss was in the Kiara Youth Club at about fifteen and at that age the kissing and groping moments really frightened me to death. One relationship got quite serious, then it split up and I was told on the grapevine that she was pregnant. My reaction was – and here's Dad's voice and humour again – 'Well, I've got a bleedin' trial at Sheffield United and I'm off.' She didn't really pursue me afterwards and I often wondered what became of it. It's fair to say that she sent somebody down to Sheffield to say that she had a child but I wasn't 100 per cent sure if it was mine or not, especially as she had wanted to end the relationship.

3

Size Can Be Everything

There is a world of difference between playing football with, and against, lads of your own age – being cock of the school – and entering the men's game for the first time. And the shocks are not just restricted to the field of play.

Although most of us grow up with the reassuring and everyday presence of a man at home, mixing with a whole group of men you don't know for the first time can be a disconcerting experience, especially in pubs and changing rooms. All that bravado and self confidence built up amongst peers and school friends soon counts for very little.

Whilst my mates and I turned out regularly for the Youth Club, I gained my first taste of the men's game on Sundays through my older brother, Ted. He played for the local transport team, as did the uncle of my pal Tiger, and we sometimes had a game with them. It was hilarious. As a kid the changing and showering was often avoided as much as possible but that wasn't the case here. I happened to be changing next to the centre-forward I was partnering and he had the longest, biggest penis I have ever seen in my life. I realised why they all called him 'Donkey' when – and this is true – he used to put his foot up on the bench next to me to tie his laces and this 'thing' was hanging down next to me. I thought, my God, mine must have fallen off the end of his.

Alan Winton was his name, and far from being a donkey on the pitch he was an absolutely fabulous footballer who then must have been in his forties. Although I was now working for a living and playing alongside him I was still a boy really, and I can picture myself amongst a group of men staring at this huge member between his legs also then thinking, Christ, is there something wrong with ME? It was the first time I had experienced taking my clothes off with other men but, ironically, the first thing a professional footballer does when he meets his new team-mates at training for the first time is undress. You automatically did that, sat down naked and then realised that invariably nobody had given you any new training kit. But you were allocated an apprentice and, standing there bollock-naked in front of twenty blokes you didn't know, you would say, 'Can you get me some kit, son,' as footballers never did anything for themselves.

Winton was an absolute gentleman who had played his entire career in the amateur leagues without ever being booked, sent-off or doing anything else wrong of any note. He really was a very good player and it seemed that everyone in the north-east knew him for what he was as a bloke and a footballer. But that unblemished record was to be ruined.

As a van lad I remembered seeing a couple of twins delivering coal by the sackful and there is no doubt that it was hard work. Lo and behold, a week later, they were playing for a team against us in the men's league. I was having a good day and knocked about five in, got a little bit cocky, and one of them literally jumped on me, pinned me down and both then started knocking seven bells out of me on the pitch. One of the twins suddenly stopped, got up and went straight to Winton and tried to explain. But he couldn't manage even one sentence before Alan, without saying anything, just planted a head butt on him – Boof! – he went out like a light.

Alan Winton, sent-off for the first and only time, having played with Keith Edwards. Word very quickly got round via the bush telegraph even then and I went home to be greeted by my brother who said, 'Alan Winton, perfect record in thirty years of football, and the first time he plays with you he's sent off so well done!'

Alan was so respected that the victim had tried to explain to him why they had done it, but Alan didn't give him a chance because he was there to protect me. We had only played a few games together by then and I don't think I played too many more after that.

We all used to meet at the Mile House, a very popular local pub which was home to about five local teams so there would have been about sixty or seventy players in there. When I go back now there might only be about half a dozen which does seem a bit strange and not a little sad because of my memories of the place in its heyday. Not many take into consideration the effect playing with older blokes had on shy young men and throughout my adulthood and professional playing career I swear to this day that I never saw anything bigger. Alan's manhood remains unmatched.

Of course, there is always banal and crude banter amongst blokes when they are in dressing-rooms and I recall Tony Kenworthy at Sheffield United after training, when he was sitting in the changing room, always fiddling with what nature gave him. When he took his shorts off his dick was like a mushroom but by the time he was ready to go in the shower it was hanging really well. That was solely because he had played with it as he didn't want to go in the shower looking as if he had a small one. When he had got it to just a nice size he would strut round the place as if it was normally like that, saying something stupid to get attention like, 'Everyone trained well?' But I usually cut him short with, 'Shurrup, tha's been playing with it for half an hour. Gerrin the frigging shower, it's not that size really.' Tony was great fun and always up for humour, as most players are, because that's all it was.

At this time with me working and Dad living in London I wondered if people had stopped watching me because scouts used to go to schools matches. Unbeknown to me they were, my name was still doing the rounds, and Wolves made an enquiry. I can't recall being approached in person but every now and then Dad would come back up and after games say something like, 'Wolves are here and talking about you.' In truth it didn't really matter to me who was watching me as long as someone was, and I did go for a trial there along with Ged Forrest who later joined Rotherham, then Southampton, and who was a very decent footballer. He lived just four doors away and although he didn't go to the same school he did represent Kiara.

We had a week, maybe two, down there, staying in a lovely house. Dad surprised me by popping up to see us and observed, 'You look just like two local lads walking about,' and it was nice to go through that situation along with somebody that I knew. Unfortunately, I was told after a few days that Wolves weren't going to take things further but Ged had done quite well. That was hard but I always remember Ged thanking me for staying with him to the end even when, in effect, I had been bombed. As far as I was concerned, I went there with him and I was going to come back with him, and at least I had seen at close hand professional players like flying winger, David Wagstaffe.

I never knew the reason I wasn't taken on and don't think I would have asked because I was shy, and didn't emerge as a character with self confidence until much later. The process of telling me wouldn't have been handled particularly sensitively either but that was the way it was then. Maybe today a youngster might be given the decision with a little more sugar-coating but I wasn't, and went back feeling a bit down and asking myself why I had been rejected.

I knew that I hadn't excelled or done myself justice and that my style of play might not have helped me stand out, although I wouldn't say that I was intimidated if things didn't quite go my way. It was difficult to get involved because I wasn't a big lad who, if things weren't happening, would say, 'Right, okay, I'll dig in or make myself heard.' Onlookers must have thought I was too timid and not forward enough to take things on. Although I became tougher because of how things had been with my brothers, maybe I wasn't mentally strong enough at sixteen to deal with the situation. Kids today are involved with clubs at a much earlier age, and for those who get a bit despondent at, say, thirtten or fouteen years old, please keep going because some lads mature later than others. I was definitely one of those.

During another trial, this time at Leeds, I again wasn't involved too much but then buried a half chance and thought that would be enough, but evidently it wasn't. Dad always recognised that at school and youth level I might score five or six times in a game but I was too shy to impose myself and take things up a notch.

Ironically, it was at Leeds when that lack of confidence thing happened again, but that was many years later after I left Sheffield United for Elland Road. I was there as a twenty-nine year-old with a touch of arrogance and a bit of swagger this time but doubts surfaced to niggle me again in training. I made a few mistakes, started to worry and it affected my game. Mind you, an error I made on my first day there didn't help because I got the wrong end of the stick and ended up being ridiculed.

They always held five-a-side games with players trying to avoid being presented with the yellow shirt for the worst trainer of the session, an idea which manager Billy Bremner copied from his great playing days there. I hadn't experienced the tradition before but told myself not to worry because there was no way I was going to be the recipient. The problem was that I didn't know how or when the 'award' was going to be made – and it was to cost me.

When the captain, Andy Ritchie, went round the group after the session, having a quick word with each of us, I wrongly assumed that I knew what was going on. He got to me and I muttered quietly, 'I'll have, err, poached eggs,' because I thought he was asking what we wanted for our pre-match meal. I had the piss ripped out of me like you have never known. Fortunately, Andy was a nice lad and told me that I should have been voting for the worst trainer, so I just picked on somebody for something totally inappropriate like having the worst hairstyle, saying, 'He was fuckin' shite, wasn't he.' I hope I also added, 'And by the way, can I still have those poached eggs?'

It was a funny incident in the end but the situation had affected me. I can go from that lack of confidence to taking the piss ruthlessly quite well to defend myself, and the memory of being a shy fifteen year-old came back to me that day as a senior Leeds player when I was intimidated again.

In the modern game most players who make it have been associated with clubs and been coached there since they were very young, say from six or seven years old. I probably went into football feeling that I had already had the best coaching in the world from my father. No-one else coached and I can't recall anyone else ever telling me that this is what you should or shouldn't do. Some just organised matches because it was their hobby, people like Freddie Branson who ran the Youth Club team and Malcolm Danby at school, but they just stood on the sidelines and there was no real coaching whatsoever. Don't get me wrong, I am extremely grateful that they showed interest and selflessly gave us opportunities, as thousands do across the country, but it might upset some people when I say that the biggest disappointment to me was the lack of coaching – until I came across Danny Bergara at Sheffield United.

I was still very raw when I went to United and you get only so far through natural ability. You learn what you can do and what you can't through the years but I suppose that, in the modern age, kids find out much earlier what they are capable of, and maybe coaches can assess them because of that. But I am still a big believer in the theory that it is too young to judge whether youngsters will make it at such a tender age because there can be a phenomenal difference in development in lads between the ages of fourteen and sixteen.

I saw so many apprentices come and go and witnessed the difference between an apprentice in his first year and then in his second. They can really grow up, physically and mentally, and develop the confidence that can carry them to one step away from the Reserves. Today, kids at the old apprentice ages might well have had ten years of pro coaching, and the ones who make it without that background are rare, with just the odd late developer.

My pathway was very different. No club affiliation and coaching, just straight from school to trials, being bombed by

Leeds and Wolves and advised to play up north by Orient. Middlesbrough dumped me because I wouldn't sign schoolboy forms at fourteen. My Dad said no because it would have tied me to one club and I wouldn't have been able to trial anywhere else which he believed would limit my options. I would never have disagreed with anything he said but at that age I probably had a chip on my shoulder because of what others would say. Jackie and Tiger have signed for the Boro but Keith hasn't.

Just being attached to a football club meant you were the bees knees because it sounded fantastic, but I didn't have that. You might ask why I went for a trial at all but it was to find out where I stood. Trials gave me good experience of playing against others from all over the area, including Hartlepool, Cleveland, Middlesbrough, just to see how I would do against them.

It amuses me to recall how different life was then, even relatively simple things such as not having a telephone handy all the time. On one occasion Dad needed to make a phone call to London about a trial so we walked to one of Steve's mates' house just to ring up – not many had phones and I couldn't even use one. When I did eventually pluck up courage to try at our Len's house he said, 'Go on then, use it.' I hesitated and eventually started messing with the dial before I had even picked it up. It sounds stupid and makes me look pathetic but I had never even seen one. I just looked at it and thought, what the hell's that?

A trial at Charlton Athletic provided another amusing anecdote. It was held on a decent pitch in a park and I looked across and saw Dad on the touchline along with his brother Reg, who was about twenty years younger than him. He was an absolutely lovely man, the spit of my Dad, and he had a Great Dane which seemed about eight feet tall. I remember the ball being kicked out of play and a little lad running off with it when this huge giant of a dog leapt out at him – the poor little mite almost shat himself and my first thought was, 'Bloody 'ell, I'm not going to make it because my uncle is going to get me bombed.' As it happened though, everything just clicked, we won 4-1, and I scored one and made three.

Here's another story about Reg but, as with all my stories about Dad and his London pals, the overall effect is funnier if you imagine the quotes delivered in a Cockney accent. I still tell them that way. Reg's dog's name was 'Kash' and whenever any callers came to collect money for rent or stuff like that, he would say to them, 'Do you want cash or cheque?' Naturally they were more than likely to reply that they would like cash, please. Reg would shout at the top of his voice, 'Kash' and this bleedin' massive Great Dane would come pounding at them. They soon changed their minds. 'Fuck that, mate, I'll have a cheque.'

I think my father must have written to Orient and asked them to consider looking at this lad who had turned Middlesbrough down because they eventually got in touch and I went down. The manager, George Petchey, was watching and he was impressed enough to say that he must get me in the Reserve side, but the game kept getting cancelled for one reason or another. I never did get the chance again because Orient were trying to win what would have been the Football Combination (Reserve League round the southern area). I was thinking, come on, get me in there, I will be on the main pitch, let me have a game, but they wouldn't leave anyone out in that situation in case it ruined their chance of the title.

By this time Sheffield United had shown interest in me and George, a very polite gentleman, advised me that he thought I would be better off up north. Dad and I accepted that as I had got a trial at United coming up and we were sort of juggling the two at one stage because I hadn't done too badly in my first Blades trial. The Orient thing just sort of fizzled out and I don't know why they said what they did because they were keen and seemed likely to take a bit of a chance on me.

I have often wondered how different things might have been if they had done because I went to United, scored goals and hit the ground running which was a huge confidence booster for me. If Orient had gambled on me and I had done the same there I would possibly have been picked up by the big London clubs because anyone showing promise at Orient invariably ended up at Spurs, Chelsea or Arsenal.

Despite the way things had gone at the clubs I trialled with, Dad and I didn't come away from Orient thinking that I had failed. The worst thing was when they would say they would keep an eye on me, but I wasn't physically big or strong enough. I had noticed at Leeds that other lads seemed about five inches taller but the Orient experience did give me confidence to keep going. I came back to the lads at the Youth Club to play again, determined to keep trying.

Len was with Billingham Synthonia and I had a game with their squad and almost ran riot over the opposition – men – but I didn't want to play for them, preferring to represent the YC. Dad was okay about it, he didn't think I would develop with Billingham and to me at that time football was also just fun with my mates.

Whilst playing trial games for United my progress was passed down the line of scouts. Ernest Cutherbertson would watch me, then it would be Fred White, then John Short and so on until the decision was made. But there would have been lots of others under the microscope and I was lucky enough to get a three month trial in the summer of 1975 when I was eighteen. I actually told my employers that I was packing in because of the trial but they were great with me and offered to keep my job on in case I came back.

It may have been a basic job but I had done it well for almost three years and earned some respect because I was one of only two lads chosen to take driving tests for the company. That meant, in effect, that the firm paid for us to have lessons with a view to us being able to drive for the firm at a later stage of our progression. Although that was a good thing my Dad became a bit worried as he didn't want my head filled with following a career path to the exclusion of football which had happened to Len. His feelings were, 'Now don't you start talking this lad into work when he still has a chance of being a footballer. If you want to put him through the test, great, but ...'

From my point of view I got on with these blokes really well and was now thinking that right, I've passed my test and although I don't have a car, I am driving a three ton lorry. Eventually I will become a salesman driver with an assistant of my own. Dave taught me his job as we went along so I was happy to carry on like that. Life had changed because my brothers had left home, I was working and there was just me and Mam together. It was nice in many ways, being with her and running errands which I was quite happy to do, especially as she had devoted herself to looking after five blokes for so long. Bringing girlfriends home was alright but once I brought an Australian girl home who I thought was absolutely fabulous but Mam wasn't too keen – I think it was the accent that put her off which was strange since she had married a Cockney.

When Dad and I came down to Sheffield for part of the trial he asked for directions from a local Sheffield bloke who naturally answered using the regional parlance. Sheffield had some tough working class fellers but for some reason they employed the word 'love' when speaking to each other. Dad got the wrong impression when he was twice called 'love' and sheepishly said to me later (Cockney accent, remember), 'I don't fink you should sign for these, son.' It must have been surreal, a lad from the north east with a Cockney father and locals asking 'Alreight, love?'

Being on trial was always a worry because of the uncertainty of the outcome, the absolute desperation to make a good impression and be asked to stay on. Everyone knew that the odds of success were very long and I saw others turned down, as I had been elsewhere. During one two-week period with United I stayed at the Falcon Hotel, Nether Edge, along with Tony Kenworthy, and remember another triallist with us saying, 'That's me down the pit.' He hadn't made it and knew what his fate was. Incidentally, when I went to that hotel I was told that I had to share a double bed with another lad who I obviously didn't know from Adam – you just can't imagine that happening today, can you? I was thinking selfishly, I hope he gets bombed as well. And he did.

On an earlier occasion I travelled to Sheffield by train where I was to be picked up by one of the coaches, David Turner. He met me at the station and said, 'It's a good job I've come to fetch you, isn't it?' I wouldn't have said anything but thought, well, what did you expect me to do, I haven't a clue who you are – you could be kidnapping me for all I know! I was a little lad lost, toddling down the steps at the station hoping that someone would pick me up, and it was Turner's job after all.

Part of the trial took in pre-season training which for some reason that season was held at the Dormer Sports Ground, just by the Jordanthorpe estate. I was a bag of nerves even though by that time I knew Kenworthy and Simon Stainrod. First up, naturally, was a fitness session and bear in mind that I had just been on and off a van for the last two and a half years. That meant I was fit up to a point but I had paid no attention to diet. I was ten stone wet through and definitely not ready for what was to come.

We ran round and round that training ground for ages. I can remember passing senior players Ted Hemsley and Len Badger, who were kicking a ball to each other in a big square, and I was getting weaker and weaker, thinking I'm going here, just before I fainted. Out like a light. I wouldn't have eaten properly and my Dad's advice would have been to get some grapefruit down first thing in the morning or something like that. Help was given, I was taken inside where Ted would have been sympathetic but Len would have just taken the piss out of me, and that was to go on for many a year. It was great with those two, I love them. They were established players in what was the top division and I was mixing in that sort of company.

In a relatively short time I recovered, got fitter, played and scored at the Ball Inn training ground for the Juniors in a 1-1 draw against Barnsley, then knocked all three in at their place in a return. They were the only Junior league games I ever played in my life.

To the Club's credit it made allowances for my circumstances by giving me those three months to see how I developed, and training every day brought improvement all round. I became fitter, stronger, gained more self belief and felt I could handle my lack of weight because I was so quick. It wasn't all fitness work, there was a bit more to it than that, and we practised crossing and shooting in drills, knocking the ball across and getting on the end of things, plus five-a-sides. I took to it very readily and when we had some kind of functional play – little sessions of decision making, knowing when and where to go on runs – it seemed so easy for me that I wondered why some others couldn't grasp it. They didn't go when they were supposed to, they would run in the wrong direction or bump into each other, but I was quite good at that sort of thing.

Off the field I was a young lad in a new environment but I wasn't short of company owing to there being others in the same boat. Crucially, although Ernie was my best pal back home, I also had older friends, usually from work, which held me in good stead because, as an example, I could walk into a pub confidently as I was used to it already. Kenworthy would go straight in and say, 'Orange and lemonade' but I would pipe up, 'Black 'n tan please, mate.' Tony's thinking was, 'I'm a footballer, I don't drink,' whereas I had worked for three years, knocking about with blokes who would drink eight or ten pints and take me to strip clubs. I felt more like a man.

I was a year and a bit older than them, feeling better about myself and there was such a difference between us in our mentality towards some things. Tony, Simon and John McGeady and the like, had come through the apprentice scheme with no experience of the real world of work and I felt I had an advantage over them. That showed in my football and although the trial was a test I thought, well, I have a job to go back to so I must have done well in that respect. I would be sitting in the stand cleaning Alan Woodward's boots, glad that at least I had something to do, pleased that it was what the apprentices did. But that soon wore off and I thought, 'Sod it, I'm cleaning my own, I don't want to clean anyone else's – and I don't care what your name is.'

Confidence was growing.

4

Off and Running

The coaches, probably conscious of my age, must have thought that they should chuck me into a few Reserve games, and the big one for me was at Coventry. I was quite nervous going there because my three months were nearly up and I hadn't yet scored at that level in quite a few games. But crucially, David Bradford played me through and I got the winner. It wasn't a great goal, I just turned and whacked the ball into the corner but I remember running back feeling relieved because I needed the goal to give myself a bit of a chance. After I had showered and changed and came out, who should be standing there but my Dad who thought I had made a decent impression.

My first memory of the Ball Inn training ground was of Ken Furphy, the manager, screaming and shouting at the top of his voice at the seniors whilst the rest of us, a mixture of senior reserves and the kids, were on the next pitch. But I will never forget him calling me over later that week. There was no fuss. He just told me he was going to offer me a one year contract on the princely sum of £35 per week. It was awesome and the best moment of my entire career, better than any goal because it meant so much. When I ran to rejoin the group the lads, who by now I had really got to know and felt at home with, asked me how I had got on and were genuinely pleased for me.

From that moment on, the north-east had gone for me. I was

on my way and couldn't wait for the session to end so that I could get back to the Lane to telephone the news. We used to sneak up to the press box to use a telephone for free but had to lie down while we did it to avoid being spotted. I nervously managed to get a connection to my Dad at work and blurted out, 'Dad, I've made it, I'm signing professional forms.' It was huge because I wasn't being just an apprentice, I was going to be paid as a pro footballer, and at the end of that trial if I hadn't been accepted I would have been back up north and returning to my old job.

In many ways it was all down to Alan Hodgkinson, a Blades goalkeeping legend who was now on the coaching staff. He had watched me train and play trial games, taken the Reserve team to Coventry when I scored, and recommended me. Alan must have been a good judge because I was playing okay but not fantastic so he must have seen something. My Dad would say about somebody that it was the way they ran, or that they had two good feet, or great balance that made the difference and whatever 'Hodgy' spotted, it was his recommendation that I will always be grateful for. I was very naïve, which was proved when I got into the first team and all I wanted to do was flick the ball on and run, and Terry Garbutt and others in midfield would go bloody mental at me.

I was aware that Alan had been a big influence on me being offered a contract. Not too long afterwards, just before he left the club, we played Forest Reserves and he said to me, 'You score tonight, son, and I have got something for you.' I didn't know what to say but thought I had better try and knock one in, which I managed to do. The Reserve team had a big picture taken in the dressing room for him and he was given the cut glassware gift the club and lads had clubbed together for. He pulled me after the game when I was with my girlfriend, Julie, and my future father-in-law who was also called Keith.

I was sorry to see Alan leave but didn't know what to say and when he presented me with a purple velvet tie I was just about in shock. I thanked him but just had to get out of the way because I don't do crying. But I went and sat in the back of Keith's Painter and Decorator van and cried with emotion all the way back to Norfolk Park. I couldn't recall anyone ever giving me anything so that tie meant so much that I was literally overcome. Ever since then I have always reminded Alan of the story which he thinks is really nice. He was a likeable coach who would come up with very snappy and inspiring words like 'panache' to get the lads in an upbeat frame of mind. For him, it was all about expressing yourself and I think he took to me.

Most of my training time was with Dave Turner who was also helpful while Alan drifted between the senior team and us, but always keeping an eye on me in the Reserves. It didn't bother me that Alan had been a goalkeeper and was now coaching outfield players as well because he was just a good coach, full stop. Everyone held him in high esteem as he had played so many games for United and was an England International, although as a young lad I didn't know too much about that. He was respected, tremendously well liked and stayed in the game coaching until well into his late seventies which was phenomenal. Alan worked with a lot of clubs and if my team played any of them I always wanted to make sure I saw him for a chat. He was the one responsible for me being given a chance and it was a great thrill to prove he had been right as Furphy himself hadn't really seen much of me.

The first time Furphy watched me was when I had just signed. We went to Preston with a very strong Reserve team that included experienced players such as Len Badger, Ted Hemsley and Colin Franks but we didn't start very well. At half-time Ken ripped into the team, bollocking the likes of Ted and Len. In those days Len would have a bit of a chirp back, Ted would mention something very complicated that nobody could understand, and I would think, 'Blimey, that's a bit tactical, what is he on about?' I had been rubbish although I had worked hard, but then Furphy pointed at me and bellowed, 'You fuckin' get your finger out or else you're on the next train back to Middlesbrough.' I was sitting there nearly filling up thinking, Christ, I didn't see that coming. Only a week earlier I had told Dad I was signing professional forms and a few days later the manager, who had never even spoken to me before, was threatening to finish my career. It was all a bit of a shock and I thought I had better score in the second-half but we were still crap and lost 0-1.

I suppose the regular first-teamers in the Reserves that night would have been bombed after the previous Saturday and, knowing what I do now, I realise that when that happens it rarely goes well. Once, at Manchester United around December 1976, Simon Stainrod and I were still kids and I was being marked by Scottish International Martin Buchan but we walloped them 4-1. It is often a case of first teamers making a point by saying, 'Fuckin' drop me from the first team and I don't give a toss.'

The relationship between senior and young players can be tricky and that is easy to understand when you recognise that both have different agendas and can be threatened by the progress of the other. That was probably truer a few years ago as players are treated more equally nowadays. At the Lane in the old John Street Stand the senior players were in the first team dressing room and the rest of us were in the shitty one. Nobody walked down the corridor there better than Keith Eddy who was a fantastic looking feller and looked just like a film star. Then Tony Currie would appear and I would think that I was absolutely miles away from them as a player. Ken Furphy would come in one day driving a massive white Rover, and the next in an equally big white Jaguar. He and the likes of Keith and TC were to me, right up there while I was at the bottom. The only way in which we were ever remotely close was in the fact that I was from Roseworth and the manager was from Hardwick. Oh, and his son was called Keith.

Senior players wouldn't all treat kids in the same way. Ted Hemsley would always comfort me, Colin Franks was nice as well, and Len Badger would be too busy having bullish thoughts such as, sod the manager. Ted was more thoughtful, would put an arm round my shoulder and reassure me that everything would be alright. He was great like that. In practice matches, if I was going down the middle, Eddie Colquhoun would kick shit out of me. If I ran down the left against Len and went past him, he would kick seven bells out of me and tell me to fuck off to the other side and play against that Ted Hemsley.

The full-backs were best mates and knew what they were doing with me. Len knew that I was far too quick for him then anyway because I was like lightning, but that was all I had. I didn't like the fact that Eddie would just boot me and mean it because at least Len would pick me up and say sorry. But Ted was the perfect gentleman so I used to think, right, if I'm going anywhere it will be down his flank because Ted helps me a little bit.

Looking back I realise that Len would be thinking he wasn't having this little twat whizzing past him on the left. I did favour that side so he made sure I didn't fancy playing out there. During those practice matches the bibs would be flying about as the coaches kept changing players from one side to the other and we would all be thinking, whoa, that's him in the first team on Saturday, and of course the opposite way round too, so we were all confused. It was a case of – get a bib on Friday, you're in the Stiffs, and if you don't get one, you're in.

It was sheer chaos. If I went past a couple and knocked one in I would think the two I had just pissed on are under right pressure now – you're gonna get a bib and I will be getting rid of this one because I will be picked for the first team. But it never seemed to happen. I used to wonder why I never got rid of the thing even if I had scored a couple of goals and it was very frustrating.

If the 1975-76 season was going to be a landmark for me in that it was my first as a professional it ended in disaster for the Club. A team that had finished sixth in the top flight – the highest position United had achieved in a ridiculously long time – faded so badly that it was relegated the next, its fate inevitable long before the season was over. With a fantastic new stand opened on the spot where the cricket ground had stood, thus ending the millstone of being a three-sided ground, expectations had been justifiably high that a place at the top table was going to be cemented.

In reality what followed was hugely harrowing for the club

and its supporters and, as with some of the women in my life, I was to experience disappointment.

The truth of the matter on the pitch was simple. A team that a few months earlier had been the best the Club had for years, contained too many players reaching their thirties at the same time and the decline proved dramatically fast. Planning and avoiding that scenario by constant reconstruction is these days a hallmark of the top sides. How many teams has Sir Alex Ferguson put together whilst remaining competitive?

Disappointing pre-season results pointed to what was to come and after an opening day home draw with Derby County, nine losses in ten games proved too much for the board and Furphy was sacked in early October. His acquisition of Chris Guthrie to add power and strength up front proved to be a limited success although to be fair to the striker he ended the season as top scorer with nine goals. However, a team total of thirty-three all season was grossly inadequate and eighty-two conceded at the other end showed that the team as a whole lacked what was required. Injuries, loss of form, advancing years and adjustment to Guthrie's style all played their part and Furphy was unable to spot the signs and act decisively or quickly enough.

From my point of view the struggle meant the possibility of earlier opportunities for the younger ones so Kenworthy, Stainrod, McGeady and I were looking at the players in front of us, wondering if we could take their places. For me that would have meant displacing someone like Billy Dearden who was a huge favourite, but I was now mixing in the same dressing room and some guys like Cliff Calvert and Colin Franks who I knew from the Reserves, were getting their chance.

It was a source of annoyance to me that although we four youngsters virtually all came through together, they all got their chances a bit earlier than I did. They were awarded longer first contracts, and received a fiver a week more in their pay packets than I did. It made me think that life was against me, still do in fact because there was to be a catalogue of instances when I thought I was treated unfairly or, at best, misunderstood. Despite the fact that they had developed as apprentices and were good players, I always felt I had more hurdles to overcome but Dad urged me to be patient and that my time would come. When it did I felt that I overtook them and made bigger strides than they did, and I was to really hit the headlines.

John McGeady, a Scottish right winger, was the first to get a bit of a run whilst Simon and TK got the odd outing later even though I was scoring regularly in the Reserves. Maybe I wasn't seen as the complete player but, as I said earlier, Dad's coaching was better than the Club's and I soon learned that it wasn't about coaching techniques, or where to run to find space, it was all really played pretty much off the cuff. That was a slight disappointment to me and I had conversations about it with both my Dad and in digs with TK. We had thought we would do more 'learning', that it would be taxing in terms of practising this and that but it just wasn't. And that is not to knock Sheffield United because I think that is how it was in the English game and you just developed naturally when you got the opportunity.

As a young footballer if your team is struggling you think, I could get a chance here, especially as a striker, so you got your head down and kept going. You didn't want the team to lose but at the same time a hint of selfishness would bubble up because you wanted that chance. A little bit of conflict would creep in from the younger ones towards the seniors who would themselves have gone through exactly the same when they were starting out. I don't think they liked it because deep down they knew they were being pushed and it was getting too close for comfort for some of them.

Don't get me wrong, not all the pros would be prickly about that and some like Billy Dearden would deal with it very well while Ted Hemsley was a help to everyone, as was Keith Eddy. One or two, like Eddie Colquhoun, didn't and I can't really blame them for that. After all, Furphy had gone, a new man was in and all of a sudden that great team had lost a lot of games and tumbled down to the bottom three. Some like Terry Garbutt and Tony Field who had been signed by Furphy would probably be worrying if the new manger was thinking of making changes.

After going through the same scenario later in my career I could understand how the senior players might have felt because we were putting pressure on them. It's a natural circle.

The Reserve league when I started with United was great to play in and we could regularly have over 1,000 people at the games. It was exciting to play at places like the old Baseball Ground and I just wanted to score because that was the thrill of it – I wanted to be able to say that I had scored at Derby County's ground. Who knows, it might have been my only chance to do so, and playing at the bigger grounds was an even bigger help because even though they were largely empty there could have been 2-3,000 there. Reserves or not, I was playing at Preston, Leicester or Stoke and things were starting to become familiar with regard to surroundings and professional ways of doing things. I wasn't really aware that I was settling into a professional way that would benefit me when I went back one day as a first-teamer.

There was no problem with the physical side of the game when I was up against seasoned pros in the Reserves because they were opponents and I had learned to take all that from my brothers as a kid. I was now a footballer and had to deal with that. It was now time to look at the positives of how I had grown up and I had something to thank my brothers for.

Easing in like that was a lovely, natural process and it was fabulous to play with people like Hemsley and Badger who encouraged me, but I will always remember how an opponent showed me a generosity of spirit as well – mind you, he was an ex Blade. It was a Reserve game at Hillsborough and I am proud to say I have scored on every occasion I have played there. I keep a check on these things because I always knew how important it was to United and the fans. Their left-back was Bernard Shaw and he actually advised me on what to do on one or two tactical matters during the game. Like Ted and Len, he was a senior professional so I just did it and probably just muttered my thanks, but what a lovely thing to do in a derby. Having met Bernard since I know he is a really nice person and I think he was very genuine in trying to help me. Brian Joicey, normally a senior centre-forward for the Owls, was playing centre-half so to score against him was a real thrill and part of the learning process.

Gnarled Scotsman Jimmy Sirrel replaced Furphy and I can't tell you strongly enough just how much I hated training under him. It basically consisted entirely of full-blooded practice matches in which nothing was supposed to be held back. In some ways it got me to know Hemsley and Badger but also to almost dislike Eddie Colquhoun because he played as hard in training as he did in a game against somebody like Mick Channon. Eddie was playing to ensure his position every week – and that was what Sirrel was looking for.

It was horrible, so competitive that players were literally battling for first-team places and there were fights as a result. On one occasion Cliff Calvert kicked Franks in the bollocks, Franks punched him in the head and the next thing Cliff remembered was waking up in the bath. Steve Faulkner was another youngster who got a chance so he started kicking shit out of his opponent. That's how it was and to me that wasn't training. Even John McGeady and I had a scrap which is hard to believe considering how slight we both were. I'd just like to say that he didn't get up, but there probably wasn't a single punch thrown. I think I just sat on him and told him not to do that again.

Meanwhile Sirrel, who to his credit was very fit, would be just in shorts and t-shirt, whatever the weather, running laps of the training ground. Nobody really liked those matches all the time and a lot of players moved on pretty sharply afterwards. Presumably, Jimmy saw them as crucial in a successful method because he had experienced a lot of success with Notts County, who included the Scottish International Don Masson in midfield, but we would literally have four practice matches per week.

By the time I started getting the odd chance in the team I was disenchanted with the aggressive and monotonous training because I really wanted to be educated and coached. When I was a bit surer of myself and the full-back got the ball in one session, Sirrel shouted, 'Close him down.' I thought no, and didn't, so he had a pop at me and sent me off. I walked from Ball Inn all the way down the big hill back to Bramall Lane in my studs, not rubbers, thinking I was going to go a right cropper in them. To me that wasn't coaching and the only way I was improving was by getting stronger and quicker. I thought I was virtually teaching myself. It was too intense, me versus him (a training opponent), in and out the team, blood and thunder and I didn't want that with people who were supposed to be my team-mates.

As much as Jimmy supported me in a difficult spell when I didn't score many goals, I disliked his methods intensely. It didn't sit well with me and seldom gave me the chance to excel. To me, crash, bang, wallop was for match day, not training, and I still think I was right and he was wrong. When the team went out on match day we were naturally together anyway and I loved it, but I hated the way we were encouraged to hammer our pals in the week.

It was the same after I left the Lane and was at Hull City when we played against United. I would sit in the dressing room knowing my mate, Tony Kenworthy, would be marking me and again, I didn't like it which made me a bit nervous. Tony would leather me and as we laughed and ran alongside each other I would respond by telling him that I would get him for that, but it didn't seem right. That feeling never altered throughout my career and it worked the other way after I had rejoined United and played against Hull. I dropped back into midfield and tackled Garreth Roberts but although I picked him up and we were pals it was awkward.

Although I acknowledge Sirrel's success at Notts County I think you have to respect your fellow players. It's like making a race horse run ten furlong gallops every single day to win. You don't, you save a bit. I never wanted to score three goals in a practice match because to me that would have been three goals wasted. You obviously had to go by people in practice and tackles needed to be made, but this was overdone. Ask any footballer from the 80s and it was always practice matches, get all the bibs out, first team against the reserves, and we would do that every time.

I used to walk off and wonder what had the manager got out of that. It was too repetitive. As a football man with an eye for a player and talent you should be able to assess someone and recognise when he has developed and is ready for that position at a higher level, or to spot that a senior player is not having a good time and needs a rest. That should be done by eye and knowledge, not through just a physical contest, and as a consequence the lads were falling out in the week. It wasn't nice. The committed, wound up stuff was fine by me, but on a Saturday afternoon when it mattered.

Jimmy would occasionally stop the practice and say the odd thing or do set-pieces but the total package didn't suit me even though I coped, largely because of the leatherings from my childhood. But there is nasty and there is cheeky. Len Badger was cheeky whereas Eddie was, without being over critical, nasty. It was all about wanting to play on Saturday and Eddie would have seen me as being in his way which I understood, but it didn't do much for the team.

If Sirrel had achieved his success with those methods he must have had a squad of eighteen tough characters, but count me out and I don't believe anyone enjoyed it. He was a dour man, a typical Scot I suppose and definitely old school. It was tackle hard, swap bibs, get stuck in, and when the game had finished in the pissing rain and cold, Jimmy would be out on his own in his shorts doing laps while I would be thinking, what are you doing, are all your thoughts channelled into just being as strong as this?

It didn't push my buttons because I wanted to work, be taught to improve and in a better atmosphere. For example, much later, after I had matured and developed more of a personality I became a bit of a comic. I was a pro footballer in the 1970s and 80s, getting paid for it so I was all for having a laugh as well as doing the serious stuff. When Ian Porterfield was managing United and running a session on crossing and shooting for forty-five minutes I succeeded in keeping my hands permanently in my pockets, never shifting them, even running in to shoot like that as well while Ian and his coaches were discussing something. I had a bet with Kevin Arnott for a fiver or something that I would get through the session like that. It was about doing it properly but with a smile on your face.

5

Firsts

When my contract was sorted I had moved permanently to Sheffield and was put into digs at 34 Donnington Road in Norfolk Park, along with Tony Kenworthy. Joan Clarke, the landlady, was great with us but she had a lot to put up with, not least from my Dad who would occasionally stay with us and got to know her. He always used to ask in his Cockney rhyming slang, 'How's Joan of Arc then?' and, embarrassed, I would think, bloody 'ell, Dad, why do you have to do it to me all the time! He hadn't got off to the best of starts on his very first visit when Joan, who had a cat she really loved, kindly offered to cook us Sunday dinner. She prepared it, we all went for a drink and when we came back she found that the cat had jumped up on the side and made a meal of the prepared chicken. Dad said in jest, 'Well, why don't we eat the cat?' The poor woman was in tears!

Although I felt more worldly wise than Tony in some way because I had worked, he was ahead of me in other respects, with shopping and dressing in a trendy fashion being good examples. When he asked if we could go around town just to look around the shops to buy some clobber I told him I had some clobber, but he said we could scour around and go to different boutiques.

I was genuinely mystified, it had never occurred to me back

home to wander around shops looking to buy clothes. What the hell do I want to go round town looking at clobber for? I agreed we would walk down Granville Road to town but I was thinking, Christ, I'll be glad when this little so and so goes back to Leeds for the weekend. I was a council lad, I didn't go shopping to buy a pair of shoes but I ended up copying him, even to the extent of once getting a pair of clogs which nearly crippled me trying to keep them on.

By now I had met Julie Reaney, a local girl who was soon to become my wife. She lived on City Road, round the corner from my digs. As Tony used to go home to Leeds on some weekends I was on my own so it wasn't uncommon for me to have a drink. On one such occasion I asked our landlady if she fancied a bevy in her local, The Captive Queen. Off we went and in there was a lass with long blonde hair and her dark haired mate. I fancied the blonde one, got my landlady to ask her out for me and on TK's return we went out together as a four – it still amuses me that the ex-boyfriend of the dark one wanted to kill Kenworthy!

Julie told her parents that she was going out with a Sheffield United footballer called Keith and that he was only on trial so he couldn't be any good. Her Dad was in for confusion and disappointment in equal measure because he (wrongly) put two and two together and thought I must be the manager's son whom he considered wouldn't be half bad – but then in walked a scruffy lad from Stockton on Tees.

By now in training I was showing more confidence in the practice matches and a touch of arrogance was starting to show through as that belief, allied to improving fitness levels, helped me settle down. There wasn't any way of changing it and it seemed that the manager was not entirely comfortable with what I did to try and catch his eye. On one occasion during training I took the ball down the left, went to cross it, but pulled inside a defender and did him that way about three times in quick succession. Sirrel, singularly unimpressed, just said, 'The boy can do him any time he wants, but why doesn't he push himself a little further? Aye, the boy's got talent, but he could do better.'

It was how I played and I would tell Dad that I seem to do so well and score all these goals, yet although I am a year older than the other young lads they all get a chance a bit before me. It didn't seem to add up but this was the way Sirrel was with me. I didn't fit in with his philosophy of dour, hard working, get stuck in type players and later in my career, on occasions, it was to be the same for me under Ian Porterfield. How many managers are like that? So many have pre-conceived ideas that if a player doesn't conform by running all the time he must be lacking something essential. For example, Tony Currie is lazy, while Chris Waddle walks back in a sloppy fashion. Why do they pick the negatives all the time and pigeon hole certain players? It took me quite a time to get my head round that because in my mind I always seemed to be fighting my corner about it.

Although I played up the middle I always tended to drift out wide because I wasn't keen on being squashed into the central areas. I liked space and room to manoeuvre because once I got an opponent out wide with grass between me and him, and a bit more behind him, I always felt that I had the pace to beat him. In training I now looked at that magnificent United back four and thought, I will destroy you now because I have moved a bit closer to you, close enough to know that I can do you any time I want. That might have been a bit of good to come out of the constant practice matches but I would have developed that anyway.

Eventually I had scored enough goals in training to prompt Sirrel into giving me my chance at Leicester in January for the FA Cup third round tie at Leicester. We weren't expected to win because of the poor league form so maybe Jimmy thought it was the right time to chuck me in, but domestic circumstances leading up to it proved less than smooth. The day before my debut, Dad came up to stay over and then travel to the match. I was rushing like mad to get to the digs because I knew Joan wasn't happy with me about some misdeed or cheeky comment but Dad beat me there, only to find all my suitcases had been thrown into the garden. I was getting chucked out on the day before debut – great preparation. It was an unfortunate end but Joan was a lovely woman who had looked after me. She was only young with a young child of her own and it couldn't have been easy looking after a cocky pair of scallywags like Kenworthy and me.

The team travelled down on Saturday to Leicester whilst Dad probably went with Keith and Ruby, Julie's parents. My future father-in-law was already a huge United fan although he watched Sheffield Wednesday as well which a lot of people did in those times. But then he started to follow my career and watched us, along with Ruby, all over the place.

En route on the team bus, centre-half John Flynn, a lovely, lovely guy to talk to, spent ten minutes just chatting and reassuring me because I was sitting on my own. That was really nice of him because it was a big coach, I had walked down the aisle and the first thing I did was wonder who to sit next to. Not surprisingly, and not wanting to annoy anybody, I played safe and decided to sit on my own and stare out of the window for seventy-two miles. Off we got at Filbert Street and the first person I saw was Frank Worthington, a real entertainer and at that time at his flamboyant best on and off the pitch. On this day he was looking like Elvis Presley and I thought, what the hell am I doing here? I shouldn't be playing in this league. But every young, nervous player has to deal with it and there were enough players there like Ted Hemsley to help me along. I have already highlighted some negatives with certain people and the occasion didn't feel as relaxed as it should have been, mainly because of the intense training we had. In a word it wasn't fun to be in such a pressure situation.

I think there were around 24,000 packed in a very tight ground and it felt as if the crowd was right on top of me. It was easily the biggest attendance I had ever played in front of and all of a sudden I was conscious for the first time of all these people shouting, cheering and booing. It didn't scare me but although I knew I could do it, I had only seen people like Worthington on television, not played against them.

Your first touch on debut is nerve wracking and my first thought on receiving the ball was just keep it simple Keith, and pass it on with a sigh of relief. As underdogs against pretty tough opponents we didn't disappoint and a poor team performance brought a 3-0 defeat and a Chris Garland hat-trick. Although I had one kicked off the line it was a pretty disappointing debut before I was replaced on sixty-four minutes by Jimmy Johnstone. The substitution wasn't pre-planned but I wasn't surprised. I had gone about my business and although a dream debut would have been great I didn't get chance to exploit anybody one on one. The important thing was that I had overcome a hurdle, played professional football in the FA Cup and it looked as if this could all get very exciting. That was it for a few games until my Lane debut as a substitute against QPR when I came on against David Webb who was reckoned to be a real tough nut. True to type, when I got my first touch he booted me and I went flying up in the air, but when I got up and jogged back past him I thought, you won't intimidate me.

Three games later when Wolves were the visitors I got my first league start, and passed up a good chance to mark it with a goal. The ball bobbled down to me about six yards out but probably through a bit of anxiety, I tried to take it too early on the up and lifted it over the top. It must have looked rubbish but it was part of my usual slow and steady progress so far although I came off disappointed after a 4-1 defeat. But I was selected again the following week which was another home loss to Ipswich this time, and although it had been a mediocre start it was good that Sirrel had kept me in for the first time.

The squad clearly struggled hugely and with only six points earned by Christmas relegation was always hanging over us and we were condemned as early as March, finishing bottom and well adrift.

But there was a bit of a change that I enjoyed as the Club slipped out of the top flight. There was less kicking going on in training, mainly because Jimmy Johnstone, the legendary Scottish International winger, had arrived and there was one ball for him and one for Tony Currie – nobody else could get it off them! Apart from being so skilful Tony was strong and would stick his arm straight out and push you away which would be a foul today but he got away with it for years. On the other hand Jimmy was so low to the ground that he just went on mazy runs, dribbling past everybody. So once again I thought, this is rubbish, it's the TC and JJ show. Put them in the same team and in an hour session they would have the ball for forty minutes. The fans' memory of Jimmy was of him in Celtic's green and white hoops, tormenting Leeds in his glory years, and he was still an exceptional performer. I could understand how he entertained people for Celtic and Scotland with the skills he had because touch it there and he was gone.

When I later moved to Chapeltown and he lived in High Green I would meet him for a drink. As a young man before starting football I was familiar with going for a pint and returning home about six hours later absolutely kettled, but Jimmy lived his life like that. I wasn't in awe of him but I liked the fact that he would invite me to join him for a trip to our local, The Bridge. I would tell Julie that I was popping out but Jimmy wanted to drink all day long. I remember him once saying, let's have a couple of pints, which we did, then the pub eventually closed and that's when he would really start drinking. As I got on better with men than women I thought, well I'm not leaving my pal, I'm staying for a drink.

The man arrived as an absolute icon but what made it easier for us all was that he was a lovely, chatty character and far from being a Billy Big Potatoes. He was brought up in a great team of players who were all pals when there was a drinking culture in the game. Then he just walked into the Sheffield United dressing room, having known no other, but remained his usual bubbly self. He would come in with all those curls one day and then the next with a skinhead. It might sound a bit stupid but it was humorous, and he blended in with the TCs, Badgers and Hemsleys who all liked a laugh. It wasn't difficult for him to become one of us, and at eighteen and a half years old, I thought it was great to say I'm going out drinking with Jimmy Johnstone. What an honour.

After United he hardly played again, most likely because of lifestyle, and I think the problem was that we brought a great player down from Scotland – where he hadn't played for anyone but Celtic – and put him on his own in a hotel. It spelt disaster because in his head it was party time.

Although Tony Currie was soon to leave for Leeds, which meant that I didn't play with him much, he was at his peak and you could recognise what a fantastic player he was. Like me, he was probably a bit disillusioned with those Sirrel training sessions, and losing a friend in Ken Furphy wouldn't have helped either. Our working routine and atmosphere altered dramatically under Jimmy. He was rigid and dour whereas it had been relatively relaxed under Ken. When he shouted it was like shouting at friends.

A bit of jealousy first appeared in my psyche around this time because Simon Stainrod was developing a bit quicker than me. He also had a bit of a matey relationship with TC who probably thought, this lad's got it, because Simon would bring the ball down and want to show off. I wanted an end product and that was the difference between us as players. But we were mates and after the pair of us had left, 'Stan' (Stainrod) to Oldham and me to Hull, we kept in touch. If he scored I would ring him and my phone bill was a hell of lot bigger than his because he would say, 'I beat this full back and then he came back at me, so I dribbled him again.' When I scored and he rang me I'd just say, 'Yeah, I knocked two in today.' End of, whereas his goal descriptions would go on forever. However, after the old guard had largely been bombed out we did occasionally have time up front together and it was great. That jealousy of his TC relationship manifested itself in me starting to get very competitive. I was up against Simon for a place and I wanted to get in and play with the likes of TC.

Simon wanted to entertain like Tony but I was brought up in no nonsense football, nothing flash. When Tony left, Simon immediately wanted the long hair and the number 10 shirt and I think he got it. I looked at it and probably should have wanted eight or ten but I wanted nine because the number nine shirt stood out for me at Sheffield United. We had our own styles of playing and, fortunately, complemented each other, especially a great spell when we were both scoring and creating for each other. I was very much wanting to score while for Simon it was little flicks and tormenting people, but that's not a criticism and in my eyes I was doing that in a different way.

In later years I have done loads of dinners with TC and he often repeats one of the nicest things he has ever said about me, and that was that the 1976 team would never have been relegated if it had contained a Keith Edwards who scored the goals like I went on to do. It is a very humbling compliment because he had obviously followed my progress when he left.

That team should have been dismantled bit by bit and not left until it went down like a pack of cards. Badger and Hemsley were now heading towards free transfers and it was sad but they are still much the same characters today, part of the Bramall Lane scene and not many people know that Ted had a huge influence on me coming back to the Club under Porterfield.

My first season had been eventful to say the least. I had started it on trial, won a contract, made my debut, got relegated and was gutted not to have made more of an impression. Although I had a two-year contract Stainrod's was for three with a three year option on sixty quid a week – a fiver more than me, and for six years. Kenworthy was the same and I thought, right, I'm gonna rip the manager's door off and I continued ripping managers doors off for many, many years after!

I'd made fewer starts than my mates and things were niggling me. I was a bit jealous of hearing the crowd chant things like 'Speedy McGeady' and I wanted the fans singing my name. To me, my pals were making progress and I was getting left behind. They had longer deals and although a fiver a week doesn't sound much it seemed a big deal to me then. Why had they done that to me? I would put my head in my hands and say to Dad, why is it always me? I was older and knocking goals in left, right and centre for the Reserves. In those days they played on a Saturday afternoon when you might get 2-3,000 at Bramall Lane. Once, the first team were doing quite well at Cardiff when the tannoy announcer gave the goalscorer as Simon Stainrod and someone in the crowd shouted, 'That's fucked you up, Edwards!'

That's how it was, Saturday to Saturday. And I loved it because you would go in on a Monday morning and hear someone ask how did the Ressies get on, to be told that they won 3-0. Then of course they wanted to know who knocked them in.

I would be in the same dressing-room when somebody would answer 'Edwards got all three,' and Tony Fields' expression would say, fuck me, that puts me under pressure. I used to think that banter was great even though it might seem as if it was a bit disrespectful to the second string. You just had to bide your time even if I felt that I was running up a hill. It was yet to really take off for me and I wasn't recognised much in that first season. After a game, everyone outside would crowd round the likes of TC so you would get away feeling that you had left by the side door.

Even though I was seeing a local girl in Sheffield which did make it easier to stay, I always wanted to visit home, stay with Steve and see all my brothers. The four of us would go out for a drink, nothing flash, and it just meant that I had to go to the bar more than them. I was halfway through my first contract and wasn't concerned about the future because another year seemed a long time and, as a young lad, it never dawned on me that they could potentially get rid of me. I had grown used to the pressure I had felt a few months earlier and grown up enough to be okay with it. But I also realised that I had to get there in my second season and not be a bit player again.

6

Making a Mark

We didn't train over the summer then, not like today when players are given fitness schedules to maintain and come back in great condition and in 1976, before our new Second Division campaign, we had kind of broken up like we had at school and the months seemed to fly by. Just as well because pre-season training was never my scene, although my wage had gone up to £55 when I signed another contract, though again I was only offered one year.

Sirrel had moved a lot of senior players on and brought in replacements for small fees in Ian Chico Hamilton, Dennis Longhorn, Steve McKee and John Cutbush. I wasn't in the team for the opening fixture, a 2-0 loss at Luton, but started the next at home to Wolves. The Midlanders had come down with us three months earlier and were destined to bounce straight back up as Champions. We went two down before the opportunity for me to get my first ever senior goal came in the second half. It was only a tap-in at the Kop end but the roar of the crowd was just unbelievable and you never forget that. What a relief. Now that the old team had gone it was effectively down to us youngsters because finances dictated a smaller squad, hence more opportunity, and to score helped me feel part of it. Hamilton got a header later on to make it 2-2.

Again it was step by step progress as I settled in to being a first teamer and now supporters were starting to recognise and stop me in the street which made me very proud. From starting as a shy little lad walking down the narrow tunnel I loved in the old John Street Stand to the little dressing room on the left – with the big one to the right – I had graduated from one to the other. I had scored, we didn't get beaten and it was just great. We finished twelfth that season and it was a real breakthrough campaign for me because after initial spells in and out of the team I really claimed the starting berth from March onwards. In all I started thirty league games, was top scorer with eighteen goals, and was voted Player of the Year. I was establishing some understanding with my team-mates and scoring a few goals really boosted my confidence. Now I was to go from being that quiet, shy little lad to the arrogant, over confident player that I became and it was to happen in a very short time, but that's how I am.

That confidence was highlighted when I went on a record breaking scoring run over eight successive league games during March and April, before which I had only scored five. I wasn't aware of Mick Jones' record until getting quite close to breaking it but when I did, boy did I want it, and I was confident that I would break it by that stage. Scoring twice in successive games against Forest and Hereford at the beginning made me more comfortable in training and I liked that feeling. Then I got another at Fulham and, like a dog with a bone, I didn't want to let the feeling go. When I got to about five the papers began to discuss my chances so although I remembered Mick from his Leeds days, I did a bit of research of my own on him and realised how revered he had been to Unitedites.

My own run felt awesome, it just blew me away. Earlier I mentioned TC showing his arrogance on the pitch in a nice way and now that feeling had jumped into me. I just couldn't stop scoring and for the first time started doing interviews with reporters who wanted to talk to me because of the goals …

The question was always whether I thought I would score the next week, and I answered along the lines of it being more a question of which half I was going to do it in. I was still basically shy but hid behind this arrogant facade which was silly and naff but I thought it was a great comment, even though I feel a bit embarrassed about it now. Against Oldham I needed to score to equal Mick's record of netting in six straight games which I achieved before scoring against Bolton and Blackpool to make it eight in a row. Ironically, the run then ended at Orient of all places when my Dad and his uncle were watching, but with so little media coverage then compared with today, it was still nice to have got a headline or two.

Stainrod and I had started to play together more, Chico was putting crosses in from the left and the great Alan Woodward on the right also chipped in with ten goals. He was a great help whilst also having to handle seeing all his mates disappear and adjusting to the new younger team. Alan absolutely drilled crosses in from wide which would bounce off my head and go in, and when he ran across to celebrate and hug me it showed he still had the desire to win, that he was okay with us upstarts and fresh faces. Maybe it helped that he was a one-club man.

Quite often it seemed that us young 'uns felt we had decent games but the Sheffield Star correspondent, Tony Pritchett, bless him, always seemed to make 'Woody' man of the match. No matter what Alan did, that's the way it was, as in everybody's eyes he seemed to have had a great game. He was probably right and it was just our competitiveness coming through. Alan was great to play with, he would ping things through, knock things about and still scored wonderful goals. He was knocking on but still doing it and I recall us both involved in shooting practice at the Ball Inn ground when goalkeeper Jim Brown would just laugh because Alan's was so powerful.

By now training had altered even though Sirrel was still manager. It had softened up a little, don't ask me why, so perhaps Jimmy thought what he had been doing wasn't working. Maybe there had been some input from coach and ex-Blades skipper, Cec Coldwell (although my main memory of Cec is of him kicking me hard up the arse and sending me round the track as further punishment). He was a lovely man but had more in common with Sirrel's point of view about training and playing.

I am not disputing their success in the game but I was thinking of when I will meet somebody in charge who is not just about digging in, grit and determination, attitude and so on, because Dad had taught me flair, to be cool, calm and collected. We didn't get that until being coached by Alan Hodgkinson and he used the kind of words that I wanted to hear which were much more inspiring to me. We were now doing things like set-plays and although we younger players were developing naturally, I believe training was becoming more effective. It was so much more relaxed and it was inspirational for us that Woody was still there after all the others had gone.

Ian Hamilton had been a regular and highly thought of player at Aston Villa and was nice to watch with a natural talent, and talk about being relaxed. He was the first man to ever kiss me. I was sitting in front of the mirror with the hair dryer because I had taken over Tony Currie's place (!) and Chico leaned over and said, 'This new aftershave's great, smell that.' When yours truly, still naive, fell for it and went to sniff, he planted a kiss on the other side of my face. When I told him to stop being a girl he put on a camp voice and told me not to be silly. It was just good fun, so refreshing and I just had to pinch that joke which I have used myself a million times since.

Sirrel had signed him and on one occasion was hammering him on the training ground but Chico said, in deliberately camp fashion, 'I've just not taken my skill tablets today, boss.' I thought, why has HE signed somebody like HIM because it just didn't fit, but it probably helped me a little bit because Ian was so laid back. He would say that he could train badly all week and play marvellously on a Saturday and I just thought, that's my type of guy. Just let it be, Gaffer, it'll all be okay on Saturday.

By the end of that second season I had established myself and was in there as permanently as I could be. Dad watched whenever he could but was living in London now and that was a shame because we often didn't do very well down there. Chelsea was one example when I was up against the giant centre-half, Mickey Droy. I used to have poached eggs for my pre-match meal while he obviously had an Alsation dog for his, and I spent all afternoon trying to get past him but he just growled at me all through the ninety minutes. Those games at Stamford Bridge were when I used to run past 'Butch' Wilkins and think, why do you smell of Brut aftershave? It just didn't seem right to us northern lads in those days.

At that time Fulham had a bit of glamour about them because they recruited some huge stars towards the end of their careers. On one visit to Craven Cottage, George Best wasn't playing but World Cup winning captain Bobby Moore was, and my proud Dad was in the crowd. It doesn't get better than that does it? Just let Bobby Moore mark me, I hoped. Who did I get? Peter Storey, the hard man, and his job was to stop the kid who had been scoring a few goals. At a corner-kick, off the ball, I punched him as hard as I could and he obviously hardly felt a thing but turned and said, 'Do that again son, and I'll fuckin' kill yer.' I drifted out to the wing a bit, came back inside a bit, went back out there ...

I had never been marked like that before and every time I turned round he was in my face. Even though people might have thought I was a bit of a softie I am not, but my punch didn't even dent him so I thought when we next lose possession I'm going to turn the tables and follow him about. Anyway, when the ball bounced off the post I followed up to score and although we lost 3-2 I had played against Bobby Moore and scored a goal so I had something to be happy about. He had stopped me with a tackle like he used to halt Pele and I felt a bit of a Wally, but it didn't become a loss of confidence as it might have once, and I felt privileged to have been on the same pitch.

In the summer of 1977 I was up for contract renewal again and compared with today's wrangles with agents and club executives there was no fuss. But I was to learn a thing or two about negotiating. Players simply sat in a room waiting to be called in to see the manager. Just before I was summoned Chico said, 'Don't forget to ask for the loyalty bonus. Have you got it into your mind what you want?' I didn't really have a clue about that and was on £55 per week but I went to face the manager.

Sirrel asked me what I was looking for, so I hesitantly replied

£90, although I have no idea where I got that figure from. Sitting there, Jimmy was quite an intimidating figure to a youngster and, in his familiar, gnarled Scottish burr he said, 'Aye don't think you've done that much, son.' Then I thought I would shock him by asking for two grand loyalty bonus. Sirrel couldn't have heard me right because he asked me what I said. I repeated that I wanted two grand loyalty bonus. I felt very much out of my depth and about two feet tall when he drawled, 'When does loyalty come into it son, you haven't shown any loyalty yet!'

I was now feeling decidedly uneasy and thinking, well Chico Hamilton told me to ask for it. But, my demands must have been in Sirrel's budget because he agreed to both figures so I hadn't asked for far too much. I still had no idea what the others were asking and didn't know if I had undersold or oversold myself in comparison. I was just glad that Chico had mentioned the bonus because I wouldn't have asked for it. You got it for every year of your contract, in this case, another three years. However, my naivety showed through again when, just as I was signing, I asked Jimmy when I would be getting the loyalty bonus. He replied somewhat wearily that it would not be until the end of the season.

I had been very nervous during the negotiating but I felt that as top goalscorer and Player of the Year I had every right to ask for what I got in the end. And I have to say, how simple was that? No fuss, just a young lad having a chat with his manager about getting a rise at a club I loved. We valued each other's position at the Club, no-one else was involved and I can't stress enough how straightforward and immediate it was. And apart from the wage increase and bonus, I now had the security of a three year deal with my wage set to increase to £108.90 in the final year.

When Ian had mentioned the bonus thing I had wondered briefly if he was setting me up, but I think I must have chatted to Alan Woodward about money on a previous occasion and he may have put me on to thinking about some kind of figure. In the end I had another couple of years playing with Alan who was very helpful and later, when I was involved in talks with

Hull, it was him who advised me to live in Beverley as it was loveley there. He seemed to have knowledge that the rest of us didn't and I went to him for similar bits of advice.

People are usually surprised that I didn't know what my mates were on but contracts were usually a private issue. I would have gone in thinking that I should now be on what the other pros were on and wanted to be treated the same as they were. I didn't care that Woody had been there for, say, fifteen years and although I wasn't asking for more, I wanted parity. My Dad would also have pressed me into pushing myself in that regard.

By now I was living at Julie's parents' house on City Road, had passed my driving test and bought my first car, a Ford Escort which cost me £450 from Pearl Motors. Julie had a younger brother and her mum was poorly on a regular basis, so I was sitting there seeing a lass who, despite being eighteen months younger than me, cooked and cleaned for everybody. It was so natural for her, even at sixteen or seventeen, to do that in those circumstances and her Dad, a painter and decorator, would come home from work and his dinner would be on the table. Here was a top Yorkshire lass who could look after somebody and at the time in my own way I loved her so the relationship seemed right for me. Within a year we would be married. When we were courting, and especially when I got my first car, my social life wasn't a case of going round town with the single lads any more.

I was a bit older than them and whilst they would be popping along to pose at the trendy Crazy Daisy pub or somewhere, I was more of a pint man. Julie and I would just drive round, have a pint at the Three Merry Lads at Lodge Moor, then another in Mosborough, anywhere in the countryside. It felt nice and very natural, the way to go, so why not? My Dad would not have disapproved although his only advice on girls was always to have a look at the mother. By now I had moved on to the older Calverts, Franks and Hamiltons of the squad for friends, partly because my route into the game had been to go to work first and gain that bit of maturity, or at least have an ease of being with older people. My life had been different and when we had bought our first house in Chapeltown I would call at the petrol station on the way home to pick up sweets – that was a night out.

Back in Stockton, Mam had been on her own since I had left but I did keep going back to see her on a regular basis. She was fine with everything and we remained close, but although I wanted to do something for her she never wanted anything from me, nothing at all. I was still the youngster of the family and was regarded as having done well but nothing really changed. Yes, I had a house exactly like my eldest brother but we weren't a jealous type of family. Ted and Len – bizarre and confusing that my eldest brothers had the same Christian names as Ted Hemsley and Len Badger! – wanted to talk about their work and wouldn't be interested in mine because they were grafters doing twelve hour shifts, whilst Steven was on a different wavelength.

There wasn't any wonderment about me making a pro career. Ted wouldn't have cared too much about it, Len was the one who just missed out so maybe he didn't want to hear about it, and Steve at that time was struggling to find work. That brought the two of us closer together so I tended to stay at his house from where we would go to the pub or to see Mam. She stayed in and I'd fetch her two bottles of Brown Ale – she was alright with that. It was easy and no-one put any pressure on anyone else although Steve was having it hard and I would sub him a few quid, no problem. Although I had flown the nest I still kept in communication with everyone, even Dad in London, and I was dealing with things on my own as I became more grown up. At the same time, I recognise now that being on my own might have led to me connecting with Julie and wanting somebody to be with.

One thing in my professional life I had negotiated (badly) and which was to become a familiar part of my life was speaking on the radio. My first was with Bob Jackson of BBC Radio Sheffield and afterwards he said: 'That was really good, now we'll do it for real.' Needless to say the 'real' one wasn't as good and I have to admit I wasn't comfortable with the experience. That is funny considering what I do now on the airwaves but you have to start somewhere. It was awkward and I would be thinking, how do I answer that? Today I try and go the other way and be laid back to counteract the nerves, just as I once had to devise a strategy to combat the problem of team–mates kicking lumps out of each other in training.

7

All Change

As the next season opened I was totally unaware of the changes that lay ahead in both my work and social life over the next twelve months. It was to start with a goal, marriage, took in a sacking, a personal loss, the arrival of my favourite coach and then, totally unexpectedly, my exit from Bramall Lane.

I had made my mark but was still relieved to be in the team from the start for the first time. We lost 4-2 in the opener at White Hart Lane but personally it couldn't have been better because Steve Perryman, the England International, was marking me and I tore him apart with my Dad and Uncle watching. To score in London at a fantastic ground was brilliant and ever since, whenever I have gone back to cover games there for the BBC, my mind goes back to that encounter. Modern day players often cup their ears when they celebrate scoring yet I actually did that back in 1977 – and I only did it because Dad was there.

But by the end of September we had won only one game and a defeat at Brighton saw Jimmy Sirrel sacked. It was the first time I had encountered that as a regular in a team, one that wasn't doing poorly, and it didn't feel good because I was desperate to do well. But it wasn't a good training ground or feeling about the place. To be fair, Jimmy was in charge of a changing team – he had replaced Chris Guthrie with Bobby Campbell – and although he was a rather abrupt man he had shown a protective side. When I had missed a few chances he came out with a few comments that protected a young player and I always remember that, but in truth he didn't appear to be a people person.

I was naive, hadn't known too many managers and unbeknown to me my dealings with him had been the start of a few rocky relationships with a lot of managers I was to come across in my career. With the benefit of hindsight now I can genuinely say, yes, I was a bit arrogant with a bit of a complex but you know what, those bosses were strange. They didn't handle people well, didn't react to certain situations and made huge mistakes. Remember Cec kicking me up the backside? It was ludicrous and they would never have survived in today's game in which you have to deal with people differently.

Management has changed massively since then. It is a lot harder now because players have so much power so surely it should have been easier then? We were just employees and didn't go in there demanding cars, houses and so on, we just wanted to play. It didn't seem as if it was difficult to handle us because, even with the players who were older and well established, managers only had to treat them with respect. Furphy seemed to scream and shout, bollocking us, whilst Sirrel was so competitive there were fall-outs all the time. He didn't get on with senior players and appeared to be a negative type of person. My most responsive time was when I first started at Leeds when I actually didn't do particularly well, but the manager, Billy Bremner was ... well, that's a story for later.

As a youngster, before agents made life difficult for managers, I was just glad to get a contract and would look around the stadium thinking, what a life I have here. I don't think I would have been difficult to handle then. I am now – making up for lost time!

Cec Coldwell was put in temporary charge and lightened the mood straight away as he understood the senior players better than Sirrel and, as part of the furniture, he would have got them to one side and said, lads, let's put this right. As a young lad coming up I found him strict and very tough, he didn't want any larking about and I knew if I did I would get on the wrong side of him. We had gone from one manager to another and although they were different characters I had still found a weakness in both to fall out about.

Under Cec we set off like a house on fire, winning five and drawing three before the first defeat. He was more relaxed but still old school and you had to work hard, and it helped that the senior players were putting performances on. The first game was 3-2 at home to Southampton and I scored the third at the Kop end which started the feeling amongst some that, dare I say it, I was the Jimmy Greaves of Sheffield United. That was because I found half a yard, got through and with the goalkeeper coming out preferred to try and pass the ball into the net. Everybody seemed to comment that it was 'stroked in with ease' and it was lovely to hear. The next game confirmed the feeling as I got two in a 4-0 win at Notts County.

Cec did a good job because he got people smiling again and turned things around, but he still dropped me later after I had gone a few games without finding the net. Whilst the first team were winning 6-1 at Cardiff I was playing in the Reserves and somebody shouted out something like, 'Cliff Calvert's just scored.' It was my bone of contention that Cec must be thinking that if Keith's not scoring, he's not doing owt. But I'm thinking, hang on a minute, why aren't I in this team? I've just come out of a cheese factory, I'm Player of the Year, you can see I'm a player so when are you going to teach me something?

Most of the time I was up top with mad Irishman, Bobby Campbell, who was a big character but difficult to understand, not to mention a bit scary with his loud, bellowing manner. I would think, just shurrup and leave me alone. The Little 'n Large style combination should have worked better than it did because in later years when I was paired with a similar character in Billy Whitehurst we did combine beautifully. Probably I should take some of blame because when Bobby came in like a big steam roller, Stainrod and I were thinking that it was us that should have been up front together. It reminds me that I will always have time for Ted Hemsley because he had regularly preached to Jimmy Sirrel: 'Put the kids in, Gaffer, it will save your job. They are good enough and scoring goals for fun in the Reserves.'

Julie's parents had been ecstatic when we became engaged and they were thrilled to bits when we married on Sunday 30 October 1977, a day after a home win against Fulham. Julie was the sort of girl who wanted to look after something or somebody. She was blonde, looked fantastic and getting married was the thing to do in those days. As it happened, she was already pregnant but we were both fine with that because Julie was good with taking responsibility for things, and that made it so easy for me to think that marrying her was a good thing to do. We were extremely young but I was earning enough to have a car and a house so, combined with Julie's organisational skills, we could cope and didn't have to wait. It was taken in our stride and was what we both wanted, although I suspect that Julie's parents had a big part to play in all the wedding arrangements because I didn't do things like that.

On my Stag night I stayed in Crookes with Derek and Vi, friends of my in-laws, after going with the United lads to the Stonehouse pub on Church Street in town, all very quiet and low key. There was no big honeymoon, partly because we were in mid-season but mainly because a house was the priority and we spent on that instead. That, and having kids, was big to Julie and we moved into a three bedroomed semi, 52 Bowland Crescent, in Ecclesfield, on the other side of the city. It cost us £9,250 and we moved over there to be nearer to Simon Stainrod.

The ceremony was at St Aidan's on City Road and the reception at the Hillsborough Suite at Sheffield Wednesday's ground which obviously surprised a lot of Unitedites. But the feller that owned it also had a big pub in the Bamford area where we used to drink and he offered us the Suite which naturally attracted a lot of publicity. Dad came up and Mam, Ted and Len came down but not Stephen who must have been working, whilst my best man was 'Davva' (David Johnstone who I had worked with on the van). Talk about a great working relationship. He was a tough character but he didn't use that to win me over. He used to have to look smart for the job but

I didn't and we used to have a kick around occasionally in the afternoon. On one occasion he was in goal for my penalty attempt and when I pushed the ball towards the corner he was desperate to save it and went full length. Inevitably he got well 'clarted up' and had to go into shops like that to deliver. It was hilarious and when I met him recently at the races he brought the story up again.

As you will hear the marriage eventually broke up and later in life I would say to Dad, why didn't you warn me about what I was doing? Considered as ever he told me that I had to find these things out for myself so why should he interfere. At his age I think I would have thought, why rush into anything, but if I hadn't met Julie and got married, would I have bought a house on my own? I had been a raggy-arsed council lad, youngest of four who couldn't do anything for himself and would probably have been getting chucked out of digs, or living in the players hostel. I wasn't forced to get married, it was just the better option and was what you did, especially if the alternative would have been loneliness. Julie was a great natural mother who had plenty of love to give more children and I was fine with that.

*****

The momentum on the pitch slowed and three successive five goal defeats in January saw Cec's reign end, although looking back the results before that were hardly disastrous. The second hammering was at home to Arsenal in the FA Cup third round and proved uncomfortable for Eddie Colquhoun who was up against the formidable English International centre-forward, Malcolm MacDonald. In the dressing room before the game, during which a young man with all those senior pros wouldn't have said Jack shit, Eddie confidently said, 'I'll look after MacDonald. He has never done anything against me, he hasn't scored against us for many years, I'll see to him.' The manager said, 'Great, you see to him then, Eddie.' Twenty minutes later and 'Mac' had knocked three in!

One or two senior players had the impression that I was

arrogant or didn't care because after that particular game I got straight off, but the reason that I didn't give a toss was because Julie had miscarried after two or three months. It was a strange and sad time for us because the pregnancy was an accident as we had been taking precautions. It was just one of those things but it was hugely tough for Julie whereas I, not a very negative person, at least in those days, thought, well, don't worry because she will get pregnant again.

After being left out or made substitute on two or three occasions, the signs were becoming clear in that we were getting beat so it must be my fault. I wasn't doing anything, nobody else scores so it must be that twat Edwards' fault, so I would be left out. The team would go another few weeks, nobody scored, so we'd better bring that little twat back! That's how simple it seemed to be to me and my frustrated reaction was, well if things are not going too well, what do you want me to do? I'm ten stone three pounds, built like a whippet and I can run anywhere you want, but you are not showing me what to do.

This is about coaching, bringing you on and improving you as a player and it was a big bugbear with me. I think back to the rows I had with managers and coaches and I wasn't going to be intimidated by them. I get in and score goals and everything is going well. Then I go a few games without scoring and it's always me who is bombed out. Managers would claim that I wasn't the only one and I would shoot straight back by telling them to hold on, let's just examine some facts here. The team's lost, there's one change and it's me. Who's the one left out here? Now, that tone they didn't like, but I was basically saying to them, tell me where I am going wrong, tell me what to do, that's your bloody job.

On 26 January 1978 new boss Harry Haslam walked in from London where he had been in charge at Luton Town, but I wouldn't have known much about him. He was a nice, jolly feller, an office manager and not a tracksuit type, completely different from Ces and Sirell. But, the little guy he brought in alongside him, this little strange talking Uruguayan chap, well, all of a sudden ...

Danny Bergara lined us all up and started doing little tricks, keeping the ball up like a magician. To be honest with you, most of the lads thought, bloody 'ell, who the hell does he think he is? But I loved it and thought, this is what I have been waiting for. Most of the players couldn't do what he could and we hadn't come across that sort of thing before, those beautiful, silky skills. He would run on the training pitch and do a few step overs, tell us not to play the ball like that, that's too simple, let's bend it round and so on. I was thinking, Dad, here we go at last, I'm alright now. Danny was just tops.

Straightaway I was the one first in the queue for coming back and doing extra training. That skinny, lazy bastard who didn't want to do anything because nobody would say this is what you do, this is where you run, all of a sudden can't get enough training. While Campbell and Stainrod etc were dubious, questioning whether to do it, I was an instant disciple and gobbled up stuff like, go that way, whip it across the keeper, and so on.

In theory it was voluntary extra training but to be fair, when we were asked if we wanted to come in you more or less had to say yes. But I was more than happy because it was totally intriguing to see this little guy, an inside forward in his day, talk about curving the ball either way. He was tiny, so close to the ground and so skilful and I took to that. And I could do it. Simon Stainrod was a skilful player but didn't take to this bending the ball stuff early on although, to be fair, he did later. Needless to say, one or two others including Bobby Campbell didn't really get up to it.

I was picking things up and learning new techniques, just like I am with golf now because I want somebody to say to me something like, 'This chipping doesn't come from the hands, it comes with a bit of a shoulder turn,' because, as I said to my golf pro recently, I couldn't have worked that out just by being a sportsman. In any sport there is a technique you have to use to improve your game and that's what I could see in Danny whose sessions were just an absolute pleasure. In practice matches I deliberately positioned myself so that my marker was directly in front of my team-mate so that I would have to bend the ball round with the outside or inside of my foot and Danny would nod his approval. In those days there were just so many people who dismissed skilful play as showboating, an attitude I didn't like. A few years on when Ian Porterfield was in charge it was all 'Square balls get cut out, don't be doing that.' Don't get me wrong, 'Porter' was great but with Danny it was, 'Bend it round him, son' and I loved that.

Even then his limited and heavily accented English was only occasionally a problem and we could cut through his peculiar blend of Cockney, Spanish and Uruguayan. It would create a lot of jokes but we could get along and understand. More importantly, he was what I wanted and what I came into the game for. For older players like Woody there might have been a natural reluctance and even embarrassment at first, that he could do what none of us could do, but then they did act positively towards him as they appreciated his ability. Danny must have only been in his late thirties so he wouldn't have been unfit. It might have been a bit showy off but if you can do it, do it, and much of the negative feeling from players was based on the fact that they couldn't.

Danny was the main voice on the training ground so I didn't get to know the manager well at all. Harry was just Harry, and he did the wheeling and dealing which was still to be respected, after all he nearly bought Maradona for United. We never saw him on the training field and he looked like your uncle, a fifty-odd year-old bloke in a light grey suit, but to be fair a lot of managers were like that then. He was more businesslike and detailed Danny to take all the training and report on who and how they had performed. For once in my life I would think I got a lot of ticks and plusses for those sessions.

Nevertheless, in a relatively short space of time I had experienced first Furphy, then Sirrel on the training pitch every day running through the snow just in little shorts, Cec kicking me up the backside and then a bloke who sits in an office all day, although I didn't really mind that because Danny was taking training. I mention those guys because it confirms my belief that because players and managers work in such an intimate and close proximity, the best managers are those that can handle individuals in the way that suits each. And I was learning that such a man would be hard to come across.

On the other hand someone like Danny could help your career with his observations. We had a player who missed an important penalty and all season I had been convinced that he approached the ball from the wrong angle. Danny had taught me to approach it in a way so that a goalkeeper couldn't tell which way I was going to go, left or right, and that stayed with me all the time. The next person to recognise that was Billy Bremner who said to me, 'You are so like Allan Clarke because the keeper doesn't know which way you are going until the very last second.'

It is about your balance and how you address the ball. It enables you to see everything around you but leave to the last minute the decision on which way you can go because the key to scoring goals is being relaxed, and disguising your intentions. In general play periphery vision is also important. When you do quick turns do you need to look up again to see what's on? No. I didn't look up, I could see the picture all the time, I could feel where the goal was because the picture was there even if I had moved. It is like, for example, tennis players hitting shots – they know where the lines are without checking. It may sound awfully arrogant but a lot of people don't see the pictures and have to deal with the ball without them.

The season petered out with us finishing twelfth but I had started and finished in the team and was with a coach I loved working with. At home, Julie and I had got over the miscarriage, we didn't have long to wait until our first child, Emma, was born and we were more than happy. The Stainrods and us had new houses, we all enjoyed going out together, and we even bought dogs. Simon had a Golden Retriever and we acquired Ben, a Red Setter, so there was plenty of walking in the woods whilst exercising them.

Life was good.

8

Hull and Back

I never saw what happened next coming at all.

We had played two pre-season friendlies in Switzerland and although Steve Finnieston had been brought in from Chelsea for £100,000, I had every reason to assume that he would be my new partner as Campbell had moved on. Steve was a nice lad, although injury prone, and with the acquisition of Argentinean midfielder Alex Sabella, I was optimistic, reasoning that if he couldn't create goal scoring opportunities then nobody could.

But I was called to Harry's office and told that the Club had accepted a bid from Hull City who had just been relegated from the same division as United were still in. I was absolutely astounded. Dumb struck. And I didn't know what to think or do. When I went back to the dressing room the older lads knew something serious must have happened and were waiting to hear what it was. When they were told it was the moment that Woody helpfully pointed out how nice a place to live Beverley was. The fact that I hardly even knew where Hull was, never mind bloody Beverley, was the least of my concerns.

Why was it happening? Maybe Harry didn't fancy me but he and Danny had been telling me that I was the ace up their sleeve and the next Malcolm MacDonald. Although I didn't know a lot of footballers then I did know about SuperMac and had been quick to get on the phone and tell Dad. I didn't blame Danny at all but I let him know how shocked I was. He naturally had to back his manager although he pointed out that I didn't have to go, that I could turn the move down and wait for a chance. My frustration resurfaced because I had gone from some nugget managers and coaches to a bloke with great skills I loved working with – but with a manager who never saw training and wanted to sell me to play someone else instead. Finnieston, ironically, became a pal of Simon Stainrod so not only did he take my place, he took my mate!

Maybe there was a need to balance the books but the lads were surprised because it seemed I had done enough to feel secure in the team. The Kop had even been singing 'Edwards for England' which had made the hairs on the back of my neck stand up, optimistic as that might have been. Simon had looked across when it happened and we smiled at each other. We wanted a partnership, it would have worked, and I believe that what we went on to do in our respective careers backs that theory up. Why wouldn't they just leave us alone?

Dad and my family were disappointed but thought, quite reasonably I suppose, that I had to go down to come back up. Yet at every level it was hard to take because I was still young, scoring goals and had fan support which also surfaced in the local paper. Nonetheless, I had a decision to make because, whatever I thought, United wanted to sell me – but did I want to go to Hull?

Off we went for talks and Julie and I walked in to this big hotel in Doncaster to meet Hull manager, Ken Houghton, and she said to me, 'Well it might be nice to be somewhere different.' She had barely been off City Road, never mind away from Sheffield but she was quite positive and I said, 'You have to remember, I get 10 percent of the fee. What's 10 percent of £200 plus grand, cos that's what we're gonna get.' Having at first been hurt and bewildered I was now thinking about dosh. Fuck it, if they want to sell me ...

My hopes rose when Houghton told us, 'Well we are taking a bit of a chance with you because we are paying a lot of money,' which convinced me that I was going to be proper weighed in.

I asked what the actual figure was that I was going to receive 10 percent of and told him he was 'avin a fuckin' laugh' when he replied fifty grand.

I had been linked with a few teams and that figure of £200,000 plus had been mentioned. That's why I thought the club had to sell me and that presumably was what I must be worth. Houghton complained that he wasn't happy about having to pay even that amount but, and excuse me if it sounds pompous, he was connected with Hull for many years as player and manager and would never make a better pound for pound signing – ever.

He had bought the leading scorer from a club one division higher for a small fee (sixty grand including add-ons) to spearhead his assault on leading Hull back up. It was a good signing for him, especially as I went into the side and started banging goals in from day one, well at least from the second game when I netted in a 3-1 win at Tranmere.

During the course of negotiations nobody at United mentioned to me that if you were going to get a payment of £10,000 from a deal you should have it added to the fee in order to receive it in cash, as a totally legal ex gratia payment. That included Harry Haslam who was regarded as everybody's friend, everybody's agent, so I can only conclude that it must have been a financial decision.

I think the evidence of what happened over the next few seasons proved that the United directors made a stupid move in letting both Stainrod and me go as he moved to Oldham soon afterwards. Why would a club get rid of two promising young players for almost nothing? I began to believe that my disagreements with staff and managers were just the way football was, and that going to Hull would be the same story with me eventually making another move.

I was also frustrated with the potential implication that I was a poor trainer with a bad attitude. I wasn't, I was just a lad who didn't understand why some things were done the way they were. Now I had a top attitude because I was working with this foreign feller who I could hardly understand but who was absolutely brilliant. Because of Danny everything had been going great in Keith Edwards' world and I wasn't a problem to anybody – then Harry wanted to let me go. And I didn't know then that I was to go to Hull and in one of the first sessions be told to hold the ball up while the manager instructed one of the centre halves to start going through me. My reaction was what a joke this football is ... and some people wonder why I have a bit of an edge about things.

City offered me 150 quid a week, plus loyalty bonus, which was a good percentage higher than I was on at the Lane, and I didn't realise until later that I was now quite a well paid footballer at that level, making a hell of a lot more than plenty of others. I was still shocked and in all honesty my first impressions of the stadium and facilities were, ahem, less than favourable. But it was my new place of work so I would get used to it and luckily I signed on the same day as a young kid who had come through their youth ranks. Garreth Roberts would soon become my best mate. The positive aspect of the move in my head was that now I was going to be a bit of a bigger fish in this pool and less likely to get dropped every five minutes if I went a few games without scoring.

The finality of the move hit Julie and I when we sold our house, having done it all up from top to bottom which actually had been great fun, and we then bought in North Ferriby (sorry, Woody). Dave Roberts, who I had played against on a couple of occasions, was being sold and someone suggested looking at his house. On walking in I immediately clocked all his Welsh caps mounted on the wall and couldn't resist joshing him with 'I know you are only twenty-one years old but this must be the closest you have ever been to me, isn't it?' I had given him a torrid time on the pitch but bought his detached house which cost twice as much as any I had bought before, and in a lovely area of Hull at the time the Humber Bridge was being built.

I was brought in to pair with Alan Warboys and initially, with him living in Doncaster and me still in Sheffield, we got the train together until deciding to car share. He was an established player but after he got bombed I remember thinking, these journeys on my own seem to be getting longer.

A hat-trick at home to Chester in the third game helped us to a promising start before we suffered a dip. It was typical of that campaign even though we finished in a respectable position, helped by a final day 3-1 win at Sheffield Wednesday when grabbing a goal was especially sweet. But I had soon begun to think that Houghton wanted to be harder on me than anyone else because I seemed to be singled out. Okay, he was a bit of a disciplinarian but I was thinking, Christ, I'm leading scorer but it's me being treated differently again. It was a stage in my life when I talked to Dad a lot and to be fair he would say, 'Well, is it you, son? He's bought you, but now you seem to have problems with him.'

Those little things in training when I was supposed to allow myself to be kicked up in the air riled me. Yes, I was learning my trade and needed to be bringing midfielders into the game but I liked to turn and be doing my own thing which was proving successful. There was a specific session which I will never forget because it involved Ian Dobson who was the most basic centre half you could wish to meet but a really pleasant lad. He didn't want to risk injuring me although he felt he had to do what the manager asked and it was uncomfortable for us as team-mates.

The animal instinct that was being encouraged was exemplified again when, as we lined up in the tunnel on match day, an assistant coach would have a bottle of whisky and offer us a swig. When I first saw him offering it to Dobbo I was flabbergasted, but when it was my turn I didn't want to sound snobby by declining just because we had a football match to play so I probably just said, 'No thanks, I'll give that a miss, mate.' Dobbo also used to put the ball against the wall and bang his head against it to psyche himself up. I could see it and hear it and cringe because it was a side of the game I just couldn't stand.

Dad and I continued our discussion about whether it was me being too touchy about things throughout the years. I could see what he was driving at but what we did in training was just ludicrous and pathetic. If Houghton was trying to toughen me up or teach me how to hold the ball up, well, I could already do that. Why couldn't we focus on something positive like working on something I was weak at instead?

Although I accept I warranted some of the blame because if things were going well I had an arrogance about me, deep down, when things were going wrong, I did feel it was mainly down to the rest of the team. I had to have that sort of self belief because I felt others were trying to knock it out of me. But they never did and were never going to because football was what I was always meant to do, and I got a massive thrill out of it.

The team managed to end that first season in eighth position and I top scored with twenty-four league goals so there was no problem in that regard. Even though Gordon Nisbet was Player of the Year I unashamedly considered myself head and shoulders above the rest and my confidence was heightened by the way the crowd got behind me.

The so-called burden of being the record signing just wasn't something I worried about, largely owing to the disappointment of it being only £60k. I was playing two divisions lower than when I started and, although it wasn't very glamorous, I was on good money and our standard of living was way better.

The privileges helped me come to terms with the situation but Sheffield was only fifty miles away and Julie was always itching to get back there at weekends. That's not a criticism because we were both still very young, growing up really in a place that we were unfamiliar with, and one of the biggest problems of joining a new club is making a new set of friends. The lads there were used to going out after a match but I wasn't at that time so I didn't really feel like one of them. I had friends but they weren't going out either, Garreth being one.

In my second season the team started badly and hardly recovered, winning only four times before Christmas which made goals harder to come by. Coach journeys often seemed to take forever and one day, at Brentford in December 1979, a new club administrator in charge of finances, obviously brought in to cut costs, did something not entirely by the book. He said, 'I'm not having this £20 for a draw business, I'm cutting it out of your contracts and will pay you per goal.'

Finances were so tight that we stayed in a really crappy hotel and at dinner a foreign bloke came into the dining room with a big potato sack. He kept digging deep, pulling out bread buns that he passed to each of us saying there's a bread roll for you. It was really low rent stuff and Gordon Nisbet, an experienced player, asked what were we doing there in that crap hole.

But we had to put up with it and, in addition, instead of being on twenty quid for a draw we were now on ten pounds a goal. We got beat 7-2 so still got a bonus! All the lads were saying that will serve him right, which I just thought was great.

That proved to be Houghton's last game in charge because Mike Smith, former Wales manager, was appointed along with his assistant Cyril Lea, who was a tough character but one I got on with. That was because you could talk to him and I respond to that in people because you get to know what they are like. Smith was an ex-schoolteacher who didn't swear and his scholastic manner didn't always help him. I recall him one day, later the following season, getting us all in a circle for a chat but he was stumbling a bit on how to express something.

'It's like bees round err ... flies round err ... err ... a honey pot.' And Billy Whitehurst piped up in his gruff Yorkshire accent, 'It's bees round a honey pot, flies round shit, Gaffer.'

Mike was going round in circles trying not to use the word 'shit' and it was ever so humorous and so typical of Billy, although Smith, to be fair, was only being himself. Billy was introduced to football at Hull when I was struggling for partners after Nick Deacy, who was brought in from a foreign club, found goals hard to come by. Somebody casually remarked that we've signed a bricklayer on Billy's arrival, and my feelings were, bloody great. Another partner but a bleedin' bricklayer, which was wrong really as I had come into the game from a cheese factory. It was just as well that I kept my thoughts to myself because then the informant added that you had better be careful with him, though, because apparently he's as hard as nails. Not wrong, was he?

Garreth Roberts had made his Hull debut in my first season

and very quickly during training we seemed to chatter away and grow close. I liked him a lot and dropped on a super little player as well. In the same way that Blades fans took to Colin Morris I think Hull people were the same with Garreth, and we looked to use each other on the pitch all the time. We were a bit naive and blinkered to start with although I was cocky enough to say to him, 'Don't bother going out there with the ball, you just give it to me.'

The relationship was as beneficial for him as it was for me because I was quick and he could impress by threading balls through. It was almost telepathic because whatever runs I made he would know instinctively whether I wanted the ball or not. He had two good feet, was strong in the air for a smallish midfielder, and as brave as a lion, an all round great little player.

When I first signed I had noticed that Malcolm Lord and Bruce Bannister would play together all the time, then it was Bruce and me for a while, and you do learn that players tend to link up on the pitch if they hit it off in some way. Bruce used to look to go short whereas I was wanting to run in beyond and I still puzzle now why I was always the one who was sometimes looked on as the lazy one. He only had to move a few yards to show for the ball whereas I was bombing on into the corners, coming back, and then going in again.

I saw him a couple of years ago and he is still a smashing lad. He had a good career, got his goals and our partnership worked, helped in no small measure by the work of Nisbet down the right and the developing young Roberts. The team seemed to take shape and get a bit better but we still didn't do much. Our occasional successes were infrequent and dampened by having mediocre or struggling seasons, and we always found points hard to come by away from home.

Smith had come to a struggling club with a team of players who were overall not quite good enough to make real progress, whilst the ones he was able to bring in weren't either. Although I got nineteen league goals we finished a lowly twentieth in my second season which was a shame because there were some positives. Chris Chilton was a very good coach and had been an excellent striker. I enjoyed working with him, including learning how to leap in the air and hold the position. He could still do it – hold, head the ball and turn the shoulders, and when I got a positive example like that I reacted to it.

Then there was being a regular in the team and linked with a lot of clubs, including Newcastle United. It might have just been paper talk but in my day the football grapevine had more credibility than today's tenuous links that owe as much to gossip or hearsay on social media sites as anything else. We rarely found anything out because you were then, as somebody once pointed out to me, a piece of meat being sold on.

Our struggles from my perspective, seemed a bit of a waste and I got myself into the mindset that, as more often than not we were going to get beaten on our travels, I was going to make sure I got a goal or two whenever possible. The struggles had not lessened my appetite for scoring but I'd come to terms with getting beaten because it happened on a regular basis, so what else could I do.

Yes, I want to get my goals for a winning team but we hardly ever won. At least I got them and therefore enjoyed some kind of job satisfaction and that's why I always sympathised with, for example, the left-backs of this world. What have you got out of that then? The team is getting beat every week and you are 'just' a left-back – and I am not being condescending. It was still a valuable learning experience alongside some good players but this period at Hull was perhaps the most arrogant period of my life, simply because of my personal success when the team wasn't doing very well.

*****

Things were developing more successfully at home because our second child, Gina, was born in 1980. Incredibly, and this seems so naive and unlikely these days, we left Emma fast asleep at home on her own for a few minutes as we rushed up the road to hospital when Julie started contractions. My Red Setter, Ben, was so affectionate that he normally bounded up to me every time I moved, but somehow he recognised what was happening and never moved from outside the bedroom door until I had dropped Julie off and shot back very shortly afterwards.

Now I had two little girls which really was wonderful and although it may have been a bit early in our marriage, Julie had always wanted a large family and we could cope, both financially and practically. Babies were Julie's business as far as I was concerned though, they were not my strength and Julie neither needed nor wanted any help. That said, I wasn't averse to getting up in the middle of the night and driving them to the Humber Bridge just to get them out of the way and give Julie some sleep. They were horrendous with regards to sleeping patterns and would be awake five or six times a night. Julie was, for her age, a first class Mum but I would never change a nappy – after all, Julie never put stripes in the lawn!

*****

Boothferry Park had a good atmosphere and a superb pitch that was a million times better than the one at Bramall Lane where the ball bobbled about all over the place. Although the ground itself was disappointing the facilities were all there, including a training ground round the back and I lived only ten minutes drive away. With Gina born in Hull I wanted to be part of the Club and its revival but we never really settled down, probably because we chose the wrong place to live.

Although we didn't have much social life I did find a real interest during my second season which became a bit of a turning point for me. I had been to greyhound racing a bit as a kid and knew a little about it but had never been to Craven Park, so when we decided to go, I asked Julie to pick a dog to bet on. When she went on to pick about seven winners I just went and stood on my own in shame.

I bumped into a chap called Ritchie Pogmore and because of those winners, went back the following weekend. So it became what I did and I bumped into him again. He was a really pleasant guy, a Hull City fan, and he became a very close friend. Ritchie owned a dog, Monard Pal, which was a bit of a favourite and had won on the previous week. It was kind of comforting to be doing what my Dad had done all those years ago when he took my brother and me. Steve would be given half a crown for a bet and whilst I had been too young then, I was now going on my own just for entertainment.

As Ritchie's co-owner wanted out I volunteered to take over his share. We had a couple of other dogs together after that and racing became a twice weekly outing. The dogs spent their lives living at the track but once I had this great idea to have one at home because it might freshen it up. It wasn't really a vicious animal but it would show its displeasure on occasions, especially as it would take your hand off if you tried to remove its food. With two little girls to be mindful of, I started it off in the garage which I decked out properly like the kennels. Gradually it went from the garage to the kitchen, to the front room and then to the bottom of the bed. Unsurprisingly, the dog loved it. When Gina would need feeding I would be lying there pretending to be asleep and when Julie got up to feed her I would say to her, 'Don't tread on the greyhound, Julie ... zzzz!' I was a sod like that.

For about six weeks I took it for some great walks on the Humber Bridge, intent on getting it really fit. Then we played at home to Blackpool when we were both fighting relegation so it was a huge fixture for both teams. I scored in our win which left their player-manager, Alan Ball, in tears at the end. I thought, great, that's my job done. Then in the evening at the greyhounds, Monard Pal whizzed in, having been looked after at my house for ages – what a day.

Someone asked me which event had given me the biggest thrill and I said flippantly, 'The greyhound, it was brilliant that.' The papers got it and I was slaughtered because the inference was that I had derived more pleasure from the dog winning than saving Hull City. People reading it may have got the wrong impression and I can understand why, but my on-field determination was never in doubt.

Having a new interest and a new friend in Ritchie was a bit of a lifesaver for me. I had been a young lad, not doing much, but we hit it off and went to Leeds dogs as well as our local tracks. I kept on with the dogs until I left and then gave them to Ritchie who was gutted I was leaving, but who understood that it had to be. It hadn't been a costly exercise, just a hobby I did instead of, for example, spending money going down town, and Julie had been great about the whole thing. I had found something that she hadn't, although she did pal up with someone across the road and they would go out occasionally. It worked for us but Hull people would see me at the dogs and Julie out and assume we weren't together, but that was never the case.

*****

One season later we were relegated and predictably, like the team, my goal output got worse – seventeen league and cup goals – but I was now a more mature player and becoming a senior figure in the dressing room. Believe it or not I was actually called up to the Chairman's massive house one Sunday and was asked what was going on at the football club. This lovely, elderly man was putting me in a hugely difficult position, comparing the club to Sheffield United and asking what people were like, what was going on, and how things were run.

I tried to be as constructive as possible and was very complimentary about Chilton. I was also fine with Cyril Lea and Mike Smith, but there were things that were missing. He felt he needed to know from someone like myself and although I gave an honest opinion, I think there were a few rumbles after that. I had been as tactful as I could but it was an awful responsibility, and I was worried that my toddlers, Emma or Gina, were going to knock something off his very expensive dining table. If the Chairman was just testing me I was confident that I conducted myself well because, basically, I was a bit scared and apprehensive about saying anything that would affect jobs.

Somewhere along the line I had got another contract and was on £300 a week with some bonuses at the end of the season on top, which was to prove an eye opener for my younger mate,

Garreth, when he volunteered to fetch the wage slips on one occasion. As everybody knows, a wage slip is a personal thing, but when he gave it me it had been opened and he gasped, 'I can't believe you're on £300 a week, that's miles more than me.'

Some people could have taken real offence at what he did but I didn't and that was down to how much I liked him. From that day on we never had any secrets about money or contracts and at the end of the season I would encourage him to try and persuade the Club to get him a car or a bonus. To be so relaxed with somebody to the extent that each knew the contents of the other's wage slip without bitchiness was real friendship. Opening my wage slip wasn't a mistake, I just don't think Garreth could resist. We were pals and that story always makes me laugh.

But there was nothing humorous in February 1981 when I allowed my emotions get the better of me during a hard fought 0-0 draw with Brentford at Boothferry Park. We were waging a losing battle against relegation which no player wants and I felt I was working particularly hard in that game. With the score goalless we were struggling to find a winner when Smith took me off. I was annoyed and upset as I had been scoring goals on a regular basis, and those were what we needed.

Trudging towards the dugout I was just a few yards away with all sorts of thoughts going through my head when I just snapped and thought, I'm not having that. Instinctively I took my shirt off, rolled it up into a ball and, as Cyril came out, I sort of nudged him aside and threw it right in Mike Smith's face. The picture in the Daily Mail the next day showed my white body and long hair in just socks and black shorts!

I went down the tunnel to the dressing room, took my boots and kit off, sat in the shower and thought, what the hell have I done. In those days the people behind the goal at Hull had to pass through a tunnel which backed on to the dressing rooms and they were all banging and screaming, ' Smith out, Edwards in' which made it worse because I was just about in tears by then. I was around twenty-four years old and wondering why I continually had a problem with managers. I needed an arm round the shoulder approach but very rarely got it.

Of course, the headlines were negative towards me and I had to go in on the Monday to apologise and release a statement. Julie asked me why I reacted in frustration all the time but I didn't know, I just knew that I was trying really hard. Smith would have had his reasons but I couldn't accept it at the time and was consumed with, why are you taking me off, I want to play. I think my pals in the team were a bit embarrassed and I wondered, Christ, Eddie, what've you done.

But do you take the striker off if you need a goal? I don't think so if he is working hard enough and capable of getting a goal – but he does rely on chances being made. I have raised this question for years and still do. Why does the number nine always jump out of that box when a sub is made? Why not the six or the eight, somebody in midfield, those who are not actually giving a striker something to have a go at? I know that nobody wants to be subbed and if I threw a wobbly other players might think, who does he think he is, it happens to us as well? But I was the sort of character to think, well, you might have been subbed but it's not going to happen to me. I believed that I had done enough and was still the best hope of a goal.

One or two of the lads might have thought, well, Eddie's not done enough today and we are getting beat, but sometimes you can give a dog a bad name and it really did stick with me. I got it in the first few years at Bramall Lane and there was no getting away from it. I suppose I got a little bit embarrassed and when I am like that I tend to defend myself by verbally lashing out. However, Smith and I sort of got over it and were fine.

In chats with him he remarked how he had similar episodes with Leighton James in the national squad. I felt like telling him that my manager at United had compared me to Malcolm MacDonald and then sold me the next week so I wasn't getting carried away by that.

Despite my fall-outs with bosses over the years they were always out in the open, sorted, and then things went back to normal. I didn't hold grudges, sulk or not try because when it came to the next game I was even more determined to play well and score more goals – it put more fire in my belly. Similarly, if the crowd cheered my name when it was read out it was a lovely warm feeling, but if I was booed at any time I got the same adrenaline rush and liked it. When Tony Kenworthy whacked me when I was with Hull, it was the worst thing he did – thanks very much, that's what I needed.

It was my good fortune to enjoy a great relationship with the Hull fans and I have to say some of the goals I scored for City were probably the best of my career. Sometimes I used to think there was no point in passing the ball and that I might as well do it on my own, feeling almost as if forced into it by the circumstances. Once, in my first season against Walsall, I picked the ball up in our own half and just went on and on, even dribbling past one bloke twice when he kept catching me up. When I got to the edge of box I simply passed the ball into net. It was one of my best ever goals, everyone raved about it and even though I say it myself, it was a super effort.

It was a time in which I almost felt that I couldn't do anything wrong because I was sharp and on top of my game, and I knew I was popular with the supporters. They play a huge part in giving confidence to any player, giving you a buzz that convinces you that you can't do anything wrong so it was strange having that in a team that was doing so badly. Both rugby teams in Hull were doing great and the city was full of talk about that, but despite us playing to only 4-5,000 spectators, I always felt assured of their support.

I needed their backing for the two fixtures against Sheffield United in that season which ultimately proved disastrous for the Blades as well as us because they had dropped into the third tier a year after my departure. Although I had faced them during the previous campaign this time, in 1980-81, there was more than a little tension in the air between two sets of vociferous supporters who didn't much care for each other. And it almost did for me in the first encounter at Bramall Lane in late December when we were already in trouble.

I was a natural worrier in some aspects of my life although I didn't suffer too much from nerves on the pitch, but when Hull were awarded a penalty at the Kop end, boy was I nervous. Oh my God I thought, I was back at the ground that had so many positives for me, all my family and mates from both teams were there, and I knew I had to put it away. But I made a complete hash of it. Former team-mate Steve Conroy was a goalkeeper I had faced many times in training, someone who knew how I took spot-kicks which was extremely unnerving and to be honest I confused myself a little bit.

Steve knew I used to bend the ball this way or sidefoot that way and must have thought, I've got him here because he always favours the goalie's left, so he decided to go a bit early. I went up and smashed the ball straight down the middle, kicked the ground and nearly broke my ankle. Striking the ball like that was down entirely to nerves because I just didn't want to miss under pressure from the crowd. I had never scuffed a penalty or sent one down the middle in my life and didn't know what I was doing, but my reaction was still ... get in!

Although Hull ended up losing, the goal was a pleasant feeling for me but it wouldn't have endeared me to Blades fans even though I was only doing my job. In the return in April we were virtually already down and I copped a load of abuse during the warm-up from United fans who aimed a lot of comments at me, as well as singing, 'You're going down, we're not.'

Now I'm a bit old fashioned and had still wanted them to like me, to applaud me for what I had done in my spell there. Wow, how naive was that. There was loads of trouble in the crowd and even though there were thousands shouting against me at that moment, the police even came up to me and had a pop at how I had conducted myself as if I had caused it. I still got letters about that from fans at United after I rejoined them.

The game was drawn 1-1 which didn't do United a deal of good. A week later I was astounded when they also went down in dramatic circumstances at home to Walsall after a last minute penalty miss. It was an unbelievable way to go down and hard to see the club that gave me my break complete the fall from First to Fourth Division.

My own career felt in a strange place then. I had established myself, the money was getting better and better, and our house had doubled in size but we were being beaten every week. I was in the bottom division like poor old Paul Garner who had gone all the way down with Huddersfield, then joined United in the top flight and went all the way down again with United. Trust me, that's not easy to take. The former Hull legend Raich Carter had been kind enough to say when we were going down, 'This is the worst Hull side I have ever seen, apart from the lad, Edwards,' which was great for me if not for the team. Raich might have been a bit harsh because we had good players in Nisbet, Garreth, Malcolm Lord and Roger De Vries.

Lots of things were going in the right direction but my football had stalled over my time up there. I would reflect on the fact that Michael Robinson of Preston had scored comparatively few goals but got a move to Liverpool whilst Keith Edwards who had scored almost sixty in three seasons for a team that had largely been struggling had stayed at Hull. Peter Barnes made the England squad, went to Leeds for just under a million quid and we met up again at Hull in my second spell, but I was their record signing. These little facts ran around my head because I had outlasted them in terms of consistency and couldn't understand why none of the big clubs had taken a chance on me. Had I not proved myself over all these years?

By this time Steven and I were very close. We fought like brothers often do when we were little but now we just got on so well. The fact that I was successful and he was then out of work didn't matter at all, and I helped him out every time I went home because he needed it. I would take him out for a drink and a laugh or go racing up in the north east which has always been a depressed area. Just as Julie liked to go back to Sheffield for visits I would nip off to Stockton and stay with Steve, popping in to see Mum who I always tried to help. But whenever I offered to buy her something – even a caravan on one occasion – it was always, 'No, I'm alright.' She wouldn't let me do anything for her because it wasn't the done thing, it was always polite to say no.

Mam was proud and set in her ways as most northern working

class women were, but it often meant she would deny herself any little pleasures and gestures that came her way, although she did allow me to take her those two bottles of Newcastle Brown whenever I went to see her. Visiting her or going to London to see Dad never caused a problem either way because they had moved on, but neither now had anyone else in their lives. My brothers and I often wondered if they might get back together when I was younger and I used to ask Mam, 'Why don't you let Dad come back now?' but I would get a very sharp 'No, I'm not having that useless bugger back in this house,' and deep down I knew that it was never going to happen.

We didn't take sides and because we saw Mam more regularly, Steve and I made the effort to go down to see Dad. I would arrange to spend five days with him in the summer break or visit when we had London games. Julie loved time with her parents so I didn't have any worries about knowing her and the kids would be looked after if I was away visiting, whereas we had all been boys so when Dad had gone Mum was left out. I still find it heartbreaking that her life seemed so humdrum and lonely.

Dad, my brothers and I really haven't been very good at handling women, and I still can't to the extent that I would like to be able to. Fortunately for me, Julie respected that I needed to go back and see everybody, and when she did come up with me she was great with them all. We all have a lot to be grateful for in that Anne, my sister-in-law, did a brilliant job in taking a leading role in looking after Mam, and eventually Dad, when he later came back to the north east.

I have never been big on holidays so Julie and I worked out ways in which everyone could do what they needed without anyone missing out. That often meant me arranging for Julie to take the kids away to Devon or Cornwall with her Mum and Dad which suited them all because they loved being away, whilst Steve and I would go to see Dad. I also made sure I spent time with Julie and the kids down south for part of their holiday, driving from Stockton to Exeter which took ten hours in those days, stopping over, and then continuing to Newquay, a hell of a journey on my own. Julie and I were both happy with these arrangements at a time when I needed to get back fairly regularly. We didn't approve of taking very young children abroad because of the sun risk, but in the end we did go to Portugal and elsewhere doing the usual trips when the kids were older.

Domestically, we had survived a difficult start to life in Hull. Fairly quickly we had both established that the house we had bought wasn't in an area that suited us, as youngsters, and it was probably too big for us at the time. We even looked too young to have a house like it and sometimes when Julie answered a knock on the door she would be asked if her Mam was in. On another occasion she was asked round to a neighbour's only to find that it was for a prayer meeting. The situation was very difficult for her and it caused huge arguments because as a result we used to go back to Sheffield every weekend. When I pointed out that we were supposed to be living in Hull, it didn't go down well and I was getting sick of it. But we didn't pack it in and eventually settled.

The problem now was that my career was stalling. We had gone down, the club was potless and my goals were drying up as the team struggled. I was a victim of circumstance and under contract so I presumed I was staying and wondered, what choice have I got. All I can do is just keep on doing what I can – we might be a bit more successful in the bottom division.

9

Golden Days

'Hello, is that Keith?'

'Yes, who's speaking?'

'This is Sheffield United. Are you interested in coming back?'

I was standing with the phone in my hand and positively tingling when I took that call early the following season whilst Julie was out shopping with the kids.

'Too right I am.'

'Right then, Ian Porterfield would like to bring you back.'

'I would love to, but on the right terms, so it's up to you now.'

'Good, we want you.'

It was a huge and exciting surprise and although United and Hull were in the same division again, a move back there made sense on so many levels. Julie hadn't come to terms with living in Hull so she would be delighted, and I was more than happy because I was aware of how Chairman Reg Brealey had recruited Porterfield and was intent on spending to get promotion.

When she came back I told her that somebody had come in for us, but then made her guess just about the whole of the teams in the Football League before she begged me not to wind her up. 'Don't tell me it's Sheffield United if you don't mean it,' she said.

'Alright then, I won't tell you it's Sheffield United,' I teased. We had a bit of fun with that but she was ecstatic. I hadn't asked for a transfer and the approach was as simple as that. In latter-day terms it may have been considered an illegal approach, a tapping up, but it was virtually the norm back then and now I had to wait to see how things would pan out.

The season was underway and I was in the City team that made an average start but I was becoming apprehensive because nothing was mentioned to me about a potential move. That was intensified because United came to Boothferry Park in mid September and I scored in Hull's 2-1 win, the first of only four league defeats inflicted on the Blades in a tremendous season. Who knows, maybe that day convinced them that they needed to make their move. If the truth be known I was a bit miffed because United hadn't been in touch with me again. I wasn't sure if they had lost a bit of interest so although doing my best for Hull was my major concern, I made my point with the goal. The transfer link, however, must have got around because the Blades fans at Boothferry Park this time around were rather generous to me. Looking back I think that the delay at that point must have been because the two clubs were still failing to agree on a deal.

When Mike Smith eventually told me that they had accepted a bid I assumed it was from United but the club was, in fact, Chesterfield, and he suggested I went there for talks. It seemed clear that he wanted me to go to the Spireites but I thought I'm not having that. I knew United wanted to buy me because they had spoken to me three weeks earlier. However, out of respect to Billy Dearden and Frank Barlow who both had strong Blades connections, I agreed to go and find out what they would offer. When Smith did come clean and tell me United were also interested I realised that Hull wanted a fee – which Chesterfield were prepared to pay – rather than go through a tribunal process with United.

Saltergate, with all due respect, was another crappy ground and I asked myself why I was bothering with talks there when United were waiting just a few miles up the road. But I had a chat with Billy and Frank and was hugely impressed with them before Billy said, 'You are going to talk to United, aren't you?'

which I confirmed. I made the right polite noises and thanked them but underneath I was thinking, let me get up that A61, and I am sure Billy and Frank would understand that. They were both great with me and I am sure when I left that office they thought they would not be seeing me again. To be fair, they must have been pushing the boat out and had a good little side, including Phil Bonnyman and a few others.

When I then went to Bramall Lane for a similar chat, Paul Garner walked past and asked if I was having talks, then it was the same when Tony Kenworthy appeared. I was already seeing people I knew and it was just so familiar to me again.

During the meeting I was told that the clubs hadn't settled on a fee so it would be a tribunal settlement. But worryingly, Reg Brealey said I would have a big part to play in it and he would tell me all sorts of things he wanted me to say when I went in, which was a bit of a daunting prospect. I was not on bad money at the time and apparently United couldn't match it but would try to balance things out with bonuses. I was happy with the terms agreed and, in a big Jag on the way to Manchester, I told Reg, 'I don't know what your problem is with this tribunal. It will be what it will be and you will be getting the best buy of the season.' Now is that arrogance or is it confidence? I was glad to be coming back home, the new stand and dressing rooms were now in full order and I was itching to get started.

But when Reg responded that they didn't want to pay too much for me I thought, here we are again, what is with me and football people and their opinions about me. Didn't they rate me? These people, none of them want to pay anything for me, but I get straight into the team, knock goals in for fun and they tell me that I am flippin' brilliant. They sold me for sixty grand and were hoping to get me back for that figure but it sounded over optimistic to me. I thought they would have to pay more and they eventually got away with shelling out £100,000 but they still wanted locking up for selling me and Stainrod to start with.

People often question why I seem so bitter about things like that and my view is, why on earth did they sell me in the first place when I was good enough to be bought back at a higher fee? Another chip on my shoulder, firmly put there by Mr Brealey who despite that, I grew to absolutely adore, was that they didn't want to pay too much, even though as a businessman he should have recognised a bargain. That phrase, having a 'chip on the shoulder' is quite commonly used but it is put there by other people whose actions and attitudes shape it.

However, Reg gave me all this spiel to say, which I almost completely forgot straight away, and although I did contribute I don't think what I said made much difference. Hull wanted about 185k, United offered 60k and they basically just split the difference which is often the case.

I think Chesterfield must have offered about 80k and were prepared to pay that which is why Hull accepted the bid rather than take the tribunal. As it worked out, City did come out of it with more than was offered but I just felt a bit annoyed that Smith had told me about Chesterfield straight away but not about United.

Completing the move was a great thrill, even after the delay which might have been out of politeness because Hull were due to play them, but it was hugely frustrating. Of course, there were no mobiles then and they would have had to ring the house number. How different that is to today, and I wonder how they got my number in the first place, yet people just did.

The deal was forced on City in a way, because they were absolutely broke and in 1981, 100 grand was worth much more than it sounds. There wasn't a huge fans backlash. They didn't want me to go but they understood why it had to happen. The real stumbling block for them was that I had gone back to United. That hurt them apparently, but the abuse they gave me afterwards was slight compared to what I got from Blades supporters when I had played against them.

*****

Back in Sheffield we moved into a club house in Intake and, apart from the fact that there was no point in me getting stuck into the gardening which I loved grafting at, it was very convenient. We didn't have to worry straight away about selling up in Hull, and the whole move felt easy because it was coming back home, even though my own real home was Stockton. Julie's family, especially Keith, was always on hand to help us out and thrilled to have us around again. I travelled back and forth for a while until our new house became available within a few weeks, but that wasn't ideal preparation for a footballer. And for a long time at Hull the coming backwards and forwards to Sheffield for weekends had caused a lot of friction because I had maintained that we had left Sheffield and it was part of our lives that was done.

We soon started looking for houses which Julie loved doing but I hated. There always had to be something going on in Julie's life and she is still like it now, so if there was a new house to look for then we would be fine. We found a place with five bedrooms and a granny flat we eventually bought in Norton which I liked, apart from the state of it. When we went through the front door and one of the kids fell through it because it was rotten, my reaction was that there was too much chuffin' work there, and I couldn't do it. But, Julie being Julie and Keith being Keith, they just dismissed it as something they could put right, and they did. In fact, her Dad was a huge help in decorating because that was his line of work.

Most important for me was putting in a conscious effort to make new friends as I had learned my lesson from staying on the periphery in Hull. I already knew Tony Kenworthy and Paul Garner and had recently met Steve Neville, who I had bumped into at Walthamstow dog track with Dad. We vaguely recognised each other from playing when he was with Exeter and neither could decide who the other was, but we started chatting, not knowing that I would soon be back at United playing alongside him.

I was to get on really well with Steve, as well as TK, Paul and John MacPhail. Whether that was the right thing to do I don't know as it led to quite a few heavy sessions at the Royal Oak on Cemetery Road, but it felt important to me then and I really enjoyed it. Steve was a London boy, so was Dad, and we had met at Walthamstow so we seemed to find some common ground. We hit it off so well that it wasn't long before he moved in with us. He had an argument with his missus, walked out and asked if he could stay with me for a week until it blew over. The trouble was, two months later he was still getting in the bathroom before me and so, under pressure from Julie, I had to tactfully ask him to move on.

Joining United a couple of weeks after scoring against them had provided me with an opportunity for a bit of a gag, telling Kenworthy, 'I scored against you again so you must be pleased that I'm back in the same dressing room,' but really I was just so excited about the return, getting the shirt on and scoring that first goal again. All I had experienced so far was defeat, getting sold on, being told I wasn't good enough and relegation to a lower division which hurt after rumours of going higher. I hoped this season was going to be a turning point.

I can't speak for the lads who had played the first five games but for me the realisation that we were on to something came virtually straight away, in my debut at home to Scunthorpe. We won 1-0 through a goal from TK which set us off, and although I was disappointed not to score I knew anyway it would come quickly in a team like that. Then there was the encouragement from the crowd and I was really touched by a feeling that I wanted to be back and they wanted the same.

Three days later on a Tuesday night I was relieved to get off the mark with two goals, as did Bob Hatton, in a 4-0 demolition of Crewe, and my season was truly underway. We were top of the table by the end of October and never had any fear about teams coming and shutting up shop because we could get the ball beyond people, and pass it as well. My first away goal was taken first time from distance at Port Vale when I made the most of John McAlle's fifty yard pass over the centre-halves which helped us to a 2-0 win, but the next fixture on the road at Bradford City was to provide an unusual story.

During a row with my father-in-law, probably over Julie and I falling out because that's what we did, some pushing and shoving finished with me falling through a glass door. My arm felt extremely wet through the bleeding and because we hadn't sold our house in Hull by then, I drove all the way back there and eventually had twenty-six stitches in the wound. I went over the road to a neighbour, Dawn, and we tried to cut off a lump of skin that was almost detached because the cut was deep. Stupidly, I thought it would be alright to do such a thing but we couldn't so I drove to hospital in North Ferriby with it wrapped up. I figured that I had been fortunate to fail in our surgical efforts when the nurse revealed that it was a good job I hadn't cut it off as I could have lost my arm.

I told the Gaffer but he and the club doctor thought I would be okay so I wore a shin pad strapped over the cut for the next game against Hartlepool. Although I scored in a 1-1 draw I fell and the arm went a bit wobbly which I thought was the pad, but in fact the stitches had burst. Afterwards, John Matthews, (another Cockney accent required!) saw it and said, 'Fackin 'ell, I think I'm feeling a bit funny' and left the dressing room.

But I played and grabbed a brace in the next fixture, a 4-1 home win against Mansfield Town and then came the Yorkshire derby at Bradford. With them also going well the fixture was televised and the commentator, it must have been Martin Tyler or John Helm, attributed the arm injury to 'tennis elbow'. Watching it back on television really made me chuckle although later I had to go for skin grafting which was a most painful experience. The specialist just skimmed off some skin and I nearly hit the roof, but it was okay from then on and I didn't miss a game.

Julie's Dad and I made up, no problem, and that is one of the things I liked about him. He was a straightforward Yorkshireman who would stand his corner, as I did, but we always talked ourselves round and he and Ruby were always very helpful throughout our marriage. The fall-out had happened probably because of the way my circumstances were changing with a new club, changing houses, maybe me starting to go out with the lads and so forth.

In order to cool off I spent about six weeks in a place the club had at Nether Edge before things settled down to what passed for normality again. But it did upset and affect me emotionally for a while and there were always a lot of arguments between Julie, her Dad and me. I suppose now I recognise that we were never really right for each other, but how were we to know after getting together when we were so young? My Dad had a way of simplifying things and explained, 'Son, you two are a couple of positives, and it don't work. You need a negative.'

And of course he was right. In our courting days I would sit there thinking, I just want to go back home, I can't cope with this. She was a strong character with a bit of a complex about me being a footballer which was a worry. It irritated me to death and caused rows because we were both sparky characters, and a football career offered plenty of scope for tensions to surface.

And they surfaced on the pitch when we took on non-league Altrincham in the FA Cup, firstly at the Lane. We hadn't lost in the league for two months, were heavy favourites and despite goals from Bob Hatton and me we were held 2-2, but for me the game was played against thugs. You have got to be able to defend yourself but the centre-half simply punched me in the head and for about an hour I was in such a daze I couldn't even remember that my Dad was there. In the replay I wondered whether to try and get him back myself, but before I could, Mike Trusson did at a corner, and got sent off. On a tight little ground we were knocked out of our stride and bullied 3-0, but it didn't halt our progress in the league and we carried on stitching wins together.

Ian Porterfield, who had been poached from Rotherham United directly after leading them out of the Fourth Division, was a new manager for me to get to work with and he was good to me. I'd had those that were a bit sharp with me and didn't handle me very well, like Ken Houghton who always wanted to toughen me up, then an ex-teacher in Mike Smith, and there was no way in which I was going to get on with him. Porter liked me and would ask, 'Are you alright mi son?'

I had always thought that Jocks were a bit dour but I was his signing, he paid a lot of money and he wanted it to work. In the cold when we were training I never overdid it with clothing, just wearing a red top, whereas others would have layers sticking out all over the place, and Ian would regularly ask, 'Are you warm enough, son?' But he could be tough with me as well, leaving me out of the side so I would be knocking on his door a few times. That being said, Ian was alright.

Hull, who were to finish eighth, came to the Lane for the return fixture and it was weird being on the same pitch but in a different team to my best pal, Garreth Roberts. Drifting back into midfield close to him during a 0-0 draw I thought, this is really strange, this is the lad I wanted to come to Sheffield United with me. He was that good and I begged Porterfield to do it but, although I believe he was interested, nothing came of it.

That was our second goalless draw on the trot, both at home, and a shock result a week later could have derailed our campaign. Colchester United at Layer Road always held the prospect of being a difficult game and as they were also in the leading pack it was selected for TV coverage on Match of the Day. Highlights of a Fourth Division fixture didn't happen very often so it was a rare opportunity for us to show what we could do.

Everything went wrong from the moment we had to wear one of Colchester's strips for some reason or another, and we had few excuses in a 5-2 loss. Although I got one of our goals when Neville crossed and I slid in, it revealed an interesting side to the old warhorse Bob Hatton who I played alongside. Bob actually said to a linesman that I may have been offside and that was how competitive he was – we were vying with each other to be top dog. But I liked that about him and don't think a bit of jealousy or competition is a bad thing. It spurs you on and I've fed on that kind of stuff myself.

Playing with Bob was genuinely a real pleasure even though we both largely did our own thing so it wasn't a traditional partnership. It was uncomplicated and you could see what a good player he must have been because he was very effective even though he was then at the veteran stage. The fans certainly respected and loved him, and maybe I got a touch of his sort of self belief. I loved the way he conducted and held himself both as a footballer and a man. He knew what to do and what to say.

As the season wore on and I was rattling goals in with regularity I told my team mates, 'Well played, guys, just keep the service going because this is no fluke.' Before then I wasn't one for storming out or saying my piece out loud in the dressing room, and I said what I did because things were going smoothly and I was in a good place. I hoped they didn't see it as arrogant because I meant it in the best possible way as I was enjoying it so much and feeling so confident, as much of their ability as mine. Maybe the lads just felt I was having a purple patch but I was appreciating what I was capable of within that group of players.

I was hugely disappointed at losing at Colchester because I only played in two losing league games for United that season – they lost two before I came back. I was twenty-four now, this was my new team with a lot of experience in it and that loss hit me, but we responded brilliantly. The following week the squad trained very, very hard even though a lot of us weren't really into that, but it was a kick up the backside we probably needed. A couple of big wins and a draw followed before a 2-1 defeat at Scunthorpe in which Neville was red carded.

That reverse, in February, was our last of the season, stretching to three months and nineteen games and we were on fire, especially as it coincided with the arrival of Colin Morris on the right wing. One of those big wins was 4-0 at home to Stockport and funnily enough on that day Julie was in the stand, my future girlfriend, Zoe, was in the away end with her then husband, David, her future husband Ted was in United's Executive Suite and I, her future boyfriend, was on the pitch – you never know how things are going to turn out!

The team was perfectly blended with the right mix of experience and ability. Bob, being taller than me, went for the majority of headers whereas I could get away from defenders. He would also drift out to the left which confused defenders whilst Stevie Neville and then Colin would go down the right. At the back we had loads of experience in John McAlle from

Wolves, Kenworthy and Stewart Houston, while we still had Paul Garner and, initially, John Ryan at right back. In midfield Mike Trusson had height and strength and chipped in with goals, whilst Steve Charles had a tremendous work ethic before Jeff King arrived from across the city. He was a hit and miss type of player but was exceptional when he was on.

With all those goals in the side you can see why the rest couldn't live with us. Four of us got double figures, including TK who also took penalties, and of course we didn't let many in at the other end either where Keith Waugh, in goal, was another expensive newcomer. You have to give credit to Ian Porterfield because he was entrusted with, for that level, a substantial transfer budget which he used wisely and largely on Waugh, Morris and me. It's inevitable that some signings don't come off and are forgotten but when you consider what he did, and continued to do in the years after to go up again, you can't escape the fact that he had an eye for players.

Virtually throughout the season I was at the top end of the scoring charts for the division and it was coming down to a battle between Bury's Craig Madden and me. There is no harm in admitting that I was selfish enough to always look out for their results and whether Madden had scored because I wanted that label.

My eye was also on the £5,000 prize for the first player to hit forty goals, a great incentive, but for me it wasn't the money but the recognition. I had something to prove. Goals came pretty regularly for me and on two or three occasions I went on scoring runs and in one, a re-arranged home game with Northampton Town in mid March, I registered my first hat-trick for the Club. It was a horrible, wet night and mistakes were made all over the pitch in a bizarre game that we won by a crazy 7-3 scoreline.

One week later a visit by high-flying Wigan loomed and the result was going to be significant for both teams as the title race was tightening up, and a crowd of over 22,000 demonstrated that. It was a big challenge to play up against Wigan's two massive centre-halves, including the greatly experienced Larry Lloyd who had played for Forest. He was a bit intimidating and must have played well against us because all I did all night was plod through, relying on the experience of having had my brothers knock bits off me. Then late, very late, Colin Morris got away and crossed for me to tuck home the only goal. Larry, who had received some stick from the start, was gutted, but although we might not have deserved to beat them we had won a big battle against a physical side. That was the way teams could beat us but if they took us on at football and advanced a bit, that was when we had the pace and ability to go past people.

It wasn't smash 'n grab but it was the sort of game when critics would say that I had done nothing all game and then got a goal. My answer to that criticism was to point out that I was able to overcome the pressure of knowing I'd not had a great game but, when everyone was watching and that one chance came along, I could say to myself, this is it now, you've got to knock this one in – and doing it. I see that as cool nerve, a strength of character as well as ability to put them away when it really did count as opposed to games where we were two up already.

In April two 4-0 wins against Peterborough with two goals in each from me, basically saw off their challenge, and having beaten Wigan and drawn at Bournemouth, we had checked the progress of our close rivals. We were looking favourites and without getting over confident turning our attention to the title. Bury, who finished ninth, were not really threatening promotion but the fixture there was one we needed to win. It was a tricky one and they also had Craig Madden with whom I was locked in a nip and tuck race all the way for the Golden Boot. In the event we both scored in a 1-1 draw.

United fans talk about my goal as if it was a bullet header and I suppose it was, but a lot of credit should go to Jeff King who was dancing about on the left wing as he used to do. He absolutely leathered the ball across at head height and I thought, you've only got to get your head to this, and it flew in, right in front of our own fans which was great for them to celebrate. It was ironic that the two games against Bury ended 1-1 with Madden and I scoring in both of them. Despite our rivalry we didn't acknowledge each other on the pitch at all, but I was obsessed with it and got a footy magazine every week to look at the scoring charts. It was the only thing I ever did look for.

The final day was Darlington on 15 May, 1982, and it was one I will never forget. Neither will the thousands of United fans who were there and had, a year previously, been shattered by the shame of relegation to the Fourth Division for the first and only time in the Club's history. This season had been a new journey that many turned into a crusade, a party with venues they had never visited before and they had thoroughly enjoyed it. We needed a victory to win the title. Although Dad was in London my brothers, Len and Ted, along with Mam, went to the game which really was a celebration.

Our 12,500 supporters, many of them in fancy dress, virtually took over the ground right down to the touchlines. Some even climbed trees to see the action. Being there was great for my Mam because the only time she had watched me before was for the England U21s at the Lane in my first spell. Paul Garner and I were in the squad but neither of us got off the bench and I felt the England management took the piss with that after attracting a lot of local interest. I remember looking at Peter Barnes and Keith Bertschin and being convinced that I was better than them as I was knocking goals in for fun.

But not as many as I had in this fabulous promotion campaign and although Bob and I got our goals for a 2-0 win, early on I thought I might struggle. When I belted through the middle the Darlington centre-half went stride for stride all the way, which had me thinking that hadn't happened all season. The bedlam at the final whistle prevented me from meeting up with my relatives which was ironic since my brother had ended his career there, an injury that finished him before he became a welder. But this was a cracking day and a fairytale ending for Bob who would have been about thirty-five years old but had a fantastic season. I may have scored more goals but he wasn't overshadowed in the slightest because he played a big part in our success.

We played that season feeling that we were going to murder the division, and with that dressing room and that crowd we were just too strong for everybody. I loved it, was whacking goals in all year and it was just so easy at times. Our style was a basic 4-4-2 but Porterfield always wanted his team to work really hard, which was one of the reasons why Steve Charles got in and helped us so much. Ian looked at the side and thought, well, this team can play both at home and away, and I don't recall having been given too many responsibilities with regard to working back. We were a strong enough team without that because it had great balance and as individuals we had better players, simple as that. And I appreciated that it was the first time that I had ever felt part of a real team effort based on the strengths of all the individuals working together.

Although it had been satisfying in so many ways, the indignation about aspects of my career and the people who affected it still burned inside at times. I think the likes of Colin Morris, Tony Kenworthy and I would have been entitled to question the judgement of the movers and shakers in the game too, because we were good players and should never have been allowed to drift to the bottom division. I mean, how scandalous it was for Colin to be down in the basement. Our ability and potential hadn't been recognised enough and we proved that by going on to play in the equivalent of the Championship and still being good players. After all the disagreements with managers and the feelings of being undervalued and underrated, I was going to prove that I had been right all along and worthy of my fees and wages.

If I needed statistical evidence I had it in the shape of a Golden Boot for leading the Fourth Division scoring chart, which I was immensely proud of and which honestly meant more than the £5,000 prize that went with it. It was a close run thing, though. Bury had gone to Hartlepool and we heard that Madden had scored one and missed a penalty while I had nipped in and got a couple which meant that I got to thirty-five quicker. Ian Porterfield wouldn't have particularly been rooting for me on a personal level and he would have played it down as an individual thing. He was all about the massive team effort in which no one person should get the spotlight, but that was his way and it was fine with me.

The Golden Boot awards were a much bigger event then which meant an evening out at a posh London hotel and the opportunity to mix with the football elite. Two things occurred which made it less auspicious for me although one of them, totally self inflicted, is one of my favourite stories. Firstly, and ironically, it was awarded on a day early in the following season. I wasn't even in the starting eleven because Porterfield had made me substitute after a few games without scoring which was a great start.

Anyway, I went down with the directors and met my Dad, who was my guest, outside this huge place with what seemed about 2,000 people in there. A stunning bird took us to our large table and I sat down thinking, well I've found my name tag, now where will Dad's be. Surely he'll be next to me? He was walking round the table looking and eventually found his spot opposite me which he thought would be alright. I looked at the name tags on either side of me and discovered that, relatively speaking, they were nobodies who I didn't know at all, but Dad had Freddie Starr on one side and Elton John on the other. I squirmed and warned him through gritted teeth, 'Don't you fuckin' speak. Don't do anything, just sit there and look at me. Talk to me, but don't talk to them.'

I'm almost ashamed about that now but I was twenty-five years old and you know how you feel at that age about your Dad embarrassing you. Although he was a quiet man with a charm about him, I was thinking he'd tell Elton John a gay joke or try and be funny in front of Freddie Starr, so I was a bag of nerves with anticipation.

Lennie Bennett, the well known television comedian was compere at the event and there I was, a bit nervous, chatting to my Dad who was also having a conversation with two celebrities which only made me more than a bit uptight. I heard my name mentioned on stage and, because mine was the Fourth Division award, presumed it would be the first to be presented. So up I got, all done up in my nice new light coloured suit and green tie and made my way for about thirty yards through all the tables towards the stage. I was just thinking that it was flippin' weird as nobody's clapping, but of course they are rude so and so's down there, when Lennie Bennett looked down disdainfully and hissed at me, 'Not now' Horrified, I turned round, trudged back and sat down to hear Dad say, 'You made a right bleedin' fool of yourself there, didn't you, son.'

Freddie slaughtered me and Elton restricted himself to polite laughter so the tables had been well and truly turned on me as regards who was going to embarrass who. This was the highlight of my career and everyone was taking the piss out of me. It was a real lesson in humility if nothing else.

The other winners on the evening were Kevin Keegan, Gordon Davies of Fulham, Ronnie Moore and Gerry Armstrong who got a special award for his World Cup exploits. Keegan came over to congratulate me later in the evening which was lovely, and I felt very brave calling him Kevin in return. My Fourth Division award was about four inches high in a beautiful little box but I did notice that the other trophies got progressively bigger. When Dad said, 'Look at the bleedin' size of those,' I thought he's getting carried away now, and I want my brothers here to march him out of the place. The pair of us just laughed ourselves silly and enjoyed a really special occasion.

It had been an absolutely fantastic day out and Elton and Freddie, who spent the whole night talking to Dad, were brilliant. In fact, when I next went to play at Watford and was just dropping down the steps on the way in, Elton spotted us and shouted 'Hello, Mr Edwards' to Dad, which was astonishing. I told Dad that I thought he would have to go down the stairs to get his ticket but he was a step ahead. 'I don't think I'll be needing your ticket, son, I'm straight down here into the Directors Box,' and that is where he went, with Elton no less.

Incidentally, when I got my second award just two years later it was a great big boot, sprayed up in bronze. After training I was told there was a bloke from Adidas here with my Golden Boot award. Oh, I thought, and went to the car park, met him, shook his hand and had a photo taken. That's it, done. It was low key, to say the least, in comparison.

Getting the number of goals I did was a big jump compared to previous totals, even though I had been top scorer at United before I left and again at Hull. The crucial difference now and what made things easier was that this was the first time I was in a side that was continually winning. I was always confident that if I got in a good side I would rattle in a canny few, and as far as I was concerned this wasn't going to be a one-off. My profile had increased and there were a couple of transfer links at a time when Watford's Luther Blissett and Ross Jenkins were both doing well, as was Bob Latchford. There were a few that managed to reach thirty plus and in contention for the five grand.

Dad absolutely loved it and my football journey before that season must have been really disappointing for him because he had done all he could to get me into it – and succeeded – but then, despite the goals, I had been axed, sold, dropped down a division and so on. He must have had his doubts about me occasionally and, at one stage when I had kept asking him why managers had seemed to have it in for me, he had even asked me if it could be me as they couldn't all be wrong.

Eventually he accepted that yes, they must have been because I kept proving it. He tried to keep tabs on me during that promotion season, following our progress in the days before teletext and the internet by listening to the results and scorers on TV and radio. It was probably one of his few sources of entertainment when he was living in London on his own, and my thoughts on walking off the pitch were often about Dad and whether he would be pleased about what happened that day.

He was having a difficult time looking after his own Mum who eventually died of Alzheimers Disease. After she died, Steve and I continued to go down and spend four or five happy days at a time with him. Steve was potless then so I would drive from Sheffield to Stockton to pick him up and then down to East London. It got my brother and me together and we still do that now, going to race meetings at places like York and Cheltenham and so on, even though Dad isn't here any more.

At Bramall Lane, though, it was party time. We had functions, drinks with the lads and wives which was a nice change, as was having a Chairman who came down to the dressing room after games to say well done which I had not experienced before. I don't know how Reg and Ian were with anyone else but they had a personal touch with me which I appreciated, and even though I would go on to have my disagreements with Ian we could always talk. Both of them needed to win promotion that season. Reg had invested heavily in players and announced a five year plan to revamp the Club, and Ian had left Rotherham after promotion to drop down again and spent the money on big signings.

It had been an important and great season for all of us.

10

Sharpshooter Again

There was a feeling within us that we might have started a run that would take us straight through another division as promotion had been won in such great style.

We had the benefit of momentum and the project set out by Reg Brealey was to go up at least two divisions to the equivalent of the Championship. Whilst the team expected a few changes and there were a few biggish signings with the likes of Terry Curran, Alan Young and later Ray McHale, we were aware of the value of continuity and already had great lads who fitted in with the dressing room.

Ray was like a club captain, a wonderful personality who would fit in anywhere, but I wasn't sure about the other two because we looked at them and thought, well, they've brought two stars in, how will it affect us? Young was our record signing and Terry was a massive favourite at Sheffield Wednesday so there was inevitably some controversy and potential fallout associated with his arrival. There was talk that the idea was to try and put about 5,000 on our attendances but knowing what we know now, that was never going to happen and maybe it was a bit naive to think a lot of fans would come across the city with him.

As much as I liked Terry and Alan it didn't work, and sometimes square pegs in round holes just don't fit. There was no doubt that Young's pedigree at Leicester confirmed he had played at a high level, looked the part and led the line but, my word, it was just one injury after another. The result was that I had no feel for a combination with him in the way that I had enjoyed before with other strikers, because he was in and out of the side. Then of course, I would sometimes find myself out of the side so it was all disjointed.

Terry's high profile arrival gave us a lift but against that we had him coming in on the right hand side with Colin Morris switched to the left and I had the feeling that it was a case of too many changes too quickly. In hindsight, maybe there was a case for the old side being given more of a chance together in the new division first, but then again you can't fault Reg for splashing out and trying to improve the team. Spending again would be what every fan would like to see but it wasn't a success with the exception of the less expensive Ray because we needed someone steady in midfield.

There was a real jolt to the system with a bad 4-1 defeat at Portsmouth on the opening day but we went on to build a good record at home and, in fact, won sixteen of our league fixtures at Bramall Lane. Unfortunately, we lost the same number away which resulted in a huge disparity in the way we picked up our points. It was down to the fact that we were based on attack and had a lot of wingers, Tony Towner came in later as well, so our emphasis was on wide play and the forwards. That was pretty good for playing at the Lane but we were picked off too easily on the road and I recall at Doncaster late in the campaign, wondering why we had so many wingers on the pitch at the same time. It was difficult as we had the right intentions but the dressing room didn't have the same feel about it.

Invariably success breeds a good dressing room and you share that togetherness, whoever scores the goals, but when you get a few new players and some move on you have to start all over again. On paper it looked as if we had the right players but it didn't work well enough on the pitch. Now I am a big believer in the fact that it doesn't necessarily have to work in the dressing room before it can work on the pitch, but it is a bonus and can be a real help. For example, when I was at Leeds the dressing room was brilliant, possibly the best I ever experienced anywhere. There was a lot of togetherness during training and that is often down to how you train as well. Billy Bremner got us all working as one and that included that bit of good natured ridicule in giving the yellow shirt to the worst player in training at the end of a session. It was the sort of fun element that I hadn't been used to before.

Our season spluttered along and I felt as if I had lost my partner in crime in Colin Morris. He didn't get as much of the ball as everything seemed as if it had to go through Terry Curran, which wasn't Terry's fault. But it seemed as if it took something away from the understanding between Colin and me because our set-up play was different and we weren't on the same wavelength as often anymore. Of course, it was well intentioned by Porter in the quest to keep making progress and you have to give credit to the Club for thinking on the right lines, but unfortunately the big signings methodology didn't work. Even though we finished what might normally be considered a respectable eleventh, the players in the squad who had been there a longish time felt, as the season went by, a disappointment because things that were successful a year before weren't quite so this time round.

Losing so many games, albeit away from home, must also have been hard to take for Porterfield because he had just enjoyed successive promotions with Rotherham and the Blades, so defeats weren't a regular occurrence. What he wasn't able to do quickly was change the team and get the new players to gel. Terry wasn't the most consistent, a one-off who could be brilliant one week and not in the game the next, and that wasn't something you could ever say about Colin. Young's constant injuries meant our partnership didn't even begin to work, as much as I liked the kid. Once the big signings had been made they were never going to get left out, whilst I was occasionally, and the attacking patterns weren't right. To be fair to Ian I think he saw that eventually but not quite early enough. Of the three big signings none played more than about two thirds of the season's games which illustrates how the side was changing. Curran and Young were good lads and it hadn't been a bad dressing-room, but something stopped us from achieving what we should have been capable of.

On the journey home from an FA Cup replay at Stoke, Terry announced that Everton and Manchester United had been watching him, and I just couldn't stop myself thinking, 'Well, I'm pleased about that for you, but why are they watching you and not me?' I played thirty-seven games and despite the lack of a successful new partnership my goals were still there, albeit only thirteen to Colin's fourteen which included penalties, but even now I wonder why the Gaffer virtually abandoned the superb one I had with Morris just a year before. I suppose in modern parlance you could say that it had been a period of transition in which things didn't fit but Porterfield recognised it, re-assessed and made sure that 1983-84 was another year to remember.

He was quite ruthless in making sure that he got rid of the ones that didn't perhaps fit, including Young and Curran, and bringing in Paul Stancliffe, Tom Heffernan, Joe Bolton, and later in the season Glenn Cockerill. We were to go from being disjointed to a balanced outfit.

Stan came in straight away as captain and although he had already achieved success under Porterfield with Rotherham, no-one knew that much about him, but he won over the dressing room and gained everyone's respect. Joe was the quiet Mr Dependable whilst the highly skilled Kevin Arnott, despite being quite deep, was well liked and came back after a loan, as did Ray McHale. The group gelled and although the facts show that the team relied heavily on goals from Colin and me, with no one else in double figures, it was a real team effort from a squad of players who enjoyed each other's company.

There was excitement in the air from the start because there were rumours that Tony Currie might be coming back and the crowd were singing his name before the opener at home to Gillingham. Feeling that I was now the crowd favourite, my insecurities dictated that I took that as a bit of an insult, and after about twenty-five minutes I curled a free kick into the top corner. The fans had rarely seen me take them before and after eventually scoring all four goals in a 4-0 win I walked off thinking, as much as I like Tony Currie, I hope that's the last time the crowd sing about an ex player whilst I'm on the pitch.

Selfish, maybe, but it was how I was and it definitely helped me with my game. Yes, I recognised TC as the best Sheffield United player in my time, but as far as I was concerned in my time I was scoring goals and there was nobody better than me so the crowd shouldn't have been singing for Tony. I took it as a negative and used it as a positive. The previous season had yielded a relatively disappointing tally for me but here were four goals in the first game on a beautiful summer's day. There wasn't any worry in Keith Edwards anymore and I had started this season with a rattle. It occurred to me that if I thought it had been a great start for me, what must it have been like for my father in London, following it goal by goal?

We were unbeaten until early October when we were walloped by, who else, Hull City who themselves were destined for a good season. It wasn't a turning point though, and we stayed on track despite Porterfield starting to make changes. Keith Waugh played the first sixteen games in goal and was then axed in favour of Paul Tomlinson, and Mike Trusson was eventually sacrificed in the deal that had brought Stan from Millmoor. I was disappointed to see Mike go because he was a good team man and versatile, but Porter must have decided that Stan for centre-half was a must.

Sometimes Truss had played up front and he worked well with Colin and me. He would think that he could get the odd goal up there but his main job was to batter the defenders about a bit so that we could feed off him, which was typical of his unselfish thinking. He didn't see it as a competition and I always benefitted from that kind of thing. Steve Charles would be a hard working grafter down the left, with Colin on the right and Mike and me down the middle and it worked, even though, for example, Peter Withe might have been a better player than Truss. That's the sort of thing I have learned more about as I got older and studied how managers try and construct teams.

A landmark for me was scoring four for the second time in three months, this time 5-1 at Wrexham in the FA Cup with Kevin Arnott also on target, yet it was something that happened afterwards that tickled me. A Wrexham journalist asked me to come to the radio point following the game to do an interview, and who was alongside me but the guy who had been marking me. The obvious line for me was to tell him that it was a shame he didn't get as close to me on the pitch.

He was being asked all these difficult questions so he did very well to cope with that. My dark sense of humour had surfaced and making that remark was irresistible, but it was embarrassing for the lad and I was cringing a bit for him. You wouldn't get a defender whose opponent had scored four times fronting up like that these days.

Our form dipped a bit when we had a wobble in January and February, until three successive wins in a week arrested the slide and happily coincided with the birth of my third daughter, Amy. My fourth hat-trick of the season in a 6-3 home win over Orient in early March came just days after she arrived so in that season alone I had been awarded four match balls – one each for my wife and little daughters.

The £100,000 signing of Cockerill in late March was a masterstroke by the manager because it brought a fresh and powerful dimension to our midfield at a crucial time. We were in the hunt for automatic promotion towards the end until Oxford and Wimbledon achieved that for themselves, and the games against them tended to show where we were short because we could be bullied. They both beat us at the Lane and we only picked up one draw in the reverse fixtures. They battered us a little bit, in addition to having some good players as well. Colin and I could be quiet on some days if we were having the shit kicked out of us but we would bounce back.

We were there or thereabouts in early May but Wimbledon got the points at the Lane and then a 3-1 loss at Bolton more or less confirmed that we wouldn't make the top two. The loss at Burnden Park was eventful because although I scored – and got an injury doing it – a lot of fans regarded it as significant. They liked to think that goal was the crucial one in us eventually going up on goals scored, but I disagree and prefer to say that Kevin Arnott's strike at Southend a few days earlier was the key one. It was a terrific effort and won us three points.

Julie, the kids and Dad were all at Bolton when I put my head in to connect with the ball even though I could see a defender about to welly it off the line. His boot smashed into my head, right on top of my eye, just as I headed in so I was out for a couple of seconds and there was blood all over the place. When I had been taken to the dressing room somebody said I was best having a shower first. Well, I am not exaggerating but it was like a scene from an Alfred Hitchcock film. Blood gushed out before the doctor came in and put about six stitches across the cut – no numbing freeze or anything, just stitched it up.

I found out later that when it happened, my family were escorted round the pitch to see if I was alright. Again, can't see that happening today. My Dad was at least as concerned about what he saw when they had been taken round the back of the goal. It was a corner kick and the players were all crash, bang and walloping against each other. 'Bleedin' ell, it aint 'alf blood and thunder in there, innit.' Despite his love for and knowledge of the game, he had never been that close to professional action before and to him, it was frighteningly physical.

Porterfield said he would drive me to hospital for another check-up which I was pleased about because I thought I would get a lift home, but my pleasant expectations were about to be shattered. I had suffered concussion about half an hour earlier which evidently didn't occur to Ian as he had music on the radio blaring away while I had a right old headache. I thought, turn it down you stupid Scottish bastard. No doubt the lads all had a good laugh at the whole thing and you can't have enough of that for team unity. I remember room-mate Kevin Arnott eyeing my unusually battered condition at that time and observing in his Sunderland accent, 'You actually fuckin' look like a centre-forward now, man.' I think my reply was something on the lines of I'd rather not cos it hurts like hell.

Five days later we had to beat Newport County in Sheffield in our final fixture with the race for third place still in the balance. Our closest rivals were, you've guessed it, Hull, who would also play their final fixture a few days after we had finished so three points were essential to put pressure on them. Fortunately I scored in the away end to get us off to a good start and Kevin added another after the break which sealed the win. We did a lap of honour afterwards, it was the only one I ever did at the Lane because the end of the previous promotion season had been celebrated at Darlington. I was quite choked, even though we then had to wait to see that Hull result at Burnley to find out whether we had indeed been promoted again.

I admit I never thought it was going to end up so close because Burnley weren't a bad mid-table side. Hull needed to win by three goals at Turf Moor to overhaul us, got one early on and later added another with still plenty of time left so it was very tense for our players and fans alike, following on the radio. But they didn't score again and we prevailed – on goals scored. A lot of the lads went to The Royal Oak on Cemetery Road that night whilst the game was on but I stayed at home because Julie wasn't happy about me going. Eventually I couldn't stand to listen to any more on the radio. We each had a bonus of about five grand riding on promotion so it was doubly nerve-wracking, but to beat my old team to it was phenomenal and just so ironic. Football keeps throwing up those crazy circumstances.

I had found the net thirty-three times in the league and had really developed now, picking up two Golden Boots and enjoying two promotions in three seasons, and throughout it all Porterfield had remained pretty much the same. He was a tough character and on occasions really quite harsh on me, but he was always kicking the ball forward in his quest to improve the team. He recognised mistakes made, did his homework and you can imagine how high he was aiming when I tell you the calibre of players I saw come and go for talks about potential moves. Peter Nicholas was one and Ray Harford another, what a signing that would have been.

Within days of going up we set off on the trip of a lifetime, courtesy of the Club, touring Malaysia, and became only the second team, after Watford, to visit there. It had been Reg's ambition to go and maybe part of it was for commercial reasons, but in any event it was my first big long haul trip abroad. I used to love Porterfield's dedication and the first night there was to provide another example. We had all gone out, had a skinful but behaved and didn't get into any bother, but the following morning dawned absolutely steaming hot. We were having a big photocall and Ian had told us all to be properly suited and booted which was just what we didn't feel like. Somebody got a bollocking just because his tie wasn't straight but Porter, who also had a skinful as well, was there with his shades on, still looking immaculate. That's dedication in my book.

The first game, on an average pitch, was won pretty easily against a Malaysian FA XI and the second match was drawn, in fact it was abandoned because of a tropical storm during which we showed how naive we were about the weather in that part of the world. During the game it had started raining which, naturally, we were alright with. It started raining heavier, and we were alright with that. It started thundering, we were still okay. Then it began flashing with lightning and we were still standing there as every one of the opposition players ran off. We looked at each other as if to say, well, should we fuckin' run as well then? Somebody said, 'Well, I'm off,' and promptly legged it so we all sprinted for it, and this was before the ref had officially stopped the game. We had been rooted there like dickheads but the opposition had been well aware of the danger and got off to safety. The memory of that makes me laugh.

The final fixture was in Peking where there were about 50,000 spectators in a massive stadium but somebody had thought it would be a good idea for us to hand photos out. They went mental, rushing and crowding us to get the pictures and it was ludicrous, never mind potentially dangerous. But what I did like was being introduced to a feller who, allegedly, was the politician who had introduced to China the law that families were only allowed to have, I think, one child. I say I 'liked' meeting him but in reality, as a big family man, I wasn't too impressed with that idea.

There were a lot of dignitaries in attendance which was to cause Reg and myself some embarrassment. It was important for us to win the game and although the opposition had a few Internationals in their side, they weren't brilliant and we won 2-1. I must have been getting a bit tired now after a few hangovers but someone shouted for the ball over the top. It was smashed far too hard and reached as far as the running track encompassing the pitch with me still chasing it before shouting, 'I fuckin' own greyhounds, I'm not one myself.' But that shouted sentence went straight down a nearby pitchside microphone and was amplified all the way round the stadium. I used to say things like that for a bit of fun but Mr Brealey came up to me afterwards and said I had to explain myself to the opposition's President. I just mumbled that I didn't know it was going to go all round the ground. It wasn't a bollocking, just a humorous telling off, but when the lads got hold of it we had some great fun with it.

My other memory was a lovely one because Reg said something really complimentary about me when we had five days in Hong Kong and Porterfield was still making us train, even though the season was finished. Promotion had been won, the tour virtually over but he still insisted we went out for a jog. We thought, bloody 'ell, you are having a laugh, aren't you, as we ran on a beautiful promenade with people there wondering what we were doing. I felt fit, happy with life and, at about three-quarter pace, just eased past a few of the lads towards the front – it was a short distance. Reg saw and commented to Porterfield that Keith just strides past the others so easily when they are flat out, which I thought was a really nice thing to say because I wanted people to recognise that I was a bit of a quickie. It sounds a bit vain now but it really thrilled me.

Malaysia was a hell of a trip. We were on and off planes going to different places and although I wasn't really a traveller, it was by far the best I had been on at that time. One of the hotels was in the top six in the world, but we also saw something of the poor conditions in which some of the local folk lived and worked.

One hotel had a hairdressing salon with a beautiful young girl working in there and although I did use it for a trim, I didn't realise until much later that they also offered massage of a certain kind. If the lads had known that and were staying longer I'm sure one or two would have been going in for more than haircuts. Typical of me, when I was having my hair cut I started having one of my dizzy spells, feeling faint and starting to sweat. I had to get out quickly so even if I had thought of getting a massage that put paid to it. Our wives were a bit miffed because the lads had held a vote as to whether it would be a wives trip or not, and the not vote won. I could never convince Julie that I was the only player to have voted for the wives to come with us.

It was a long time to be away from them and children and there were a few tears at times, especially after a few sherbets, because we were a whole day away on the other side of the world. I wasn't one of those that used to telephone home during every away trip, in fact I didn't ring Julie until we were a couple of weeks into the trip. I just wasn't like that and most probably got a bollocking but I did miss the kids a lot.

This was really the first time we had the opportunity to sit with Reg and Ian in a stunning location and get to know each other better. Derek Dooley, a prolific Sheffield Wednesday striker of the 1950s who tragically had his leg amputated, was there chatting to us as well and even used the pool. He took his wooden leg off and just swam round and round. The three of them had good stories to listen to and it was the first time I had ever really relaxed and sat down with people like that on a social level. As for the lads, the banter was different class and I'll never forget being on a coach and Steve Charles, the brightest kid on the block, saying that we must do the Great Wall of China. He was almost pleading with us, shouting to me, 'Eddie. Great Wall of China?'

Well, the rest of us were pretty bolloxed so I said hands up for a beer at the hotel. There was a unanimous response as all the hands went up so I told poor old Charlo that he would have

The whole family on the east coast. Dad probably had a football somewhere nearby

Roseworth Secondary Modern team with Gerry Forrest at back left, my mate Ernest Kilvington at back right, and me second right on the floor – I didn't go there very often!

With a monkey on my back during early courting days with Julie … I'm saying nothing more!

Wedding Belles – my Mam on the left, and Julie's mother, also called Ruby, on the right

Making my mark with awards in my first spell with the Blades
© Sheffield Newspapers

Who says I only did tap-ins? I could do spectacular when I wanted to

© Sheffield Newspapers

Richie Pogmore and me with Monard Pal (right) at Craven Park, Hull

Taking the plaudits from Joe Bolton after scoring against Blackburn Rovers at Ewood Park in 1984

© Howard Talbot Photography

Bob Hatton scored his 200th league goal whilst at United and I claimed my 100th

© Sheffield Newspapers

With Julie and (left to right) Gina aged three, one-week-old Amy and five-year-old Emma, with the four hat-trick match balls
© Sheffield Newspapers

Reunited with my boots which 'disappeared' during the celebrations that followed the Blades' Championship winning fixture at Darlington
© Sheffield Newspapers

Kenny Burns can only watch as I lob my second goal in a 3-1 win over Barnsley in October 1985

© Sheffield Newspapers

Thought I'd include a picture of me heading the ball – I scored with quite a few despite people thinking otherwise. However, this one against Walsall wasn't one of them

© Sheffield Newspapers

Colin Morris – what a player. Talk about being on the same wavelength
© Sheffield Newspapers

Division Two Champions Norwich City hammered us in 1986 but I netted our goals – here's the second which Steve Bruce (left) can do nothing about
© Sheffield Newspapers

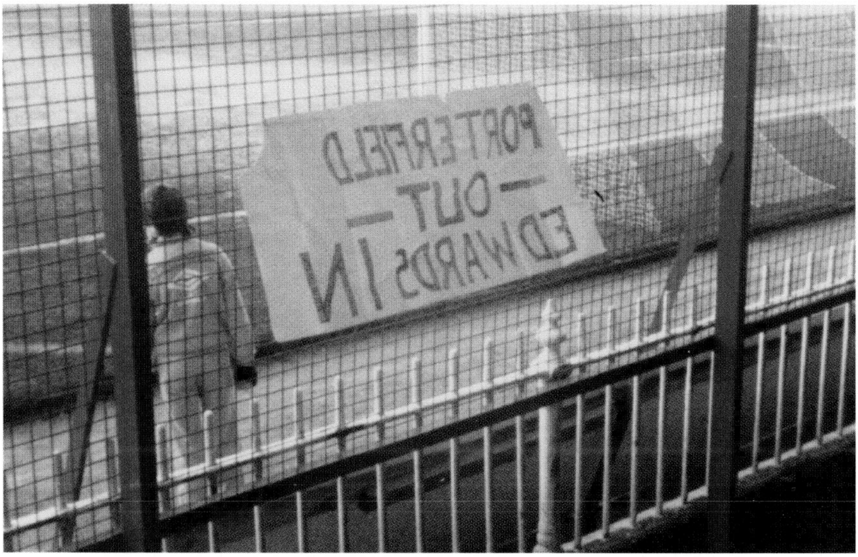

It was always nice to have the fans on your side – and kind of them to hang this poster in a way that I could read from the pitch!

One of my favourite goals for Sheffield United against Bristol Rovers. When the ball came across I dummied the goalkeeper, Pele style, by allowing the ball to run past us both. The difference was, Pele missed!

Signing for Leeds United and Billy Bremner. He was a top man, and a Gaffer who really knew how to manage his players
© Varley Picture Agency

Up against old Blades' team-mates Martin Pike and Paul Stancliffe very early in my spell at Leeds
© Sheffield Newspapers

The team photo at Hull City for the 1988-89 season. Eddie Gray took over as manager and was a real gent

Courtesy of Hull City FC

Big Billy Whitehurst was so unselfish on the pitch – that's one excuse for not scoring as many as me!

Courtesy of Hull City FC

They put me on the programme cover for our FA Cup clash against Liverpool
Courtesy of Hull City FC

Knocking one in for the Tigers in the FA Cup against Liverpool. Always good to give the 'big teams' the run-around!
Courtesy of Hull City FC

My third Golden Boot Award was probably my most satisfying because of my age and the fact it was achieved whilst Hull City struggled that season

With my brother Steve outside our childhood home in Stockton

Courtesy of Blades Photography

Still got it – at my old school, Roseworth Secondary
Courtesy of Blades Photography

My pal, Aidey Sidall, with one of the big trucks we drive at work for Sheffield Insulations

Not everyone can close a motorway for hours but it wasn't an experience I remember fondly

From goal scorer to the family dog-walker-in-chief. Here I am with my son Eddie, along with Stan, Nellie and Millie

At Norton Lees Golf Club with playing partner, John 'Swordy' Wilkinson, and pro Andrew Rossington

I taught young rising star Holly everything she knows about the game. Not!

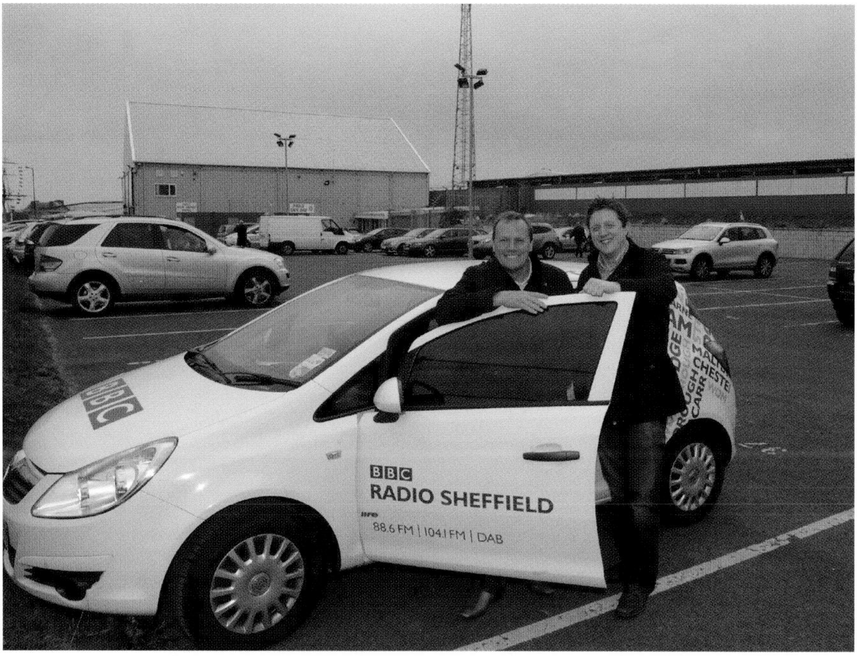

Back in the north-east, this time at Hartlepool United with Radio Sheffield's Andy Giddins

On air at Wembley with Paul Walker as the Blades lost to Hull City in May 2014

to wait another bleedin' year!

Steve, who used to call me 'Zico whilst I nicknamed him Syrup because of his dodgy barnet, was a great lad who wouldn't be offended, and it is safe to say that the rest of us were not culture vultures like him. But I was going to need him when we got back to England so he, deservedly, was to have the last laugh.

On another occasion we were all going to the horse racing in Hong Kong and beforehand Reg came to see us in the hotel lounge wanting to know who were the betting men. Everyone looked at Ossie Arnott and me. The Chairman said, 'There's six hundred pounds, get so much from the lads so they can put into it as well and we'll have a joint bet, but it's up to you two to get it done and pick the horses.'

We got to the track and I was quite excited because six hundred quid plus contributions from the squad was a lot of money. All of a sudden Ossie told me he wasn't feeling well to which I replied, 'Fuckin' tops, I've got six hundred quid in my pocket, I'll make all the decisions then.' Suddenly Kevin felt a bit better which pissed me off because I felt loaded.

We trooped off to the track but didn't really know what we were doing when it came to choosing where to bet because there were queues about eighty yards long. I soon sussed that the smaller queues were for the bigger bets so I quickly suggested we put a bit more on than we were going to. In the end we had a win or two, gave Reg his stake back and had about six hundred to share out with the lads so we all ended up pretty even.

There was a postscript to that story after we had got back to the hotel when the lads from the north east, Joe Bolton, Kevin Arnott and me, were tormenting Derek Dooley who was getting a bit tired and needed to rest his leg. He retired to his room, unscrewed his leg as he always did and, well, I'll let Derek finish the story. 'I sat on the bed, shorts on, lovely day, magnificent hotel, flick the telly on and the first people I see on it are flippin' Keith Edwards and Joe Bolton, walking a horse in at the races. Those two, along with Arnott, have been winding me up and I've come back to my room to get away from them – and two of 'em are first up on the box.'

Every player was paid an allowance of £50 a day on tour which I thought was phenomenal and the whole trip, although hard work in some respects, was fantastic. We flew home and the Club wanted to put on an exhibition at the Lane of all the photos the lads had taken with their fancy cameras. They were to be mounted on a big spread so that the fans could come and view them. Well, for my trip of a lifetime on the other side of the world I had managed to bring back ... six pictures of a racehorse! Julie went ballistic. 'I bought you a camera, the kids want to see where you have been for three weeks and you bring six pictures of horses with little, tiny jockeys on – and that's all you've got to show for three weeks?'

I went back into the Club the next day and asked Steve Charles to get some of the photos that he took and put 'em on my little bit of the display, otherwise I was going to look a right twat. 'Just a minute Keith,' said Steve. 'I remember you voting not to go to the Great Wall of China, and now you want my photos?'

'Oh, come on, Syrup for fuck's sake, gerrem over 'ere – I've got you promotion!'

11

So Long, Ian

Football is so familiar to everyone in our country that as a result everyone seems to be an expert, no matter what level of experience. Managers and players fall out over team selection, chairman and managers over performances and transfers, whilst supporters pay their money and therefore have little hesitation in saying their piece about all of it. Now we have an increasing influence from overseas and whilst I am not necessarily suggesting that foreign management or ownership is always a bad thing, it does throw another factor into the mix about any club's decision making.

To spend or not to spend – and on whom – is a key area that managers and chairmen have to get right. Reg Brealey and Ian Porterfield got it right in 1981-82 when we won the Fourth Division, but then recruitment and letting important players go maybe restricted our progress the following season – or perhaps it was sensible consolidation. That's where opinion can differ and armchair experts and people within the game will always argue the toss about who got it right or wrong. Certainly Porter hit the right balance with his personnel changes in securing our second promotion a year later, but considering 1984-85 and beyond, I reckon the jury will still be out on how he and Reg assembled the squad back in what is now called The Championship.

Again, momentum wasn't maintained, one or two of

us including myself missed games through injury, and for whatever reason there didn't seem to be money for signings. Experienced goalkeeper John Burridge was brought in, plus striker Mel Eves on a free transfer, and later ex-England man Phil Thompson, whilst quite a few lads who had contributed to one or both promotions were moved on. Porterfield was rebuilding a side for the higher level but we won only three fixtures in the Autumn up to the turn of the year, after which we eventually climbed to a final position of eighteenth.

It took us the best part of a poor season in which, basically, we didn't spend enough. Burridge did okay and was supposedly great for the dressing-room but in most people's eyes he was a complete and utter lunatic. That's been said before and will be said again but in any event, with Waugh and Tomlinson, we weren't too badly off in that position anyway. I couldn't understand the move for Eves who was a nice bloke but wasn't a target man or a quickie although he had scored a few at Wolves. Although he did well with us it didn't really work between us.

Someone once said to me that when we were in the Fourth Division we thought like a First Division Club, and when we were in the Second Division we started to think like a Fourth Division club, and I remember thinking it was a spot-on judgement. I doubt you or I know why the Chairman and manager embarked on that policy and perhaps there was a good reason. Maybe this was when Porterfield started looking at the likes of Peter Nicholas and Ray Harford to strengthen the team, players of that calibre he wouldn't have been able to attract if we had been lower down. The money might have been drying up, who knows, but we can all chip in with our 'expert' input.

It was a bit of a stop-start campaign for all of us, similar to when we went up from the Fourth and immediately had a mediocre season. That might, I suppose, have been fair enough in terms of adapting but the expectation levels were always that we would run through the divisions. Oxford managed it, though, winning their second successive title with Birmingham and Manchester City immediately below them

I hurt my neck during pre-season in Sweden when somebody

ran into the back of me which consigned me to wearing a brace for a while. Ian set standards that he expected us to maintain and when we dropped below them he could be lenient with certain players but very ruthless with others. I mean ruthless to the extent that he actually sold some, whereas with me he was of a mind to crack the whip by leaving me out, believing that by doing so I would come back bursting with pride and energy and start scoring goals. Naturally I didn't agree with that theory and we had regular chats when I used to knock on his door to tell him what I thought. Ian believed it was the way round my head but I told him all he was doing was making it harder for me to be top goal scorer.

As it happened my contract ran out at the end of the season and I had talks with Middlesbrough in the summer as their boss, Willie Maddren, had I believe about a quarter of a million pounds to spend. Willie actually knew my brother Len, but told me that because Porterfield wanted 200k or thereabouts I would take nearly all his budget up which he couldn't afford, so he spent about 25k on Gary Rowell instead. We never got as far as talking terms because the fee ended the interest anyway, but to have talks with what was virtually my hometown club was a bit strange.

It never sat well with Julie either because she knew I would be out with my brothers and although, deep down, I was excited about it, I was never really convinced it was the right move as there would indeed have been too many distractions. There was a part of me that always wanted to play for 'Boro, it being the closest club to my hometown of Stockton, but I didn't have the slightest problem with returning to the Lane because I now regarded Sheffield as my home and United as my Club.

But United, again, had been prepared to let me go and didn't take me to America on the end of season tour because I was in dispute and virtually a free agent. Porterfield put up the sheet with the names of the lads going to the USA, minus mine, and scarpered, and I was very hurt to miss out on what was basically a jolly. I wasn't invited just because I wasn't happy about something, so effectively Ian had decided to deprive me of a trip with my pals by not taking me to America when we had already seen the value of bonding in Malaysia.

A lot of us, including Porter, had shared a great journey and I had certainly done my bit but this was a knock I didn't think was warranted. It wasn't unusual for me to have disputes which we'd get over and I would get back but then – bang – there would be another one and it got to be a bit tiresome. I had done more than enough to warrant a new deal, re-thought things and part of my decision to stay was that we were going to sign the likes of Peter Withe, Ray Lewington and Ken McNaught.

The club had made huge efforts to get well-known players, some of them Internationals, who they thought would be good for the club, but maybe were in danger of forgetting those who had helped get them to where it was in the first place. Without wanting to be over critical they turned out to be probably the most disappointing signings of my career as so much was expected of them. McNaught was a lovely feller but by the time he arrived with us he was honest enough to admit he had lost his pace and his way a little bit.

In today's game players tend to find their clubs wanting to tie them down to new deals well before their contracts expire, whilst back then Ian and Reg seemed quite relaxed about things like that. But it was at the heart of the complex I had about how I perceived the way people responded to me. They probably felt they could be like that because, I think I am right in saying, they could still put a fee on a player who was out of contract. Despite my indignation it would be wrong to say that the situation affected me unduly. Although I had only netted thirteen league goals during the previous injury-hit and mediocre season I wasn't worried because I was a confident player by then, used to pulling on the shirt and well established. In the end I settled on a new one year deal after Reg told me I couldn't go wrong with it because I would just score goals again and we would renegotiate next time around. I saw the logic of that because if I did the business I would be in a strong position and if I didn't then United would potentially still be able to sell me.

Looking back to the Middlesbrough link it was fairly unusual then for players to hear of interest in them. Today there are so many channels of communication, including agents, that a player can spit his dummy out if he wants to leave, get the issue in the open and force a move. There was less chance of distraction by rumour, although I did hear from the Gaffer once when we played at Birmingham that Manchester United and Newcastle United were watching me that night. As it happened I cursed my luck that on such an important occasion I was up against big centre half Noel Blake, but I still looked at it as an opportunity and wasn't overawed. I maintain that I had done enough to get an opportunity of a big move because players like Ian Rush had managed a move to Liverpool by scoring goals for Chester, so it didn't seem impossible. But I stress that I wasn't looking for a move and that sort of talk never affected my attitude in a United shirt – or anyone else's for that matter.

*****

On the face of it, season 1985-86 seemed promising as the team eventually finished seventh, which was a huge leap up the table, yet it was to spell the end for Porterfield and me, at least at Sheffield United, and I almost ended up playing abroad.

Ian had ostensibly strengthened all three outfield areas of the team and with Colin still there, I thought a new team was being built, presumably with me as the piece of the jigsaw that knocked the goals in. So what does Porter do? He leaves me out right from the outset. The start was average but not disastrous, and I think Colin played about fifteen games up front with Withe in a new partnership, while I was sitting on the bench wondering, where the hell do I fit in.

I certainly had respect for Colin's ability to play alongside him but I had a long chat with the manager in which I told him, 'All you are achieving is to make my season more difficult to be leading scorer at this football club, making it as hard as possible for me to bang twenty to twenty-five in. You will eventually see that, and when you put me back in you will do what you do best and say that the rest has done me good, and that you have brought the best out of Keith Edwards. But in effect you are pissing me off, I am not playing and you have cost me about seven goals in about fifteen games.' I said that because that is what I averaged and I still ended up getting twenty-odd and being top scorer.

Looking back on my career, especially at Sheffield United when I appeared to be at odds with the management and say I was not playing for them again, and that I wanted a move, it was because I felt they were indeed trying to make things difficult for me. I had scored so heavily for them that when in training I was thrown a bib to wear because I wasn't in the starting eleven, I couldn't help but think what the hell I was wearing it for as I had scored tons for them, and I was better than that lot – so why was I being treated so differently?

That was my bugbear and I have tried, along with friends, to analyse why I was like that for a long time, so perhaps it makes sense for others to come up with the answer. Maybe it's because there were occasions like the one when I spent shooting practice with my hands in my pockets, and still knocked a few in. I didn't always take some things too seriously but to me football was fun, the greatest game ever, and I loved being a footballer and there were laughs to be had. But when we were doing proper fitness sessions and there was seriously tough fitness work that needed doing, I would always do it properly.

I looked at myself as a good trainer and never wanted a day off in my life, but there always seemed to be a stigma attached to me. If we had lost we would be coming off the pitch and I would think, I know what's coming here, I'll be sitting down and Steve Charles will be told that he had worked hard and the others would also get a slight positive, but the manager would get to me and it would be a total negative. I would just smile because it was so inevitable and maybe my reaction was interpreted as a bit blasé.

I saw a defeat for what it was, as I did when I had a set to with Jim Dixon, our trainer, after a Reserve game against a very strong side from the top flight that beat us about 7-3 and won the league that year. At some point I stood up and said we had done well under the circumstances but Jim went mental and tried to give the impression that he cared about it more than I did, to the extent that he just went over the top and followed me to the showers. I had put my towel down and was about to go in when he barrelled up and wanted to scrap about it. We were having a swing at each other, I was bollock naked and he had on all the padded coach's gear in the world.

Here we go again, I don't know why I attract this stuff. Surely it can't be just because I spoke up and said that I thought we had done alright because that Everton team would have beaten us nine times out of ten, in fact it would have beaten our first team. Some players get the emotion all out on the pitch, go home and the wife doesn't know if he has had a bad day or a good one, but I would spin it around my head for days and take it all home, despite how it might have appeared.

Porterfield brought me back eventually at the end of September and I stayed in. I was now about twenty-eight years old, established but confused as to why I was having all this bollocks with how I was. It seemed strange considering I was supposed to be the finisher, the bloke to win you the game, who puts the ball in the net and bums on seats. Okay, the fans might get frustrated with me occasionally if I didn't appear to be doing much, but that was usually when the team was struggling. What was I supposed to do then, head the ball off my own line or kick it clear down the field for someone else – we couldn't all come back.

Colin's pairing with Withe worked on the opening day at Stoke and Morris got a couple so I could see that to the manager it would make sense to carry on with it and, as much as Colin and I liked each other, playing up front and getting off the mark was like a new lease of life for him. He would tell me that the quicker I was back in the team the better, but he did think the team was playing well so it was obvious that it was going to be hard to get back in. Naturally that wasn't good enough for me and my frustration was that the system, despite the team containing a lot of defensive players, was working and the results were okay. Whilst some fans were always encouraging to me, I am sure others would have looked at things logically and conceded that the team was doing alright without me in it anyway.

Then, in mid October, Glenn Cockerill joined Southampton which was a personal disappointment to me as I enjoyed his company very much and he and his wife used to socialise with Julie and me. He was a really good pal and very humorous. When he joined he said he had looked through the team and thought, I bet Edwards is the bloody awkward one in that lot. Although he lived in a different part of the city we met up regularly and had great times together.

So now I was up front with Withey. I bided my time before making a judgement because I respected what he had done in his career, but after three or four games I was screaming and whingeing at him, which was what I did when I wasn't happy with what I perceived wasn't working. To be fair, Peter didn't lose any sleep over me doing that but what I couldn't get to grips with was that he just seemed to foul everybody all the time. It just meant that play broke down and as the last piece in the jigsaw, I didn't get a kick.

Despite all this we actually hit second spot for a while in the Autumn and I ran riot in one five game spell, scoring a hat-trick against Hull and on three other occasions getting a brace. A dodgy December set us back, including a 5-0 hammering at Wimbledon when Withe and McNaught were red carded, and then inconsistency set in. But a spot of largely unexpected Spanish sunshine provided Colin and me with an opportunity neither of us would normally have even thought of.

Seville had a coach who fancied taking the pair of us and a game was set up in early March over there for them to see us in close-up action. The trip was a blast, at just the right time for a bit of a break in the season, and we went out there with our wives regarding it as relaxation, a bit of a late season piss up. All parties knew why the fixture was being played and Colin and I got together with the wives and asked ourselves if we fancied it. There was an opportunity to play abroad and the potential deal being for both would make it easier for us.

Seville had a fabulous stadium with a moat round the pitch, although there were not too many there for a friendly, and Colin had an absolute stormer. I came up against a centre-half who kept dropping off me which was marvellous as it gave me space to play in and attack him. We won 3-1, I scored a cracker, made one of the two penalties that Colin knocked in and, as we walked off, Ken McNaught tapped me on the shoulder to say that he thought I had done myself a bit of good.

Back home later the wives, Colin and I got together to discuss things. Reg Brealey, who was behind a lot of the deals, thought it was great chance for us, but don't ask me why because I was as dumbfounded as anybody as to why they would want to sell us. We were then on £300-400 per week, plus bonuses, whereas Seville's offer was something like £160pw, which I wasn't impressed with, but with an £80k signing on fee for me. Colin's lump sum wasn't as high which understandably disappointed him a bit and maybe affected his decision making. Although Colin and I agreed we should give it a go, the coach who was initially interested eventually got the sack anyway and the move didn't happen because the new man brought in Alan McInally, now of Sky TV, instead.

I had never felt from the outset that I was particularly excited about going and was always worried about how the deals would be structured financially. Not getting any answers was a concern, but we both wondered if we needed a new challenge after three or four years at the Lane and we spoke to United about the finances. I was equally happy either way, despite my little run-ins and grievances with United, and our wives were open-minded about the whole thing.

What I was convinced about was realising that I wouldn't ever have coped if Julie and me had gone on our own because learning the language would have killed me. I would have been the typical Englishman abroad wanting to know why they don't speak English, or asking if they knew who I was, while on the pitch it would be 'I don't need to speak Spanish, just the look on my face will tell them where I want the ball.' No doubt when I got as far as saying, 'By the way, where's the nearest dog track or what is Spanish for Ladbrokes?' that would be when poor Julie would have wailed, 'I knew we should never have come out here! You haven't changed.'

Overall, just being linked with Seville was something I regarded as a compliment, especially when Danny Bergara, who had played there, confirmed that it was a great club and an opportunity not to be missed. But it didn't happen. We tore them apart so it should have done but somehow it became a chapter in my career that wasn't to be written. I like to think that I handled it all really well because it never disrupted our performances for United, and it annoys me these days when you hear trotted out that a player is 'not in the right frame of mind' to play when a move is imminent. What have you been training for all week?

Just three weeks later Porterfield was sacked and the lads, virtually to a man, were stunned. Even by today's standards of rapid discontent on the terraces and in the boardrooms it was harsh, so imagine the impact back then. We were doing alright, more than comfortably placed in the top eight or so, and had won two and drawn one of the three previous matches. But we were spanked 5-2 at home by the eventual champions Norwich City, and Ian was replaced by Billy McEwan, our Youth Coach, until the end of the season, during which time we won three, drew three and lost three, finishing seventh.

Given the results you wouldn't have expected the sacking and when we heard of it in the car park after training our collective response was, 'Based on what? We're putting a team together. We're not struggling but heading in the right direction on the fringes of the promotion race.' To this day I have absolutely no idea why it happened and you would think that his achievements in his short managerial career by then, one promotion with Rotherham and two with us, deserved better.

A lot of people will be surprised but I was sad to see Ian go. When I went on a goal run he was always very reluctant to hand me too much praise, preferring to spread the credit to the whole team which I see the merit of, but he was generally nice to me and loved me as a person. He was someone who stayed in touch with me after he had left and when he was in a hotel in Sheffield with Chelsea he rang me and invited me round for a cuppa, which I was happy to do. I never did that with any other manager, even though a lot of people probably thought we were always arguing like mad because of our spats – but that is all they were, and the proof of the pudding is that when he got the Aberdeen job he bought me again.

He was someone I could talk to and respected because we would have our disagreements in the open and be very honest with each other, which was important to me. Porter would always be on about attitude and I remember saying to him once, 'Well, explain to me what attitude is then?' which initially stumped him a little bit. I asked that because I thought I had a great attitude and cared as much as anybody. 'That's why I am sitting in your office now instead of in the betting shop, Gaffer, asking why you aren't playing me – that's a good attitude!'

Even when I was saying that I felt like I had during the Sirrel saga when his reaction often seemed to be that 'as the result 'didna' go our way we'll leave Keith out.' It just seemed so easy for him to rationalise things like that and Julie, her parents and the kids would often wonder why the number nine always came out on the substitute board with twenty minutes to go if we were not doing very well, yet when we were doing well everyone was singing my name. Even the kids had noticed. But it was different with Ian. When I disagreed about being left out I would go along to his office,and he knew what I was there for because of the speed at which I came through the door. But he would say, 'come on in son, sit down.' The way he used the word 'son' just killed me and that was good management because he was a bit of a pal as well.

So for him to be replaced by someone who he had brought in to do some physiotherapy and then take the Youth Team was such a strange step. No disrespect to Billy because he did well with the Youths, but while shouting at kids might work at that level, it is not the same as doing it to established pros who know the game. I'm not saying Billy was the bullying sort but he was used to being very firm in his coaching with youngsters who wouldn't question anything, and he then found it more difficult with us when anybody did. I was one who questioned some of his methods and recall one little trip when Billy told us he wanted us in bed for 9pm. As far as we were concerned he was having a laugh with that because this was a bit of a break, and to illustrate that it wasn't only me who thought that it was too severe, I had the support of Ray Lewington among others.

Ray, later Assistant Manager for the England national team, was the nicest man you could ever wish to meet on a football field and even he had a pop at the decision. It was an over the top, 'I'm the boss, I am in charge, you are getting fined and we will all be in for 9pm' sort of management. Now some supporters might think that was the right way to go about things professionally, but we weren't dancing around Stringfellows until three in the morning, we were just talking, having a beer, and there was nowhere to go anyway.

For me it was back to the business of telling me what to do again and I didn't respond to it. After all, I was a father, and if you have children you are used to telling them what to do for the best, for their safety, but here was this bloke doing the same to me as a grown man. I am not saying that I couldn't be told what to do in certain circumstances, but to tell me when I have to go to bed at thirty years old just did my head in.

I said to Ray who was skipper, 'Tell him to fuck off or I'll tell him,' so that was basically the end of my relationship with Billy. He knew where I stood with him and vice versa. A lot of the lads didn't like being managed like that which was a real shame because there was nothing wrong with his ability to coach, to work a team hard and get it organised. I would never question that but Billy's way would be to have everyone with a smart haircut, all dressed the same way and highly disciplined like an army camp. In short, some people do it for you and some don't, and Billy didn't do it for me, basically because, like Sirrel, he had one way only.

12

Billy's Boy

Billy McEwan's team building over the summer of 1986 indicated that he was intent on lowering the average age. Whether or not I fell into that category I don't know but I was on my way out of Bramall Lane before the season had kicked off, after playing only another friendly at home against Seville, which was presumably part of the original arrangement.

Derek Dooley simply pulled me in and said, 'I never wanted this to happen, I have been fighting it for weeks on end, but we have agreed a fee for you with Leeds United.'

'Fair enough, and thanks for trying to keep me,' I told him. 'Taking into account the ups and downs I have had here, I will accept what you are saying. Maybe this is the time to leave and I have been bordering on thinking about it for some time because I have been in and out of the team which is not acceptable to me at this stage of my career.'

I did wonder about the ramifications of leaving, about how it would be greeted by some Unitedites who had lamented the loss of players like Mick Jones, Alex Sabella and Tony Currie, also to Leeds, over the years. But, from my point of view, it was a most convenient switch of my place of work to forty miles up the road without moving house ... and it was Leeds United. They were in the same division, looked stronger and better prepared than us, Billy Bremner was now in charge, while

Tony Philliskirk was emerging at the Lane and there were a few younger ones coming in so it made sense.

I had suffered so much negativity from Sheffield United with talk such as Seville want to speak to you, Middlesbrough are in for you and let your contract run out. I was out of the team and then in, so that sometimes it seemed an up and down relationship, even though I had been there five years, scored all those goals, won two Golden Boots, broke records …

Almost convinced already that the move would probably be the right one I told Julie to get the kids in the car because I wanted us all to go up and be part of the decision after I had finished the talks. I put on my suit, got to Elland Road, left the family in reception and was shown through to Bremner who was sitting in his office in his training gear.

'Keith, how are you?' Billy asked.

'Alright.'

'I think you will make a difference to us this season. We need a natural goal scorer and you remind me very much of Allan Clarke and I want you in this team.'

Allan was a Leeds legend and England International so I was obviously flattered by what Billy said, and I agreed that I would like to be part of it. I knew how big Leeds had been and could be again. It took about five minutes to agree terms which went along the lines of Billy throwing some figures at me very quickly, then me hesitating out loud to try and get more and coming up with a higher figure of about £700. Billy smiled and said, 'You're not that good' which made us both laugh. He offered me £500 plus decent bonuses but also told me they would give me £25k if I accepted there and then. That was legal tax-free money as part of the fee that I would get when I went back down the M1 to United and Derek Dooley

Billy wanted to know if it was a deal, but I was quite enjoying the wheeling and dealing because by now I had done a bit of it over wages. I had never met Billy before but was impressed by his positivity so I shook his hand on the move there and then. He was likeable from the start and we did the deal but then his assistant told me to go to the dressing-room, get some kit on and join in training.

I thought they don't know me very well and told them that Julie and the kids were waiting.

'They'll wait for you, Keith,' he said and I was gutted, thinking I had got myself a day off.

Off I slunk to the dressing room to get into the training gear, deciding at that precise moment that I hated training after all the years of never missing any. It was really just the thought of putting strange kit on and running out there, not knowing anyone, which made me not fancy it. I was sitting there doing it very slowly like a mardy kid, contemplating saying that I wasn't going to do it, when I realised I had only just signed and was already causing trouble.

Just as I had my shorts on and was pulling on the second sock the assistant stuck his head round the door to tell me the Gaffer had said I didn't have to train until the day after, so I could get off home. Well, you have never seen anyone get dressed so quickly. I dashed into reception and told Julie to hurry up and get the kids in the car again as I had signed, but she asked what the rush was all about. All I could get out in my haste was, 'Come on, hurry up, back to Sheffield, I've got a cheque for £25k to pick up, love – let's get back.'

We literally went straight to Bramall Lane and I headed for the office in which Derek was waiting. He was amused by how I kept the small talk to a minimum because all I wanted was to ask if he had the cheque. 'Yes, I knew you'd be down straight away so here it is,' he smiled. I thanked him, put it straight in my top pocket and jumped back in the car but Julie immediately stuck her hand out and said ... 'GIVE! There's two Ladbrokes shops between here and home. GIVE!'

'Oh, alright love.'

She knew what I was like and as I reluctantly handed it over I acknowledged it by suggesting that we could get a right greyhound for that but she swiped it off me and put it straight in the Bank, I never saw a penny. I always make a joke of it, even now, and the kids love it even though their main concern at the time was whether or not we would have to live in Leeds.

We didn't and I was happy to commute.

When I went back down the Lane later to say goodbye to Derek I went into the Social Club where I saw Steve Foley and some of the other players to tell them I was going. Most were pleased for me and sorry to see me leave but they wished me all the best because it is understood within the game that moves happen and you all just get on with it.

When news of the move broke I told a reporter in all honesty that I would always be a Unitedite because I had loved it there and your first club is always immensely special. When Sheffield United went on to say that they had offered me what Leeds had offered, it wasn't quite the whole version of events because that didn't take into account the signing on fee. I thought that was slightly misleading because a lot of fans, perhaps in anger, would therefore accuse me of not being a Unitedite because I had still gone. In any event, I think that by settling in the city and doing the Blades related coverage on the radio since, more than proves that I was telling the truth back then about my football allegiance. It was just time to leave for a new challenge.

Reg Brealey had always been great with me and he must have okayed the transfer so there were no hard feelings there, and the move gave me a great lift. That said, three games into the campaign United came to Leeds and won 1-0 through a goal from Philliskirk and whilst I was chuffed to bits on a personal level for Tony, I came off that field absolutely choked. I was competitive and wanted to bang goals in and although I had dealt with a similar situation before when switching between Hull and United, on this occasion I was devastated.

Initially I travelled with Ian Baird, then later John Pearson joined us and we took turns to drive. My first few weeks at Leeds were exciting although to some extent there was a return to the slight lack of self confidence I had suffered earlier in my career, and the first few training sessions didn't go very well for me. Nerves got to me a bit even though I got on with the lads and they had a great dressing room with the likes of John Sheridan, Ian and Glynn Snodin and so on. In one pre-season fixture at Halifax I whacked two in which made me feel better but it wasn't quite right just yet and Billy told me I was probably working too hard. That was a nice change and I thought I would have to sit down because I had never heard that before!

The goals weren't really coming for me but Billy, bless him, wanted things to turn in my favour. He didn't lose faith and kept me in for almost half the season before pulling me aside and confiding that he was going to leave me out. I remember saying to him, 'That's fair enough. I know I'm not quite doing it for you. It's taking me a while to adapt to the style of play, this initial slow build up with me not being the end product all the time – and you have other options. Often the ball goes to Andy Richie when it could come to me, or by the time the ball gets into the box there is just a huge muddle of bodies in there. At Sheffield United we played a bit deeper and I got space to run into as a result.' Billy told me that he did understand, and telling me face to face like a man was something I respected him for.

He would also come out with good comments which appealed to my sense of humour, even when they were at my own expense. Once at Ipswich, when he told me I was back involved as a substitute, I was chuffed and knew I needed to go on a run for him. He told me not to worry because I was going to be in the side for the next six games, but I only lasted two!

Probably for the first time in my life, I was alright about it, and on another occasion when he pulled me in to chat I said, 'Look Gaffer, this is not working out here in many respects. When the ball goes out wide, instead of it being crossed for me in the box it always goes back to Sheridan and Snodin – its driving me barmy.' Billy thought, then smiled impishly and replied, 'Hmm, yeah, but I don't think I'm going to swap them two for you, son.' I liked that. It was hurtful but it was honest and delivered with humour so I went away and thought, I'm not going to fall out with him about it because eventually something has got to give, which it did eventually.

The style was all based on midfield, not back to front, but it would invariably end with a cross to the far post and then just a big scuffle which didn't play to my strengths and even John

Pearson once commented that I never seemed to get it early. It was rare to receive a through ball and if it was bouncing about and I had trouble getting it down and holding it up for the midfield, then it inevitably looked as if I wasn't playing very well.

The daft thing was that when Bremner did drop me to the bench, it turned for me because he would put me on for the last twenty and things would happen. The way of playing when Baird and Pearson were in the side didn't suit me but when I started coming on for one of them I scored a few. On the downside that led to me being tagged 'Supersub' which was a label I really hated. Overall, my goal tally was down by my standards but my performances were good and people never questioned them. I had gone from being a big fish to a much smaller one where it was all about good players like Ian Snodin and Sheridan, and when my touch wasn't as good as it ought to have been I found myself getting bollocked. 'Shezza' was a lovely guy off the pitch but on it, like me, he demanded high standards and whinged a lot, so when I told him that 'whingeing' was my role we just laughed about it and got on famously.

Later in the season, before it came to a climax in which I was involved, the Gaffer told me that he had accepted an offer of £90k for me. It was from Allan Clarke at Barnsley which meant that he could more or less get his money back on me and so I thought, bloody 'ell, I'm on my way again.

When I got down to Oakwell for talks Clarke was really nice. I was back to my usual negotiation stance by starting the discussions off with how much can they afford. Clarke responded by saying that I could have my twenty-five grand signing on fee. I thought, this is great, can I move twice every year? Although he couldn't also match the basic figure I was already on, I thought, alright then, to be fair I can live with that. Off I went back up the M1 thinking I was set to leave but Billy told me the deal was off. He told me that he had been friends with Allan all his life but he had a huge fall-out with him. Apparently the fee had been agreed between the two of them but then Allan tried to reduce it to accommodate my signing on fee. So my potential move had broken a very long relationship.

Billy needed his money back for me because I had only been there six months, and he didn't blame me at all for wanting my 25k, but he insisted that Allan had gone back on his word and should have financed my part of the deal on top of the fee. The significant thing, and a measure of how comfortable I was with Billy's management, was the way in which I just calmly accepted it. Fair enough, I'll get on with it.

My situation was made easier by the Leeds fans being great with me throughout. They didn't see a 'non trier who scores goals,' they saw me working hard, trying my best and I think they were pretty sympathetic because I wasn't missing chances, I just wasn't on the end of things in that system. Driving back to Sheffield after games was my reflection time and I would ponder, I'm just half a yard from getting there or the ball has just dropped behind me rather than in front, whereas at United I would just walk on to it, control myself and knock it in – goal.

At Leeds it wasn't happening and at almost thirty I occasionally wondered if I was just unlucky or maybe was starting to lose it, especially as Leeds had already highlighted stiffness in my right hip during my medical. Having had the Asa Hartford 'hole in the heart' episode they weren't going to miss anything again and my own medical was probably the most thorough I ever had. It was playing on my mind and subsequent years have proved me right as anyone who has seen me limping about since will testify!

But I got through the confidence issue and it all happened well for me when I became kind of comfortable with being a substitute, and making an impact from there. The lads were playing well, we were in the top four or five every week and although I wasn't over happy with my performances, we all got on and had some laughs, as I was always up for those.

One that ran for a while and I enjoyed was when Andy Richie was obviously unhappy with what he had been offered and signed a week to week contract, every week for about eighteen months which was unheard of. I would go in to training and whisper to somebody something like, 'I've heard Sheffield

Wednesday are after Andy' just so Andy would eventually get to hear but nothing would come of it so it would wind him up. Then a few weeks later I would chuck another in, like having a mate on the board at Newcastle and that they were now fancying Andy. I would watch it go all the way round the dressing room to him and he would whisper to the guy who had passed it on, 'Where have you got that from?'

'Keith said it.'

'Where's Keith gone?' he'd shout, just after I had quietly slipped out of the room – I got him every month!

It would infuriate him and he fell for it every time but we had great banter between some good guys, despite my overall disappointment about my contribution. And it was always good to come on and do something for Billy who seemed to have a bit of a bugbear about rivalry with Bradford City for some reason. He told me once to get on against them and straight away I knocked in the winner which I had a happy habit of doing against Bradford. Billy hugged me when we went down the tunnel and I thought, you know what, I'm alright with this because there was somebody there who understood me. I knew I hadn't filled the gap they wanted me to, but I got a buzz out of him doing that sort of thing for me because I had not always had it. He was straight down the line with me and I liked that.

Billy had played his ace card when he suggested I might be a half an hour player at the end of games in that set-up because by then, if we were losing, we would be a bit more positive. That's what happened and I benefitted by settling down and getting some important goals at crucial stages of the campaign. In fact, I got nine league and cup goals so it wasn't as bad as some might have thought. We finished fourth in the league, qualified for the play-offs for the current Championship, and faced Oldham in the semis. Joe Royle had built a good side including Denis Irwin, Willie Donachie etc, and although it might seem strange now, Leeds and Oldham were massive rivals then.

In the first leg, at home, when we needed something because the high ball to the back post hadn't worked, I came on and Shez played the ball in to the near post for me to head in the only goal. I thought, I think I'm proving my point now and, in the return at Boundary Park where the atmosphere was immense, we were in trouble, two goals down and facing elimination until I went on again and nicked another so we went through on away goals. Charlton then got the better of us by the odd goal in a replayed final but we had also battled our way to the FA Cup semi-final when I managed to get another giggle out of the manager. It was against Coventry at Hillsborough of all places and I was very disappointed not to start even though it was not entirely unexpected. After about three and a half minutes play I said to Billy, 'I think John Pearson's having a mare, Gaffer, and I think you should bring him off. I'm ready.'

It was such a great occasion with both sets of fans generating a nerve tingling atmosphere and we drew first blood through David Rennie. When we went 2-1 behind the Gaffer went a bit more direct and summoned me off the bench in search of a goal. I can't tell you how good it felt when I flicked a header from Ritchie's cross into the net and had another effort kicked off the line. It was one of those moments that could have made a difference to a club's destiny. Our style of play had to change when I went on because I needed a bit of space behind defenders to exploit, and Billy was the cute one because he recognised the value of switching styles, and knew when to do it. In the end, although we got done in extra time by Dave Bennett after Brendan Ormsby didn't kick the ball out for a corner, the pain was worth it just to have experienced those moments of sheer joy.

I had my family there watching, including Julie who was eight and a half months pregnant. During the match, I was thinking, please don't have it here at Hillsborough of all places, get your legs closed, pet. Thank God, it didn't happen but our son, Eddie, duly appeared not long after that momentous day. It had been a great game, one that many people said was one of the best they had ever seen and I was absolutely thrilled to bits that I had scored, but gutted about the result. Spurs and Watford played out the other semi in a dour contest but all four teams had been involved in a lot of media stuff beforehand in the event of getting through. It included television appearances, meeting Terry Wogan and was a big deal for those days before 24/7 coverage – and the Leeds lads were on ten grand each just to get to the Final. That was a lot but clubs were happy to pay it as bonuses because, win or lose an FA Cup Final, there was money to be made.

That has, rather sadly I think, been put in perspective now as I have just read that the FA Cup winning club now receives £1.8 million whilst the team finishing bottom of the Premiership gets £60 million. No wonder priorities have changed.

The 'magic of the Cup' was brought home to me immediately after the final whistle of our game. I couldn't see the point of hanging around and I never was a big waver to the crowd, so after I had respectfully done my bit I headed for the tunnel. But none of my team-mates seemed to be going off and as I wandered back towards them I could see that about half a dozen were standing there crying. I wasn't emotional like that so it was awkward and although I mumbled, 'Come on, it's alright, lads,' seeing them like that did upset me a bit. Eventually the Gaffer came over to take us off because a lot of the lads were sitting on the pitch and the crowd wouldn't leave. Everybody was still bawling but I was edging towards the tunnel thinking, bloody 'ell, how long are we going to stay out here..

When we did finally make it back to the dressing room my first thought was, who's got some shampoo because I haven't got any. But when I asked Dave Rennie who was sitting opposite for some he just 'boo hoo' blubbered as well. I couldn't believe it and, honestly, started rubbing my face in my hands to rough it up and make it look as if I had been crying, just in case Billy came in and thought I wasn't bothered. I really wanted to shout, 'Av you got any shampoo or what?'

I don't mean to offend anybody when I talk about being less emotional than most about something that is very special to fans and players alike, but it isn't really in my make-up and it makes me uncomfortable. So when I asked Billy if I could get off as I was more or less at home and he said that we were all going back to Leeds for a big reception, my thoughts were, great, thirty-five miles up the motorway for more blubbering and then thirty-five miles back. We had lost, I didn't want to dwell on it and even Julie wanted us to nip away quietly, although I appreciated that it was important for the fans and off we went. There were loads of supporters and we were told that we were going into the Reception and introduced one at a time. I predictably thought, well I'll get a reight (sic) cheer, cos I scored – but the lads all started crying again. They were undoubtedly a lovely bunch but they didn't just sob, they were really crying and I will never forget it.

It had been a memorable day for experiencing how disappointment can be so sudden and total. In comparison, getting relegated is a drawn out affair so I had never before experienced such a level of disappointment based on one game. Everybody from Leeds was there, it had been on television and the whole local and national media build-up, the occasion, game and reception were unbelievable – the only downside was the result and we were to suffer more as the season ended with defeat in the two legged Play-off Final which went to a replay at Birmingham. At St Andrews we went a goal up through John Sheridan's free-kick but got beat with just minutes to go by a Charlton side that was coming down from the top flight so, in a sense, we had done well to go so close.

I look back on it as a good season, a learning curve during which I had enjoyed the company of some great guys, found a manager I was almost completely in tune with and perhaps most significantly, a way in which to cope and accept when I was not in the team. Although I think I would have turned a corner if I had stayed, I was soon to play my last game for Leeds because I was destined for a new and unexpected move.

13

Border Raid

Part of the fascination of being a professional footballer is that, more than in most careers, it throws up moves to other parts of the country that often come as a surprise and which players don't always have full control over.

Sometimes they want to go, sometimes they don't, and the reasons why can be many and varied. Dressing rooms can be volatile whilst working relationships with other players, managers and coaches can make or break a player. Friendships can be made or snuffed out in an instant when a player moves on.

He will know that he is likely to be leaving when he is listed, at loggerheads with someone, out of contract or attracting interest that will further his career. He can't always know what a manager is thinking whilst trying to juggle a squad, generate finance or assess the value of a player according to what he will get out of him in future. That being the case, sometimes transfers can come out of the blue.

I started the following season on the fringes of the squad, appearing mainly as a substitute but playing a full ninety minutes at home to Hull City in a defeat in September which proved to be my curtain call at Elland Road. Quite soon afterwards Billy got me in and said, 'As much as I like you it hasn't quite worked out and I have the chance to get a few quid back. But don't take it the wrong way because, if you don't go, you are more than welcome here and will always be in my plans.'

When you hear sentences as honest as that you can't fall out with someone, can you? He told me that my old Gaffer was in for me and I wondered who that would be because I had sort of forgotten about Porterfield in that way by then. It's fair to say that when he told me it was Porterfield my response, only half jokingly, would have been that he must have needed someone to drop because that is all he seemed to do with me. I suppose I ought to stress that although I go on about not liking the Jocks it is in a good natured way because Ian, Billy and later Eddie Gray, were all good for me.

I liked it at Leeds but thought about it and accepted that I was always running with that bit of disappointment at how I had not quite nailed it. Ian had taken over at Aberdeen which really was a bit of a hike from Sheffield, or even Yorkshire, but when I discussed it with Julie and the family I said that we should base the decision on the same financial basis that we had gone to Leeds. If it didn't work out then the option would be to move again.

I didn't turn down too many moves in my career and when I heard of other players doing that I just didn't get it. Going to Aberdeen wouldn't be like the Blades move to Leeds because although that hurt, it did make sense. This was different as Aberdeen was the third best team in Scotland and I could go there, maybe knock a few goals in and who knew what could happen then. As usual I figured it was worth going for talks anyway as I had done when I went back to Sheffield United from Hull when Chesterfield were also interested. I had chatted to Frank Barlow and Billy Dearden then because firstly it was a respectful thing to do, secondly, it was the right thing to do and thirdly, I was communicating with people in football. They knew I would probably sign for United but hopefully, by taking the time to see them, they would form a favourable impression of me as a person. It was bearing in mind that later on in my career they might need me and vice versa.

I hadn't asked for a move from Leeds but it didn't occur to

me to turn it down and ask for a transfer in the hope of getting somewhere closer. To me, that would have been wrong and I am certain that if I had it would have struck a sour note with Billy who insisted that I was in his plans. He wasn't pushing me out, just telling me of the interest. The fact that he was prepared to accept the bid because he could see I was struggling a bit, was a respectful gesture on his behalf. On the occasions when I had reacted sometimes in a slightly immature way at Sheffield United – asking for moves when I didn't really mean it – they had really only been empty threats because I was a young and frustrated professional. Billy treated me like an adult and I reacted like one because I never asked to leave or fell out through knocking on his door asking why I wasn't in the side.

I could see for myself why I wasn't fitting in the team. It was doing alright without me and I accepted it, so when supporters jump to conclusions and say that a player is a mardy arsed twat and so on ... When I was at the Lane a headline that had hurt me was, 'I'll never play for Sheffield United again.' My gripe had been the result of not being treated or understood properly, more a case of me saying, this is doing my head in, it's probably best that I move on.

After a rollercoaster of success I was being knocked by the club and I hope people will realise just how many times I was either blamed or not encouraged to forward my career in a better way. Instead, I would just be left out and fans would ask why I wasn't playing in those periods because they knew what I could do. I didn't cause Billy a problem at that stage so you have to ask why not. I kept going in to work, stayed cheerful with him and recall Julie turning to me and saying that she had never known me as happy when I was not playing. I told her 'It's a good dressing room, I love the manager and the training, and I can understand why I am not in. I'm just struggling to come to terms with why I am not being as effective as I was.'

That was especially so as I had got off to a nice start in pre-season with a goal or two and thought this is ready made for me. But deep down I could feel that the style wasn't really going to suit me.

When I first told Julie that Aberdeen had come in for me she never had a negative thought about the place seeming to be about one million miles away because it never really bothered her. As much as she was a Sheffield lass and disliked the moves at first, I think she fancied the idea of moving a long way away, and she was a real support for me in that regard. She still loves her holidays and would always organise ours because I was useless. It's a wonder how I manage to live on my own now.

Her response when we once went to Portugal is typical of her excitement at getting away. We were driving down to Heathrow and I thought, what the bloody hell are we driving all the way down here for when we could save ourselves the trouble and fly from Manchester or Leeds/Bradford? She said that she liked that bit of the holiday. To her it was part of the build-up she loved, it was fun and probably stemmed from going to Cornwall with her parents and stopping off for an overnight in a cottage to break up a seventeen hour journey. I wasn't brought up like that because the furthest I ever went from Stockton was Redcar, fifteen minutes away by car, and even then, three minutes down the road, I would be snoring my head off.

*****

I might as well have been asleep for how attentive I was on my way up to see Ian for talks. For some reason he had wanted to keep the possibility of the transfer quiet and as a result wanted me to fly up to Aberdeen under an assumed name. If that wasn't bizarre enough because this was hardly a record-breaking move, wait until I tell you the name which I had been booked under because he had arranged my ticket and hotel. If you are travelling in Scotland in the 1980s and not wishing to arouse interest, never mind suspicion, you wouldn't choose the Scottish name of a famous television detective, would you? Readers of a certain age will identify with the name Taggart. Yep, that's what I was to be called for this top secret assignment!

It was fraught with the potential for a problem, not least my inability to remember that I wasn't called Edwards any more. I was sitting in the airport lounge whilst Flight ABE 397 or whatever was first announced, thinking, what am I doing dragging the kids all the way up there.

'Will Mr Taggart please make his way ...' asked the PA announcer. All I was thinking of was the name of Aberdeen's bleedin' ground.

'Will Mr Taggart PLEASE prepare to board ...'

Look, I'm nearly thirty years old, I'm still fit and I think I can play in England until I'm about thirty-eight.

'WILL MR TAGGART ...!'

Oh, for fuck's sake, they are asking for me. I fair sprinted to the flight desk and gasped, 'Sorry, pet, I'm flying under a different name because of this daft football manager up in Scotland.' Fortunately, she understood and I got on the plane with everybody looking at me with disgust, tut-tutting away, but almost by the time we set off we were virtually there anyway.

Waiting to pick me up in a Range Rover was a big fat director who was nice enough but didn't say much or try to sell the move to me. At that time Aberdeen was a big club, the team that competed in Europe having been built by Alex Ferguson, and some of his successful squad were still there. With McLeish, Leighton, Miller, Simpson, Bett along with Davy Dodds up front it was certainly a good team.

I like a familiar face because it makes me feel more comfortable so it was lovely to see Porter again. He had put me up in a beautiful hotel on Queens Road on the way out of Aberdeen, the Granite City, which is gorgeous and the nicest place I have ever lived. When we began talks and he started wavering about not being able to match what I was on at Leeds it was here we go again time. I teased the Gaffer by asking if he wanted to borrow a couple of quid because I had a few now, and was that the reason he wanted me up there.

He laughed and said he could give me another twenty-five grand, knowing I'd had that amount a year ago when I had left Sheffield United. That enabled me to make my joke yet again, that I quite liked the idea of being able to keep moving every few months with another twenty five grand in my back pocket.

We compromised with Ian upping the wage from £500 to £550 but with the signing on fee and bonuses on top.

My first league game was a debut off the bench and I managed to get on the scoresheet against Dunfermline, and I also recall playing against Clyde, who were semi-pro, in the Cup when we were on £750 bonus to win, on top of basic. Ian said we wouldn't lose to them and he was right because we beat them by five and I scored. Jim Bett played me through, I took one touch and got a few headlines when I rattled the ball into the corner. As the media were building up a potential rivalry between Ally McCoist and me for top dog in Scotland, it was nice to get a good start and I felt comfortable.

Our stadium, Pittodrie, was lovely and, I am led to believe, the first all-seater stadium anywhere in the British Isles. There was a pleasant crowd reaction, a few English lads in the camp, and our wives and kids all got on which is important. Ironically enough, Peter Nicholas was there so Porterfield had finally got his man, having tried to take him to Sheffield years before. Peter remembered and told me he had really wanted to sign but just couldn't agree a deal and it petered out. Despite having been awarded something like fifty odd caps for Wales, after games he would inevitably feel compelled to ask if he had played alright, as if he needed re-assurance. I would laugh at him but that was just how he was.

We had a very good side but my overall view of the game up there was that we would have eight easy games and then play Hibs. Alright, we would brush them aside but we also had to play Celtic and Rangers so there was this inevitability about many of the fixtures. But what I hadn't fully understood the magnitude of was the sheer scale of support for Celtic. When they came to Aberdeen their supporters just totally took over. The town was a mass of green and white and with a guaranteed full house it was quite intimidating as well as exciting. On one occasion we played them at home and half an hour beforehand the game was called off owing to heavy rain. The Celtic fans went absolutely mental. They just didn't want to leave and we were stuck in the ground for two and a half hours because of the commotion outside.

When I had first joined Leeds and wore the famous white strip I was struck by its history and how special it seemed. You couldn't help but think, God, there is something about this kit, and I felt the same about the red at Aberdeen as they had done so well in recent years. It somehow turned my horizons potentially to European competition and naturally I wanted to do well, but unfortunately, during the week, we trained at a local park – more like dog-shit alley – where coach Jimmy 'put the cones out' Mullen' would set things up . Afterwards we would come back on a sort of minibus and, if I am being honest, there wasn't much talking going on as they were such a quiet set of lads and normally strangely silent.

During the sessions I would stand there while Porter was talking and would be thinking about how slightly weird it all was. It's true that I never listened too intently and would be wondering what horse or dog was running and where that afternoon, or when Julie was coming up with the kids, but I used to look at all these Internationals and think, that's a good sign because they weren't listening either.

Ian was very enthusiastic and in fairness to Jimmy, there probably wasn't anything else to do but put the cones out because Porter would do just about everything. Footballers don't listen very well, or didn't back then, because they just want to train and play, but the Millers and McLeishs were all experienced Internationals and knew what to do. You reach a stage in your professional career when training is just about keeping fit, you don't need the coaching. For example, Jim Bett was normally very pleasant and laid back but on match day he would be nice and edgy because he wanted to do it on the pitch.

Although Ian wasn't given a negative reaction from the squad he was intense in a 'let's get this one done' kind of way which is quite common in the game. He had been like that at Bramall Lane when everyone would listen intently to what they had to do, apart from Kevin Arnott and me, so now I reverted to type again. McLeish and Miller weren't disrespectful but Ian wasn't going to teach those two new tricks about playing centre half. They didn't run the club but they had an awful lot to say at the right time and were extremely professional in what they were doing.

It was like when I later played for Eddie Gray at Hull and got to thirty-two or thirty-three years old. He would say at the end of training, 'Right, we'll finish off with twelve laps' but then to me and Peter Skipper, 'You two just do six,' because he recognised that we didn't need it. The pair of us, like those Scottish Internationals, had done our bit and by then less was more for us. Miller looked after himself to the extent that he would virtually tell the Gaffer when he needed to train. Big Alex was always prepared to get stuck into anything really but the pair of them would control their own tempo without taking advantage and being slack. Davy Dodds was also sensible when he was protecting an injury and that is always fair enough as well.

Younger players coming through needed the full training works but accepted that the older ones were not being allowed special treatment just for the sake of it. It was the same at Sheffield United when Bob Hatton used to come up from Solihull or Peter Withe from Birmingham and were often allowed two days off when the rest of us had just the one. Mind you, it was even more acceptable if they were really likeable characters. When Porter played Dodds in front of me I would say, 'You are joking aren't you, I can score goals for fun in this league.' But really, I had done my fighting and falling out and I wasn't going down that line again.

Aberdeen was still a big enough club to land high profile names, despite the usual predominance of Rangers and Celtic, and the arrival of Scottish International Charlie Nicholas was a great signing. He flew in wearing a Bono hat and within a week most of the rest of the Aberdeen population was wearing them. He was like a Superstar so the first thing I did in training was nutmeg him because I thought, I'm not having this. Seriously though, I was pleased and was looking forward to meeting him because he was staying in the same hotel. In the dressing room he was a breath of fresh air because he wasn't like the quiet ones, he was a top bloke with an ebullient personality and I knew we would get on.

However, it didn't take me long to commit a mistake after arranging to meet up in the hotel. We were breaking the ice as you do and Charlie innocently asked, 'Fancy a bevy, mate?'

'Aye, might as well.' There was me, thinking I could hold my own.

'Couple of pints, please,' Charlie ordered.

We had downed four or five before Charlie asked if I fancied going out.

Well, actually, I was about ready to go to bed but I was weak enough to give in, and maybe I didn't want to lose face, so off we popped. It was pint after pint after pint, I was wobbling and slurring and every time he asked me if I was alright I just nodded and drawled 'yerssch.' Charlie was good company, a top drinker, though not over often, and he certainly didn't carry on in a Jack the Lad sort of way as you might have expected from his reputation. No, he was very clean living, trained right and we enjoyed spending some time together as we were in the same boat in some ways.

It was quite humorous when Julie and the kids had made noises about coming up for the weekend but I was half hoping they weren't so that I could share a glass with Charlie. At the slightest hint of a possible complication for her visit I would ring to tell her and ask if she was still thinking of travelling, expecting her to cry off. But she would stick to her plan, confirm her intention of coming up, and leaving me to plead, 'Err, are you sure love, the weather's really bad up here!'

I'd bought a big Volvo Estate so she could cope with the kids and the drive after we had used up our free flights from the Club, and although it was a heck of a long way she made nothing of it. I now had four kids and Julie staying for the weekend with me in a massive hotel room and we had a great time. She met Charlie and thought he was just wonderful, a lovely personality, and made me feel even worse by saying something along the lines of him having charisma. I just lied and countered with, 'Well, sod that, he's a crap drinker – we went out in midweek.'

They were relatively infrequent flying weekends but it was really great to see her and the kids, and, after a short while, the novelty of hotel living wears off and you miss your loved ones. With that in mind I grasped the nettle, unusual for me, and sorted out a beautiful bungalow about eight miles out. It was also right next to some stables which was perfect as Gina was now into horse riding, and I even found places at schools close by. Frankly, I was very proud because I had managed this all by myself – well, with just a bit of help from ladies in the office as often happens at a football club. I couldn't stop being a tad smug and thought, you know what Keith, Julie thinks you are useless but I've done a top job here, I've done really well. But when I rang Julie and told her everything, apart from the golf course next door, she was really put out.

'What's up with you, you will absolutely love it?' I challenged with some indignation.

'I'm coming up this weekend.'

'Why? What's up, like?'

'Err, I'll come up to sort things out.'

She came up and straight away I told her and the kids all about what I had arranged, really laying it on thick to impress them. Within what seemed only about ten minutes she had cancelled the contract, found another house somewhere else, cancelled the riding lessons and schools and we ended up living fifteen miles further out.

A hissy fit was surely called for and I threw it. 'That's why I never do anything, I just sit back and do jack shit while you do it all. You ask why I don't do anything, well, it's because whenever I do, you just whack it back in my face.'

To be fair to her she found a better house in a better area with a better school. The only thing I got right was finding the stables because we still used it for the riding lessons. Every time we went there I would stir it by telling the kids that we'll go this way round. 'We could have lived in that bungalow next door to the stables but your mother wouldn't let us.'

As usual, she was right. Her parents used to pop up for weekends, my sister-in-law's sister lived not too far away and my plan was always for them to visit so that we could all meet up together. As I said earlier, I was never a fan of hotel life for more than a few weeks because it was too easy to overeat or have a drink and I did miss family life. I thought it right to commit to a football club and settle properly but things hadn't been going smoothly for me on the pitch. I was in and out of the team although Porter did bring me back in when we played Hibs and old mate, Andy Goram, was in goal. Our meeting was to have an unexpected and unwelcome outcome.

When I said Goram was a 'mate' I meant that whenever I played against Oldham and he was in goal I scored, so I was looking forward to it. Sure enough, I knocked one in but then, when we were drawing and I was one on one with him, I took a touch, went by him and then – Boom! He took me off by the knee and although I didn't blame him because he must have been sick of me, it was the first time I had been out injured for a month or so in my entire career and this was bad. Training on my own and having treatment was a new experience and maybe I was getting a bit bored and feeling sorry for myself. For the first time ever I got a bit unprofessional by having a drink during that period, and when I did get back in the running for a place the Gaffer told me that I wasn't selected. That was okay as I wasn't going to entertain conflict by then, but what I didn't want to accept was the alternative.

He told me the news on Thursday, I trained on Friday and then the Reserves played on the Saturday against what was virtually some local farming team. I wasn't having that and, in the manner of Miller and McLeish who took control of their football lives, I thought, well, I'm thirty and I'm not staying in Aberdeen for the weekend. My plan was to fill up the car and head south until I got out at Stockton while Julie and the kids went on to Sheffield. They would pick me up again on the way back at the end of the weekend. Not turning up for Reserve games was something I had never done but now it happened on several occasions, although Ian understood. He was very good about it when I explained, 'Sorry, Gaffer, but I can't stop here if you are not going to play me, it's doing my head in up here at weekends. It's too far away for me to play for the Reserves and still go home. You know what I can do and what I can't do, so if you are not going to play me, don't expect me to play in the Reserves every week.'

I did play in some and rifled a few in to prove a point and ironically, it was in one of them that I scored one of the best individual goals of my life, beating about six men before putting the ball in the net. Okay, it was at a lower level, but the following day I heard one or two of the senior lads who had watched, talking about it in glowing terms which was quite nice because we had never really gelled. Up there we even had tea and cake after matches – give me a pint afterwards any day! When I told Julie about the tea and cake she just said, 'That's what you should be doing at home instead of drinking wine.' God knows why I live on my own ...

That injury period was a miserable one and I plodded on trying to get fit again, but another concern gnawing at me was that my eldest, Emma, was unhappy with her school. She had gone from a lovely school in Sheffield to one that was, admittedly, much further advanced but which had an open plan set-up. When she would say, 'Dad, we're all in the same class, all in the same room,' I couldn't really knock the system because it worked, but I do remember telling her not to worry as we wouldn't be there for long. I wasn't prepared to potter around if I was in and out of the team. I knew I still had something. But when my youngest, Amy, came home and said in a slightly Scottish accent, 'Daddy, when do I go up to the Academy?' I vowed then to leave because I wasn't having a daughter speaking with a Scottish accent.

Don't get me wrong, there were aspects of being with Aberdeen that were beneficial for us. We were winning games and the money was good but it was something entirely different that made an impression on me and which might be of significance when examining why I didn't really settle. I vividly recall doing one particular PR presentation at a school which I didn't mind doing at all and was well capable of. But on this occasion the school then wrote to Aberdeen complimenting me on how well I had spoken and represented the club. I was quite taken aback because it wouldn't have been the first time players had done that, so maybe it was again down to the lads being so very reserved. After training they just went home and never did anything so I naturally put it down to the tea and cake. I'm sure that if we had all sat down and drank four pints after training all would have been fine.

An episode that comes back to me about my frame of mind at that time. I was sitting at home thinking, I'm lost, I've got no pals here, because there wasn't a Kenworthy, Neville, Cockerill, Shez or Pearson to suggest having a beer with or a get-together. I was left with Julie suggesting that I go to Asda with everyone. But as the kids also asked me, I hatched a plan and went along with them all. Once there I just messed about like you've never known, buying everything, eating all the way round and making the kids laugh. We had a great time and best of all, I reckoned that Julie wouldn't ask me to go shopping ever again.

If that was a slightly daft thing to do it summed up my confusion and, I suppose, feelings of isolation, but then spending Christmas up there shocked my system further. At New Year we went to a sports do and to start with I did my usual trick of buying everyone a drink whilst forgetting to buy one for Julie, even though she was teetotal. Then she was up on the floor dancing away with the Jocks whizzing her round, having a great time, while I was sitting there like a miserable old twat. Maybe it was good for her to get away and enjoy a few distractions but it didn't suit me, and I decided that if I was patient I would get my move back to England.

I think I knew my number was up with Aberdeen once I turned up on match day and the feller on the car park wouldn't let me in. I tried the old cocky line I have used countless times since in Sheffield, 'Do you really not know who I am?' but he just shook his head, sniffed and wearily said no.

Eventually I went to see Ian and said, 'Don't suppose you'll let me go. It's not really working out and I've had that bit of an injury.' Knowing what I meant he was as good as gold, and as I was now used to the transfer market scenario I followed up with, 'And I don't suppose you will let me go on a free will you?' That would have helped me get another signing-on fee but it was never going to happen because the Chairman wanted his money back on any move.

Ian and I always talked things through and he understood when I told him, 'It just feels like a bit of a waste of time, Gaffer. I've scored 200 and odd goals but am I going to be forgotten, am I going to have a year in which I play about six games, because you know what I'm like about that. It's the same as when we were at United and you left me out, and I'm not coming up here so far from home and doing that again.'

'Okay, I will make a few enquiries,' he said, and the following day he called me in to tell me that Rotherham had made an approach. I wasn't too impressed, and they weren't paying wages that were tempting either, so I said, 'No, Gaffer, I may be desperate but I'm not called Dan.' That's not being disrespectful to Rotherham but at the time it would have been too big a drop for me both in league status and wages. In any event it didn't take long for Hull to come in but just before they did, at around the time Dave Bassett came to Sheffield United, I had actually spoken to Danny Bergara and Derek Dooley, putting feelers out about a third stint with United. Derek told me he would love me to do that and would make enquiries. I would have jumped at the chance because I was totally convinced I had something left after overcoming the injury.

I was probably at the biggest club I had ever been at in Aberdeen but it just didn't feel like it.

14

Happy Returns, Then ...

So, on Transfer Deadline Day in March 1988, I made my way to Old Trafford, Manchester, to complete my transfer. What, you don't believe me?

The signing part was true but a move to Manchester United wasn't – as if you didn't know. I really can't remember why I had to get to Old Trafford from Aberdeen to meet a Hull official, just that for whatever reason, it was the closest place for us to meet and use a fax machine to register the move in time. It didn't stop me walking in and thinking, if only ...

Hull, then in the equivalent of today's Championship, paid a fee of 60k and the transfer meant a cut in wages for me to something like £400 from £550. This time I didn't get a 25k cut, more like 20k in staged payments, but I wasn't greedy and was prepared to take that drop of about one third in wages. When Porterfield told me about having had an offer from an old club of mine I have to admit that I had hoped it was from Sheffield United, but I had no issue at all about returning to Hull. After all, Roberts was still there, it was a place where I had been successful and where the fans had been great to me. Brian Horton was now manager but Dennis Booth was his assistant and I knew him from my previous spell. Although Aberdeen was a lovely place to live and a good experience, I was looking forward to playing regular football in England again.

After starting off with reasonably lengthy stays at my first two clubs it did feel strange, almost gypsy like, to then have three moves in a relatively short time. That thought amused me as I was driving back to Westhill in Aberdeen to tell Julie and the kids that we were on the march again. The little ones wanted to know where we were going and that's a facet of life as a footballer that most people don't take into account. There can be a lot of upheaval, especially when you have a house, wife, children and schools to consider, in addition to friends and other family.

But I was glad about this move and teased Julie by asking, 'Who do you think has come in for me?'

'Oh, come on, Keith, there's ninety-two clubs.'

'Well, it might be another one in Scotland so there might be a few more to choose from!'

Julie hadn't been instantly happy when we moved to Hull the first time so then I asked her where she would like to go or not go to but she didn't like playing games so I couldn't spin it out much longer. We agreed that it was still a good opportunity, plus we could move back to our house in Sheffield which we had let out but which had been left in a disgraceful state. I had always maintained an immaculate garden with striped lawns and Julie was very house proud, but the tenants had left it in such a mess that we took them to court. It was mortifying to see it like that and I even took a photograph of Emma and Gina standing in the garden to show how high the grass was. When we employed a company to come round and sort the whole garden out properly again, one of the lads who did it, Adrian Siddall, was later to become a fellow lorry driver with me at Sheffield Insulations.

I was so grateful to come back and be playing again and I scored on my second 'debut' at Leicester, then followed up with two at Hull against Huddersfield a few games later. The crowd had given me a big welcome which made me feel at home again and I picked up my partnership straight away with Garreth, who was also my tennis partner. But in the first game at Leicester, Horton had come in at half-time and screamed his head off throughout the whole of the interval. I was sitting next to Peter Barnes, the ex England International winger, and when I glanced at him he raised his eyebrows and said, 'The game's fucking gone, hasn't it?' And that is all he ever used to say. I made an excuse to get out for a piss and he followed me, muttering, 'Game's bloody gone, hasn't it?'

'Yeah, he goes on a bit, doesn't he. Is he like that every week?' I asked.

'Every week without fail, he just screams and shouts. It never stops – even at three-nil up.'

After the game I went back to the hotel and Horton came in and said to me, 'Having a drink, lad?' I was just thinking, here I go again with another bonkers manager, when he added, 'Don't worry about me ranting, that's what I'm like all the time.'

'Yeah, you were a bit full on, weren't you? They did get a bit of a bollocking but, by the way, that won't work with me, I've just watched McLeish and Miller!'

To be fair, Horton was fine with me and I knocked a few in but he wasn't there much longer and was replaced at the end of the campaign by Eddie Gray. Any change of manager is a concern for players because it's about timing and it can make or break you, but I was quite excited about the new season.

In training we were doing free kicks and I said that I would take them from this side. That was okay and when we moved across the pitch I said that I would take them from that side as well. One of the coaches got really pissed off with me but my reasoning was that I was not being above my station, I was just keen to get involved. I reminded him of the situations in which players don't put their hands up and suggested that, as I was experienced now, he should be looking at players like me to take responsibility. In other words, don't knock me for that.

I didn't know Eddie but I got on well with him and liked him right from the start. He was a lovely, very polite man who respected the senior pros, and almost annoyingly, he was the best in training every week – what a stunning player he would have been at his peak. Pre-season was effective and sharp, very much about the ball, and I felt good because I was fit and running better than for a while. We started encouragingly when my goal saw us to an opening day win against Manchester City but although I got on the scoresheet regularly, draws and losses both exceeded victories in the first half of the season. The running of the team was such that I could see us making a bit of progress even though we were in the lower reaches of the division. Richard Jobson was a good player, Billy Askew had a beautiful left foot and, of course, you know my thoughts on Roberts.

Out of the blue one day Eddie called asking me what progress had we made. That he did so I took as a genuine compliment because he wasn't testing me, he was valuing my opinion and equally truthfully I replied, 'This is a million times better than it had been under Brian Horton. I know the results are not great but that is because we don't pick up much on our travels.' We did climb a little bit but the truth was that we had three or four individuals who basically just weren't good enough, and if Eddie could have replaced them we wouldn't have been a bad side.

This period of my career, coupled with the fact that Eddie was to part company with City, could have been very significant because if things had worked out differently my life after playing may have turned in another direction. He asked me if I fancied staying behind regularly after training to do an hour with the seventeen and eighteen year olds instead of getting off home. That bit of responsibility in training and helping coach the kids did make me feel good. It inevitably increased the regard I already held him in and could have resulted in me trying to stay in the game after I retired. Circumstances conspired to put a stop to it and I didn't pursue that option when perhaps I should have done later.

Despite our lowly league placing none of us felt Eddie was under pressure as it seemed to me that he was slowly putting something together. He did leave me out once which pissed me off a bit and I asked him if he knew how many times he thought people like me score in the last ten minutes, which he accepted with good grace. I also accept that most likely he left me out because I wasn't playing very well, and the good thing was that we spoke about it without rancour and moved on.

Incidentally, I have a bittersweet recollection of a couple of events that occurred at the same time in December of that season. We were fortunate enough to be taken on a mid-season tour to Bermuda when there was a weekend off from our normal league fixtures. It was a huge perk but we flew back home on the same night that the tragic Lockerbie air crash occurred in Scotland and as we were made aware of that before taking off, our own flight had a distinctly eerie feel about it.

Life was pretty good on a personal level on the field as we reached the halfway point of the season but my equilibrium was to be shattered when I lost Mam. From the age of fifty-seven she had suffered from Alzheimers, spending some time in a care home, so I had made sure that I kept visiting her on a regular basis, and Dad had moved back to the north east into the family home. My brothers and I made the decision to ask Dad to come back and I think he was glad to do so. Ironically, his own mother had died of the same illness and he had endured a torrid time as she would occasionally go missing in the middle of London.

Whilst Dad and us brothers, as kids, had done things together, usually sport, Mam had been in the background doing all the household things that mothers do as well as being a school cook. She was fairly quiet, a tough character and absolutely first class for us, but she would never let us do anything for her, even though she had four sons plus a husband she didn't really get on with. I bought her a beautiful coat for Christmas once and she gave it to Steve's missus, Anne, because he was out of work and they were having a difficult time. Mam would only permit herself a couple of simple pleasures such as playing bingo and staying in a caravan occasionally which she loved. But although I could afford to buy her a caravan she wouldn't let me. She was a woman who wouldn't take anything from her family, apart from that couple of bottles of Newkie Brown when I visited.

On Christmas Day I got the call saying that she had died at sixty-four and I was mortified. Steve had left it until tea-time before ringing so that I could have the day with the girls, so I straight away went for a huge walk to clear my thoughts before telling them. Christmas was never going to be the same again.

There was nothing good about the way her life had petered out and I wasn't happy with some of the people who had been looking after her in the Home. On one occasion she was being pushed in a wheelchair and her foot was dragging underneath. Being responsible for her was the first time my brothers and I had to deal with anything like it and we weren't very good at it. Steve and I have talked many times about whether what we did in terms of the care home was right, because when she used to go missing it was just so scary. And I felt a bit disloyal because we had done so much with Dad whilst Mam was really the backbone behind everything. That was probably the way it was for thousands of post war working class families but it was of no consolation to me.

When we were growing up we had always known that Mam and Dad weren't right together. When he was a lad he really loved his mother and wasn't fussed about his Dad who left for another woman in Colchester. To Dad, nobody could measure up to his Mum and in those days you tended to marry the first person you really went out with. Lo and behold Julie, the woman I married, was the first girl I had really met.

The news shattered me but we had a game on Boxing Day at home to Bradford City and although I really loved playing and wasn't an emotional softie, I was thinking that I shouldn't play. It was so tough dealing with my mixed feelings but I held it together for the kids, even when Julie told me to let it out. The girls were a different proposition for me though, and they cracked me up because they were gutted for me.

The decision was reached that I would go and play but I told nobody about Mam, not even the young team-mate I gave a lift to. It was 1.30pm and I had been sitting very quietly in the dressing room when I realised that I couldn't go through with it. I felt so tired it was unreal, and nobody knew about this woman who had missed out all the time, or the guilt that the rest of the family were feeling that she had been so alone even when we were all together.

When I went and knocked on the Gaffer's door I just lost it

and burst into tears. Eddie was obviously a bit shocked by it all when I told him, 'I can't do it, Gaffer, I'm really sorry. I know it's a big game.' He was absolutely fantastic and went on to tell me about a personal family tragedy he himself had suffered. To be honest, I didn't really want to hear all that because this was my own private little grief, but the way he handled it was as kind and thoughtful as it was possible to be. Then he told me to get myself off, taking as much time as I wanted. I felt as weak as a kitten but I wanted to see my brother and check how everyone was.

I thanked Eddie and made my way out but there was another difficult hurdle to negotiate. As I mentioned earlier, at Hull there was a big tunnel outside the dressing rooms where the fans used to walk past. I had to go down the tunnel in the opposite direction to the expectant supporters coming in full of the joys of the season, slapping me on the back, and they must have been wondering where I was going whilst they were greeting me. That walk was such a difficult thing to get through because my head was in bits.

I missed that game and the next one at home to Ipswich which was also drawn, and just literally stayed in Stockton feeling too weak to play. Then, prior to the funeral, my brothers, Dad and I were asked if we wanted to see Mam for one last time. My brothers decided not to but I did even though I had never seen anybody laid out like that before. She looked beautiful and Dad guided me through it all which was nice given what had gone on before.

In fact, I came to watch the second game and everybody at Hull City was fabulous to me, but I was taken by surprise when Eddie came in and told me to get a bit of kit on and do twelve laps with a bit of a run round. I thought, back to normal, you are having a laugh aren't you asking me to do twelve laps. But I did them and they seemed to take about three weeks because I felt as if I hadn't trained for a year. I was absolutely shattered but it didn't occur to me until much later that it had most probably been the right thing for Eddie to do. I had to regain my sharpness so I put my back into it.

Dad had been very calm about the death because he was a calm man anyway, and he was seeing us through it because he had lost his own Mum. We had persuaded him to move back up as he had been sitting down there in London with people breaking in on no less than five occasions. I was so pleased he came back and he never left, moving eventually to a bungalow.

*****

Mam's passing had coincided with the arrival of goalkeeper Iain Hesford and Billy Whitehurst who returned to Boothferry Park like me for a second spell, and I was really glad to see him back because our partnership was always going to work. As he was so physically intimidating everyone saw him as this rough, tough character but he was also very nice when he had to be. That was evident when I popped into the dressing room before the Ipswich game just after Bill had signed. He spotted me and said simply, 'Alright, Keith?'

'Alright, Bill.'

'Sorry about your Mam.'

'Cheers.'

That was all but we hadn't seen each other for ages and it was typical of Bill. He had his ups and downs in life but I judge people by how they were with me and my partnerships with him and with Colin Morris were the most effective I ever had. That season was phenomenal for me and I can't overestimate the help I got from Billy. I used to say to him, 'There is only one thing failing in this partnership and that is I am not making enough chances for you.' Then I did create some for him and he kept putting them over the bar so I changed tack to tell him that now he was getting chances but the difference was that I could finish and he couldn't!

Talk about smash 'n grab! It was mainly about getting the ball to Billy and me feeding off him, but that became a bit of a cop-out so we developed a little more subtlety as well. Garreth knew what we both needed in terms of different service so that helped, and Billy and I combined by playing to each other's strengths. And talk about looking after me throughout the game just through his sheer presence. Of all the people I actually played up front with he was the only one who defenders were 'worried' about. They were concerned about me, but they were worried about Billy because of his physique and bravery. I used to tell him I took advantage of what he represented but Billy didn't give a toss because it worked for both of us and, as with Colin Morris, there was no jealousy. Bill accepted it like a man and knew his role but, more than anything, we used to have so much fun.

We went to Sunderland once and as Billy used to play for Newcastle we knew he would get more than the usual stick so, just before the warm-up, Billy being Billy said, 'Come on, we'll get out early and go to the Roker End, just to piss 'em off.' He told Hesford to go in goal and me to set him up with some shots at goal as if he was really trying. When we did he purposely kept on blazing the ball over the top, much to the delight of the home fans who gave him dog's abuse, totally oblivious to what was going on. He was trudging back looking all disappointed and I would say loudly, 'Come on, Bill, try again.' He did, and WHOOSH! the ball went miles and the crowd went mental but I was almost in tears through laughing.

Bill thought it was great and said, 'You watch, I'll shut them up when we start because I'll rifle one in.' The game began, I managed to set him up and WHOOSH! the bloody thing went miles over the bar again! I said, 'Bill, the fuckin' game's started, you are still taking the piss.' When he got a bit too carried away later and managed to get himself sent off, my helpful and consoling comment to my vital co-partner was, 'Bill, don't get sent off, you will be suspended for two games and what am I going to do then.' He was great fun. Eddie had brought us back together and if he had added a couple more decent players things could have turned out differently. We clicked from day one and although every game was a bit of a battle I was to thoroughly enjoy that season.

*****

I came back with a vengeance and a real sense of determination after Mam had passed on and got two goals at Barnsley on my return. That was the start of another run in which I scored twelve times in league and cup, equalling the eight game scoring sequence I had achieved for Sheffield United. The eighth fixture was at home to Liverpool in the FA Cup fifth round and I was desperate to score because to me it was all about my Mam. As the opposition included the Beardsleys, Grobbelaars and Barnes I couldn't help but think, it would be Liverpool, wouldn't it?

The game went quite well for us, especially when Billy scored but Liverpool levelled through Barnes. That was meant to signal the Reds assuming control but when Billy won another high ball I got in behind two defenders and clipped it back across the goalkeeper to regain the lead on the stroke of half-time. I was in heaven, having gone from the lowest point of my life to equalling my record, one which, unashamedly, I had considered to be phenomenal for such a young player. Now I had equalled it as a thirty-three year-old in my first eight games back. Talk about feeling proud. I had an effort kicked off the line late on and wished we had drawn 3-3 instead of losing 2-3 because it would have been lovely to go back to Anfield.

Nevertheless, it had been a great occasion with Boothferry Park rammed and a lot of TV coverage and signing sessions. The highlight for me, though, was what Eddie Gray said about me and I will never forget him going on TV beforehand and stating with such conviction and style that he had never worked with the lad before but goalscoring is an art – and he has got it off to a fine art.

I had watched that and thought, bring on Liverpool. Man management is about little things like that, comments that inspire and stay with you. Eddie was very professional but I admired him not just for that but for the way he handled my worst personal moments. Sometimes you get people at the wrong time in your life but I tell you what, in Eddie I got someone who was just so right at that time, caring for me in a difficult period.

Allow me to digress for a moment as it is appropriate to talk about an episode that caused me distress because it inadvertently put another great man unfairly in a bad light, although the real measure of him eventually shone through again. Upon leaving Leeds I had done a story with a Daily Mail journalist, mainly because it was part of the job. When I was asked what went wrong at Leeds I answered by saying that it just didn't work out although I was not too bothered about going down that line. But he didn't let go, saying that there must have been something.

I considered whether to accept the interview and eventually, because I do have opinions which I am getting paid for now on the radio, I agreed. I explained that Leeds didn't really play to my strengths and it was all about midfield. The story came out with a headline along the lines of ...

'YOU'RE GETTING IT ALL WRONG, BILLY'

It was the first time I had ever done an interview like that and I was distraught, feeling as though I had been stitched up, even though the journalist would not have been responsible for the headline. I had explained how I really liked Billy and was happy working for him. Moreover, it had been the only time I could stand there, not be in the team and be able to say that it wasn't due to any fallouts, but because I was either going downhill or just out of a bit of form or whatever. If anything I had let them down.

Desperate to atone I sent the interview fee off to charity and wrote a letter to Billy, apologising to him and the Leeds Board. I had never done anything like that before or intended what I said to be construed like it had – almost insulting to the manager. It had never been my style to leave anywhere on bad terms so it was hugely disappointing and I was very careful in interviews after that.

Billy was Billy Bremner about it and didn't fan any flames but I didn't get a response from him or bump into him again until I was at Hull. Eddie called me in and his great pal Billy was sitting there. It was a little unnerving but after we had shaken hands, I again attempted to apologise and tell him that

I had been misrepresented. Billy just accepted it and dismissed it out of hand because he knew the score and that is why we would never have fallen out. The episode had really upset me at the time because I had heard that Billy had been annoyed, but he didn't blame me and we continued to respect each other as friends. There was no grudge – he was brilliant like that.

*****

My support for Eddie made it tricky on occasions because it was difficult to take somebody like Billy Whitehurst to task occasionally in training, but I did because of wanting it to go right for the Gaffer. Can you imagine me now running over to fetch the balls back whereas before I wouldn't have dreamt of it. I felt loyalty to the manager and Billy could occasionally piss about but he was great for the majority of the time. We just had a laugh as when Billy and I both talked like Tommy Cooper all the way through a match that we won easily. I think Dennis Booth, who was a real character, started us off and the opposition defenders were so baffled by us doing something so ridiculous that it unnerved them, and it clearly worked to our advantage.

I wanted all the lads to like the Gaffer and they did, by and large, although Andy Payton, who went on to become a very good player, did have a bit of a negative with the dressing room. My take on it was that maybe he wasn't too keen on me scoring plenty of goals, and one or two players had overtaken him, so he had a bit of a whinge. But I did sympathise because I remember thinking, well, that's how I was earlier in my career. Funnily enough, much later when I was back once at Hull doing a radio programme, Andy rang the station which surprised me because we hadn't always seen eye to eye. He had wanted to score the goals and be the best player as I had wanted to years before, so I was a bit wary when he first came on air, but he was very complimentary which I much appreciated.

For all my hopes and confidence about what Eddie was building we won only one of the last eighteen fixtures so it is no real surprise that we finished just above relegation in twenty-first spot. Obviously as a team we weren't a winning combination so, in my opinion, to top score the whole of the division with twenty-six league goals made winning my third Golden Boot one of my best ever achievements.

Ian Wright finished second and Kerry Dixon third with Palace and Chelsea, respectively, and both of those teams went up, which sort of proved a point to the likes of Aberdeen, Porter and those that I crossed when I was left out of a side. I had my whinges at places like Bramall Lane about being dropped and now, in my mind, I could say, well, that's what I was on about when I said I was better than those who were put in instead. Ideally I would have loved to have been as successful for Billy at Leeds, because that would have been extra special but, nonetheless, I was pleased to do it for Eddie.

It may be considered controversial to hold this view but I genuinely think that great players often see things straightaway that others don't, and can see strengths and weaknesses better than others. In any event I definitely believe their personalities and man management methods appealed to me and made me want to do well for them as well as myself. There was never a problem with either which is quite telling. Maybe people will come to the conclusion that I was just a mardy arse sometimes which makes good gossip rather than consider what might have gone on behind the scenes.

If returning to Hull was good for me because I rediscovered myself as a player following disappointment at Leeds and Aberdeen, going to Aberdeen had been flattering because Porterfield had made me feel needed again. But that didn't work so it is ironic that the move to Hull was the only time I ever signed for a club almost purely on the basis of finance. When potential transfers are offered a player has to add up all the pros and cons and then justify the decision. I factored in that Julie could go back to Sheffield and her family, the kids would be back home and if that just meant me travelling to Hull every day, so be it.

Now I look back with fond memories of the place and it is

so strange that now one of my lorry drops of plaster board in Hull is at a housing estate which was built on the old ground, and the delivery note is even headed Boothferry Park. My route there is just the same as it was, except I drive my big articulated lorry straight through what would have been the dressing rooms right into the middle of where the pitch was. On a recent drop I was standing there looking around and a bloke asked me if I needed anything but I just said, a little misty-eyed, 'It's okay, mate, I'm just reminiscing.'

He probably thought, what the hell is he on about but it was sad for me – and what a beautiful pitch Hull had, by the way. As at most clubs there had always been some negatives at Hull. They were potless when they had to sell me the first time but I absolutely loved that second spell.

League position apart, everything was going great. Eddie was in charge and looking to strengthen the team, I was a Golden Boot winner again, I had extra responsibility for the first time ever, and we were all looking forward. But it was all to end in disappointment as Gray was bombed in the summer.

15

The Bitter End

It might be a generalisation but footballers today are often associated with a lifestyle of male grooming, celebrity shows and the glitzy glamour of the red carpet. Before that some of the highest profiled stars shared ownership of racehorses and could be seen rubbing shoulders with the great and the good in top hat and tails in the swanky areas of Ascot and Cheltenham.

I liked greyhounds.

That is some way off being flamboyant and speaks accurately about my being a council lad and regarding myself as a pretty basic sort of bloke. I have never tried to betray my roots or make myself out to be more than I am, and the theory came home to roost when a dog I gave a home to later turned out to be more valuable than I was.

Its usefulness outlasted mine as a professional footballer, but the first I actually owned was called Carrie and belonged to a friend of Joe Bolton during my second stint in Sheffield. After watching it run a fair race at Doncaster, Joe, Paul Stancliffe, Tony Kenworthy and me bought it between us, but it soon became my best pal because she ended up in my care.

The four of us had watched it run at Owlerton and afterwards we all got bladdered on Ecclesall Road and started talking about which one of us should keep it. Joe seemed the obvious choice but as he already had three it fell to me. I don't think keeping her in a centrally heated garage did much to help her become a racing snake and she didn't run much after that. The kids loved her and Julie, as usual, obligingly fell in with the idea for our sakes.

At Leeds I was able to keep her but the transfer to Aberdeen threw up a problem so Steve and Dad looked after her and she became more of a pet than a racing dog. Upon returning to Hull I decided to tread that path again and bought another, already a racer, from Aughton, near Sheffield, for the tidy sum of £1,200. I wasn't knocking about with the Hull lads because of living in Sheffield and my former United team mates had moved on, so it became a little hobby that was also enjoyed by the family, particularly the girls.

The week's dog activities consisted of two nights of racing, then on Sundays watching the trials or helping the dog called Peg, get fitter. Although it is not really a girly thing my daughters would tell you even now that they loved helping out. We gained a nice group of friends through it and although I raced the dog and had a little flutter, it was only ever a kind of plaything for us. It would be easy to be labelled as someone with a bit of wedge spending this and that on gambling but that wasn't the case at all.

The attraction for me was looking after Peg, training her, maintaining her weight and managing injuries pretty much all by myself. The two eldest girls became quite competitive in a small way about betting, I'm talking coppers here, not pounds, and Emma became very annoying because she was always winning and Gina wasn't. I had to try and put that right with my expert knowledge which rarely worked!

When Peg wasn't in season she would usually race at Brimington, Chesterfield, once or twice a week, which was good fun and just what I needed to perk me up at a time when I was feeling a bit on my own, largely because of the travelling to Hull every day. Having been used to Julie putting me at the bottom of the pile after the kids I thought, well, I'll show her, I'll get a greyhound.

That was another decision that backfired because I soon lost my place at home to the dog as well, effectively relegating myself to sixth! But it was credit to Julie and typical of her that she embraced the idea even though she probably didn't approve of it in the first place. However, she won't be happy to learn from this book that the dog had cost me £1,200 because I had told her it was only £200!

Peg did alright, won a few races and on the occasions when I felt she would win I would bring Steve down for a visit to put a few quid on it. I sneaked a bit more out of the bank without Julie knowing again and, with a couple of good wins, basically got my money back on the price I had paid. Steve had seen my relatively comfortable lifestyle and was perhaps a bit intimidated by it, so on one occasion when we got back from a race meeting and were bedding the dog down in the garage I played a trick on him.

As he was counting up the winnings I barked urgently, 'Bloody hell, put it all away, Julie's here' and he panicked, all fingers and thumbs, as he tried to bundle it away. When I told him I was joking he gave me a right telling off as he had to count it all again and there were £20 notes all over the garage floor. The pair of us do look back at that and laugh but Steve earned a bit by coming down and putting the bets on, rather than me which might have looked a bit dodgy. It was what you did on those flapping tracks, all part of the game and you weren't guaranteed to win.

I do wish being involved with greyhounds didn't carry a label of 'he must be a bad lad spending all his money at the dogs' because I didn't go mad. There were no flash cars, Julie had whatever she wanted and I just enjoyed getting out of the house with Peg for walks and training. It stimulated many good conversations with Billy Whitehurst because he knew his dogs and that, along with my friendship with Garreth, was another reason for me enjoying that spell at Hull. That dog had cost me 1,200 quid and was worth its value, but less than a year later it was me that was on a free transfer.

Being asked by Eddie Gray to do a bit of coaching had given me such a lift and I was aware that players who retire and stay in the game usually start at the bottom in that way. Being involved with that part of football for the first time was a bit of a buzz and I had found the enthusiasm to want to stay behind and help. Who knows where it might have led but I went up to the north-east before pre-season in the summer of 1989 and heard the news that Eddie had gone and Colin Appleton had been appointed. I was shocked and very disappointed in Hull City as training had been fabulous, there was a good set of lads and positive signs developing but the board lost patience.

I rang Billy Whitehurst who knew Appleton from a previous spell and asked him what the new man was like. He said simply: 'Dour. And tha'll not like him.' He was right. I walked into the old changing rooms after the summer and there he was doing the ceiling, boarding out, or tidying up because I think he was a joiner by trade.

'Hello,' I ventured.

'Alright.'

'What'ya doing?'

'This dressing room needs tidying up.'

'Oh, that's your job then, is it?'

I had never met him before and thought it was a strange thing for him to be doing, although I suppose you could say fair play to him for mucking in. We started pre-season training which, although a necessity, never really inspired me and is something I regarded as a bit of a ball-ache. The best I ever had was with Eddie because it was always with a ball, achieving fitness gradually, and I was fortunate in that I never felt unfit and always got back on track without too much trouble.

By now I was thirty-three years old and putting a few pounds on as you do but I certainly felt okay. For his first session the new man got us all together in the main stand, stood on the track, looked at us all and said, 'I will only keep you for twenty minutes because I know footballers can't concentrate any longer than that, so I won't waste my time.' An hour and a half later he was still babbling on. Unfortunately for me, I was the type of guy to say, 'I thought we couldn't concentrate after twenty minutes – we've bleedin' well been here an hour and a half.'

Showing my annoyance didn't get us off on the best footing but I maintain that some people are very fortunate to get their opportunity in football management and I don't believe it is as hard as people make out. To be perfectly honest, I thought it was a complete shambles. He probably didn't like the way I trained and thought that I didn't give a toss, that I didn't have to train, which wasn't the case at all. I was just basically looking after myself and by the time the season started I would be as fit as anyone for my age. That is logical and, taking into account the fact that I had scored twenty-six league goals in the previous season, I think it warranted a degree of respect.

City always trained round the back of the stand and I went there for the afternoon session, but for some reason that day it was being held on the main pitch so I was delayed. It wasn't like me as I don't do late, but he walked up when I got there and said, 'Piss off!' I was quite shocked, and peeved enough to think, yes, you know what, I think I will. Sod you then. After changing I decided not to go straight back to Sheffield but instead spend some time in the bookies before going back to the ground at the end of the session. Garreth, one of the nicest blokes in the game, knew what I was like and asked if I was alright because he thought Appleton had been a bit over the top. I agreed and, probably emboldened by his support, went to the manager's office to see him.

Now I am what I am in certain situations, which can be right or wrong depending on the way I am perceived, but I stood in front of him and said, 'What the fuckin' hell are you doing, telling me to piss off not only in front of everybody but to a thirty-three year-old father of four. I've obviously gone to the wrong session and I apologise for that but we had always trained round there. And then you come round and say that to me. I am fairly laid back but I'm always punctual and I'm a senior professional. Do you not think that overall, you are a bit out of order with that?'

I wasn't trying to undermine him but I couldn't take a liking to him in any way whatsoever, and he didn't like my way either so it was uh-oh, here I go again, in a conflict situation.

I had just enjoyed good rapport with Billy, Porter and Eddie but now I was back to somebody who couldn't deal with me or get the best from me. I could tell he wasn't going to play me and I don't know what he said to the board but it wasn't long before they told me they had accepted a bid of sixty grand from both Stockport County and Scarborough. Strangely enough, or perhaps not because they knew me, my old pals Danny Bergara and Colin Morris were at those two clubs, respectively. At the eleventh hour Colin rang me at home and asked me to go there, but I had to tell him that I had given my word to Danny at County, even though there was a cut in wages. Colin did offer me good money but owing to my respect for Danny stretching back to the late 1970s, I felt I owed it to him to honour my word.

My time with Hull City just crumbled, ending in friction and I could never see us getting over it. The fans had been through me leaving before and didn't take it very well, but City had got their money back so they might well have believed they had done the right thing. I never found out whether the deal was done for financial reasons or because of Appleton's influence.

Stockport was run by Sheffield businessmen, Howard Stephenson and Brendan Elwood, and at first I looked at going there as being a bit of a drop because I looked back to just a few months previously and wondered what might have been. I'd just had a great season but right at the start of the next one the feelgood factor and optimism vanished straight away. That, as the saying goes in cliché world, is football.

Maybe I should have told him that I was staying there, just to get on his nerves, but it would have been time wasted because I really wanted to play. Presumably my name would have been circulated so, had I been patient, other clubs might have come along but I was optimistic about joining up again with Danny and enjoying the way he felt the game ought to be played.

My focus had to be to play every week and not become a player happy to just sit there and pick up his money in the Reserves. Throughout my career there had always been players challenging for my place and I had to keep scoring goals to see them off, that was the competitive element I always liked.

To not have that and sit in Hull's Reserves after rowing with a manager who wasn't going to use me, and to then decide I would just toss it off was not for me. There wasn't time at my age, even though I willingly took a pay cut and there weren't too many other clubs knocking on the door willing to pay sixty grand which was a lot for County.

Stockport put a lot of work into getting me, their record signing at the time, and it represented a bold move because although I had recently scored freely, you never know when age could become a real factor, or a move not work out for whatever reason. But in David Frain, Chris Beaumont and Darren Knowles, they had players I knew from Sheffield which at least helped for sharing the travel, but it was exactly that kind of thing that landed me in trouble with the law further into my Stockport days.

The Club took us on a short trip during which we stayed very close to Gibraltar and Danny told us that cars were available for us to use to get into town. A few of us took the opportunity to do that and relax during a bit of a drinking session. I was wearing a green top, similar to one worn by a lad who was driving through the centre when he lost control, whacked into one stationary car, then another and then a third, although not at a speed that would be too dangerous.

Stunned, probably through the effects of alcohol, he sat there blinking before opening the door, saying, 'I'm fed up of driving, I'm not driving anymore,' before getting out and leaving the handbrake off. Yours truly, quick thinking as ever, jumped out and into the front to pull the handbrake on just as the police arrived. They saw me in a green shirt like the driver, and locked me up overnight. The squad had been told to be back at our hotel at a specific time for an official function and Danny could hardly believe it when Darren Knowles raced in to tell him that I was in prison.

The following day Howard Stephenson got me out and after a rather Mickey Mouse type court hearing I was fined £200 but given no penalty points. We were walking back through town with me apologising, saying that it hadn't been my fault as I hadn't been driving, when Howard said, 'Well, how much are we telling the lads you got fined, seeing as you've spent a night in prison?' to which I immediately responded that it will have to be at least £600! There were about six of us and they got off totally free so, although we didn't do them for as much as that, we took them for a few quid. Call it compensation for taking the rap.

Joining Stockport was definitely a shock to my system, beginning with entering the tiny little dressing room. Someone suggested that I get changed in a particular place and I had just started when this big lad came in and said that's my place, I've used it for the last five years. Oops! Then I was told that we had to take our own kit home to wash. 'What? Are you having a laugh? The missus won't be happy with that'

But I thought the ground was fine for that level and the fans were a bit excited because, and I am not being big headed, this transfer was what they had always wanted – a player with a record of scoring goals coming in from a higher division. Funnily enough, my first game was a win against Scarborough and I knocked the only goal in, which is a good habit on debut, but other signs weren't so encouraging.

The hip stiffness diagnosed at Leeds was getting worse. I wasn't as mobile and all of a sudden Danny shocked me a bit because we were lamping the ball from back to front into the corners and I couldn't get there anymore. This was a real turnaround because at that stage of my career I wanted the thing coming into feet but it was going long. Age and injury dictated I should be trying to adapt to what I could still do and this was the first time I began to realise that those factors were catching up with me. Danny would have understood that because he had been a player but I told him that it seemed as if he had changed his ideas of years before and changed to English style football. I couldn't get on to the ball but there was a big lad up front with me in Brett Angell who did benefit. He was a good finisher and I was outscored which was possibly the first time ever when I had played regularly.

Although I did manage some good games and goals,

including a couple against Cambridge, I wasn't consistent. I couldn't turn like I used to and felt more sluggish than during the previous season. The best bit for me was some nice touch football with David Frain and I did okay up to a point with ten goals in twenty-six starts. Indeed, when we watched the game videos afterwards the lads were very complimentary, saying how they could see why I had played at a higher level because of my movement and so on. That was great for me but I couldn't do it on a regular basis.

I had to come to terms with the fact that I couldn't be as effective any more so I tried to play to other strengths, but I was going downhill and when you get older you find that your good games are still good, but your bad ones are very, very bad. It always hurts when fans give you stick, which is fair enough because they have their expectations and don't always know the circumstances, but that was to become harder when I slipped into non-league.

In my own mind I had always felt I would play professionally until I was about thirty-eight but the years I had from about thirty-three showed a rapid decline in what I could do. I was in agony at home with my hip aching all the time and it wasn't like having toothache because that can be cured. The pain was there now for good, despite the physio loosening it up a bit which never lasted very long. In confronting the fact that I was irrevocably declining I reasoned that my decision to move on from Aberdeen and Hull to play regularly had been justified because by doing so I had squeezed as many senior games in as I could. If that had meant dropping a hundred quid a week to play then, as long as I had some in the bank, I'd live with that.

Danny stood by my inconsistency for so long and then, towards the end of the season, loaned me out – up a division – to Eion Hand's Huddersfield Town who finished just outside the old Third Division play-offs. Leeds Road was a good old football ground and in Ewan Roberts up front I had a big target man to feed off whilst Iffy Onuora was pretty swift on the wing. My first game was in the Reserves with a lad called Robert Wilson who just played one-twos with me all through the match. We both enjoyed it and for me it was because our play was more patient which gave me chance to get up there. I thought, this could be alright.

Hand mainly put me on the bench to start with but I got in eventually, scored twice against Rotherham to start a personal run of four in five games, and the loan had gone quite well. However, I don't think I was quite as dedicated as I ought to have been and maybe being as relaxed as I was about my football and training had caught up with me. That struck me when centre-half Peter Jackson later came to Huddersfield. We had faced each other a lot when he was at Bradford City and it was fair to say that I looked upon him as not being particularly fit or agile. But as he got older he trained his socks off, focussing on being very fit and it showed. I am convinced that I should have done that to stay nice and sharp for longer, but that was down to me again. I liked a giggle to lighten the mood during the hard sessions.

It was soon to come to an end, really through lack of movement in my hips. I had been naturally fit and was still sharp over ten or fifteen yards but age and wear had done for me now. Jacko, now superfit, had really got stuck into it because he had recognised earlier on that he needed to do that. I go back to when I was playing alongside the veteran Bobby Hatton when he had a great season, even though he would probably have been around thirty-five. We were winning and scoring and although it may have bugged him that I scored more, he got his share by adapting his game as he grew older. I had that in my mind to do but if you are playing in a struggling team it is much harder, and six months after leaving United and joining Cardiff, Hatton retired. United fans loved Bob so much, but in just months he had gone and football can do that to you. I hadn't known at Hull that it was to be my last season of quality, of turning and moving to give myself the space to score with relative ease. I had finished above Ian Wright and Kerry Dixon in goals but a few short months later, in pre-season, I had fallen out with a manager and then, gosh, didn't things go pear-shaped quickly from there.

When the loan finished and summer was over I was back with County for a good pre-season with Danny and Roger Wylde, and I was really touched by how nice the fans were to me. Having not really justified being their record signing I had feared I might be in for a bit of a roasting but they were fine and gave me a warm reception. The return was short lived, however, because it wasn't long before Huddersfield came back in to buy me for about £30k, and Danny accepted the situation which seemed fair enough all round.

Given that I was moving back up a division, and to an environment I was familiar with, it should have been all the incentive I needed to enjoy a real swansong to my career, but it proved to be a disastrous and thoroughly distressing finale. Critics who believe that a breakdown with another manager was an appropriate ending to my time in the game might derive some joy from my demise but the reality was humiliating and entirely unnecessary.

Although Eion Hand had seen fit to buy me it didn't take long at all for him to somehow decide that I was a bad egg. Doing the journey up there for a while by train inevitably resulted in, on rare occasions, being unavoidably late for training which you know I hate. But it meant I crossed the manager because he reckoned it was a contributory sign of me not trying a leg. That wasn't the reality, even when things weren't going too well for me. I was never a sulker and would think, well I'm going to work, I'm not in the team at the moment but I can still have a laugh with Jacko and one or two Sheffield lads there such as Chris Marsden. They could remember what I used to be able to do and to an extent I was living on past glories but I was coming to terms with it. The physio did his best for me when I was telling him that my hip was screaming but he knew in the end that there was little he could do.

Because I was quite jolly most of the time, Hand thought I didn't care and was a bad influence so he fell out with me and made that clear very aggressively during a one on one in his office. I asked what could I do as I was struggling, but he was accusing me of not wanting to do it. What would I have to gain by that when I wanted to stay in the game as long as I could? You normally got a bit of leeway if the manager had brought you in so maybe with my performances not being great, he thought it reflected badly on him.

It wasn't intentional and I recall a hard relay session during which the individual legs we had to run were each a full lap. Fortunately, the team I was in was winning when it came to me on the final leg, but it was very competitive and I belted round using every ounce of energy I had, just managing to hold on. But to do a full lap at pace at that stage of my career took it out of me to the point where I was physically sick and dizzy afterwards, although nobody knew. I felt like death but wanted to prove that I was a trier and not backsliding.

There was another opportunity for me to do that when I accepted a month's loan at Plymouth Argyle over Christmas, before Hand and I really fell out in a big way, but it was destined to fail. Manager David Kemp needed a bit of a goalscorer but even on the train on the way down I was conscious of how far away it was, and unbeknown to me then, I had started this process of frustration with football.

Julie tried really hard to make it easier for me by visiting with the kids, despite the distance, but I was staying in the same hotel as a big lad who played up front and he asked me out for a bevy. I did and we had about a dozen which didn't get things off on a great footing. We played at Oldham on my debut where I just about touched on a cross and claimed the goal because I thought at least I could say I had scored. Eventually I was made sub and, to be honest, I drank too much down there but I was on my own and this guy kept asking me. Ironically we went out and Tommy Tynan, who had a good spell at Sheffield Wednesday, was in the same pub. It was an inauspicious loan and didn't spark a glorious return to Huddersfield.

Whatever I did cut no ice with the Gaffer and in the end he told me to, 'Go and fuckin' train on your own.' He was killing me off but I went with the kids first and then on my own. The first team would go one way, the kids in the other direction, and one of the coaching staff would tell me to go and do laps.

That was round a park and I did it but then I went to the empty ground and just ran, completely on my own to try and keep fit. I looked around and thought, well that's me done now, this is all coming to an end, and we were only three quarters through the season. I couldn't avoid thinking back to being a little lad wanting to be a footballer, hearing about Denis Law who had started his career at this same ground. There were all these little memories of wanting to be a player crowding my mind and it was all disintegrating during those token laps.

When Hand told me he wanted me out of the club and would be paying me off I said, 'Okay, but I don't know why you have such a negative with me and why you think I don't want to try.' He had stopped listening by then but we agreed on a settlement. It was when the free transfer lists came out that it dawned on me that the dog had cost me £1,200 but I was being given away for free!

It had been vindictive and horrible of the manager to make me train on my own considering the career I had, and when I make comments on some of the managers today it is through an awful lot of personal experience of how some go about their work. I would go home and almost be in tears, wondering why this man disliked me so much that he would do that to me. It was beyond my comprehension because he must have known what I had been capable of. Lo and behold, there was a little spell when I actually got back in the team which I just couldn't weigh up, so I assume that somebody must have been injured. It was at Reading and I scored what was to be my last ever goal as a professional when I ran in between defenders and half volleyed past the keeper from eight yards.

It was a thrill because I so wanted a goal to prove to him that I was trying but that my body wouldn't let me in the way it once had. There is no shame in that and it should have been accommodated properly. I had worked very hard in that fixture to the extent that fans who really knew Keith Edwards would probably not have recognised me, but none of us knew it would be my last goal. And with only a handful of away supporters at the evening away fixture it wasn't exactly a fitting end. In celebration I put my hand up, relieved because I wanted to make up and get back on track. There was still a real desire to be respected and given another chance to prove I was worth keeping. Although Hand eventually subbed me and I was totally bolloxed on the bench, I thought I might have turned a little corner and be kept in ... but it didn't happen.

It was a difficult situation to deal with and I thought, for God's sake, just pay me off because my relationship with football just wasn't the same any more. Without doubt, it was the worst time of my career. Training should be fun and I always thought that as a striker you needed to get on with the lads because you wanted them to make you goals, so I had banter with them. If you weren't liked by your team mates it would show during a game because you wouldn't get the ball, and that wasn't the case with me. It got to a stage where I went see him to try and turn the situation round instead of rowing because it had almost got to fisticuffs on a couple of occasions. That was something I hadn't experienced before and I thought it was pathetic.

The effort to try and reason with Hand probably paid off. I told him that I really admired the fact he stuck by his team, that in the previous seven games he had kept faith in his strikers who hadn't done very well. Bear in mind that I wasn't in the team so I wasn't currying favour on that one, in fact I had tried to highlight a strength of his to turn our relationship around. Hand came back to me the following day to tell me that he thought Cork might be interested in me as he had spoken a few words with them. All of a sudden he had made this effort for me to go over to Ireland to play, then he threw Halifax into the mix as well and genuinely tried to get me fixed up.

I'd like fans to know that yes, footballers can be a bit temperamental but sometimes they have a reason for that. Maybe there is an injury or other players haven't taken to them, but a manager should recognise those issues and help his players. Telling somebody to go and train on his own or wanting to fight him is not management, and in that heartbreaking three month spell at Huddersfield I just completely lost my love of the game. Sheffield United fans might ask what I should expect from wearing blue and white stripes.

I went home after being paid up and thought what am I going to do now. How does a manager who is aware of how much it means to become a footballer in the first place, feel about ending someone's career, albeit for his own reasons, just by saying, that's it. Even though I had tried to make him feel like a complete twat by trying to turn it around, the way it was done was still a mystery to me.

For a couple of weeks I sat at home hoping the phone would ring, whether from Cork, Halifax or somewhere else, but it didn't and I was mortified. Even though I was disillusioned, if somebody from a club had asked me to come with them I would have jumped back up and gone, not because I needed the money, but I just thought that in the right environment, admittedly with the right team and the right manager, I could find it again. After all, it wasn't two seasons ago that I had been taking the piss out of defenders in the Championship and winning a Golden Boot, so surely I could play again.

Fans of Huddersfield and Stockport had seen glimpses of what I could do and I felt as if that could come back at any time. I was still fighting the fight in my mind even though I knew it was coming to an end, and I suppose anybody playing sport feels like that unless they retire before they start to decline. It was awful and it can't ever end well because you find yourself having to accept that you are not good enough anymore. The silence from the telephone was deafening and I knew that the longer I went without training the less likely it was to happen. I thought, this is me done.

16

Break-Up

It wasn't golf that finished Julie and me.

There were enough other issues in our relationship that contributed to its demise and maybe the way I struggled to adapt to life without football accelerated the process. It would be fair to suggest that I didn't see our time together coming to an end although I wasn't naive enough to think that everything about us had been rosy in the later years. My pre-occupation with golf didn't start until football had finished and, although it was soon followed by divorce, I am thankful that my hobby gave me a new passion which helped me negotiate an awfully difficult time and begin to rebuild my life.

Danny Bergara had introduced me to the game at the Norton Lees Club in Sheffield but I didn't play regularly until making friends of others who did. Then it began to replace football for me even though I was pretty average when I started. It was a challenge that intrigued me to the extent that I would play twice a day, having become a five day member in an attempt to become competent enough to eventually compete at a decent level.

After leaving Huddersfield I had fourteen months off but came to terms with packing in within a few weeks because I knew that when the new season started, I would have been out of the game too long to expect to get back in. It was painful, but it was done and I couldn't do anything about it. Dad, now in Stockton, was quite philosophical about me finishing, reasoning that I had enjoyed a good career and scored a lot of goals and so on.

But he didn't like how I initially sat around literally waiting for somebody to give Keith Edwards a call, and I confess that I am a bit like that, instead of going out and making things happen for myself. But I believed in fate and that certain people come into your life when you need them so I was prepared to let things happen. We had savings and policies so were getting by, the kids were okay and even though Julie and I weren't getting on too well I believed we would last forever. Although I don't think Julie divorced me because of my finishing football, it was awful timing given my state of mind.

She was patient at first when I was out of work but after a while I was sitting in my chair in the house once when she came in, put her head round the door, and said, 'Not got a job then?' and if looks could kill I would have been stone dead. Although I have never been, and never will be, a drama queen I honestly admitted that I was lost and scared to death.

That's when the Golf Club seemed to be a great place to meet people who might offer me something as far as work was concerned, and to be fair I would have done anything. Julie was a morally upright and decent Yorkshire lass and probably expected me to get off my arse and find a job, and she was probably right to expect that. But it was tough to know she felt like that about me, after all, she had given me four kids – and I had provided everything that she and the children had needed. She knew I was devastated about my career ending and gave me some leeway to search out a new career but on balance, I took it too far in delaying finding a new job.

I wasn't quite done with playing, although at a lower level, and within just a few weeks of finishing might have moved back to the north-east following a potential offer of a job with ICI, combined with playing for Billingham Synthonia. Oddly enough, my old schoolmate and fellow pro Ged Forrest went up there with me on the same basis, and although nothing materialised I was given an astonishing demonstration of personal support going all the way back to my Sheffield United days.

Warming up before the special game they had set up against Newcastle United Reserves my attention was attracted by Dad and two of my brothers in the small crowd. Walking round just before kick-off my brothers had spotted a bloke, with a couple of his pals, wearing a tee shirt with my picture in Blades kit on it. 'Isn't that our young 'un?' they said to each other incredulously. They could hardly believe that anyone should take such trouble to travel up there for a meaningless game, that didn't even involve the guy's own team, just because I was playing. Dad was really thrilled and we made a point of thanking who I now know is Bill Brearley, a fanatical Unitedite known to many supporters and obviously a particular fan of mine.

It made me feel so proud that he had driven from Sheffield to Billingham despite my having left United several years earlier. Although I would have said hello and thanked him, I hope I conducted myself properly because I was truly shocked, and I will always owe Bill for paying such a tribute. At that time I had not long retired and was missing it a little bit so for him to bring it back to me in that little way was pretty special. In bumping into him once or twice at functions since and chatting to Bill I have learned also that, despite his regard for me, he never latches on and makes a nuisance of himself. He just isn't that type of guy. In fact, he will probably be embarrassed about his inclusion here but it's nice for me to be able to repay the kindness.

What nobody else knew during that game was that I was given a sharp reminder that my playing days were likely to be numbered, even at that level. One of my opponents annoyed me when he caught me a bit late and out of character I have to say, I had a bit of a lash at him. When he retaliated and lamped me in the chest, my God it was painful, and I thought, I think it's time to pack it in, Keith, they are starting to hurt!

Another flirtation with non-league football involved a brief reunion with ex-Hull colleague Dennis Booth as his brother owned Stafford Rangers at a time when former Wolves defender George Berry played for them. In my first game I'd scored a tap-in and still felt I wanted to carry on playing because it was plain difficult to pack in, and I still wanted that little buzz that scoring gave me. Admittedly, I didn't have a great game and as I walked off around half a dozen fans yelled at me, 'Get some mud on your shirt, lazy git!' Without thinking I turned round and said, 'Why do you have to get mud on your shirt, just to run around. Aren't you supposed to play on your feet?' Despite the brief high of scoring it was another example of me thinking I'd had enough because it was a case of now that I can't actually run. You want me charging around like a headless chicken?

But I still had one or two more stabs at it. Several months on, back in Sheffield, and coming up the eighteenth at Lees Hall, I spotted two men mending the roof on top of the clubhouse. Unperturbed I knocked the ball close to the flag and one of them, who turned out to be Paul Mitchell, the manager of Alfreton Town FC, said to his mate that I looked fit. His mate replied 'Yes, but can he still play?' They shouted over to me, got my number and gave me a chance to play for eighty quid a game which I decided was at least worth giving a go. But when I did it merely confirmed the earlier realisation about my good games being good and the bad ones, horrendous.

I knocked a few goals in during a decent start for the team, which included a lot of lads local to Sheffield, and I didn't mind training on Tuesday and Thursday nights, but my experiences were mixed to say the least. A hat-trick against Worksop Town encouraged me to think, this is an alright decent team, but in another we were awarded a penalty and when I shaped to take it Mitch shouted, 'Don't let him take it, he hasn't done owt all game.' He must have been having a laugh because I popped the ball on the spot and put it into the top corner. Afterwards he told me he didn't think I was going to score which surprised me because you don't lose skill as quickly as you do fitness. Other than that, Paul was great with me and although it may have been something of a coup for him to say that he had brought me in, the truth was that I was bolloxed and couldn't be a blue-arsed fly any more.

I would most probably have been better off dropping into midfield, trying to influence the game from there, but managers hoping for a touch of scoring magic would never have seen that. Instead they would think, you are joking aren't you. Keith plays up front and will solve our goals problem. I got that in charity matches in later years all too often as well. 'Go up front, Keith, we'll knock it into the corner for you. Hello! We would get hammered and I would walk off wondering what the point of it all was. In one such fixture for BBC Radio Sheffield against Sheffield Steelers Ice Hockey team I was up front with TV sports presenter, Damian Johnson, and the evening proved both lively and productive.

Bored, I ran back and clattered Steeler Tommy Plommer, a good footballer who had played at a decent level in Scotland, as well as starring on the ice. He was feisty and, rare for me, I was up for it as well so we had a bit of a scuffle, nothing too nasty. After the match when both teams changed and got together to socialise I met up with the hockey lads, including Ron Shudra and other Canadians, and found them fabulous company. Along with Tommy they were great and asked me to join them for golf on the following Sunday. They were to come back into my life later following a chance remark I had made after that football match.

Aware that ex-Sheffield Wednesday player Lawrie Madden had done a bit of summarising at his old team's matches on Radio Sheffield, I asked the radio boys why there was no pundit covering Sheffield United games in the same way. They suggested I gave it a try and my broadcasting career started. It was also to lead eventually to my third serious relationship.

My marriage was deteriorating as I floundered around completely lost but oblivious to the signs of how things were going to change between Julie and me. She was trying to keep things together, bringing in whatever money she could, and it probably looked to her as if I wasn't trying to help out. I was doing my football but that didn't bring in much and I think Julie was falling out of love with me in that period.

The amateur football fizzled out but, largely through PFA funding, I decided to take driving lessons to be a heavy goods vehicle driver. I don't know if there was some kind of weird genetic thread going on but Dad's father had driven trucks, one of my elder brothers had been a diesel fitter and, of course, when I first started working for the cheese factory I was delivering on the van. Driving was something I enjoyed so that, plus the element of being my own boss to some extent, made a job driving big trucks around seem appealing. Lessons were twice a week for about four hours a week and although I was knackered because it was intense I loved it, especially having done little for so long. I duly passed my test at the second attempt.

One of my old mates, Joe Bolton, still lived at Baslow near Sheffield and Julie and I had often gone over there for a drink and a chat. As it happened he was also a tanker driver and as we had stayed in touch he had told me to give him a shout when I had passed the test. When I did he rang and asked if I fancied helping him out the following day as he had a difficult long run and might need me to help with a bit of driving, to help with his hours. I jumped at the chance and asked what time he started but he wasn't impressed when he asked me what time I got up and I said, that it was usually, about 10ish. He was picking me up at six in the morning so it was a bit of a shock as prior to that I had only ever known one six o' clock in the day, and that was teatime!

It was lovely to see Joe again as I jumped in this big tanker and we just fell straight back into the old football banter very naturally because he was a real down to earth feller who I got on with. After a few hours I asked for a go, which was a bit of a risk because although I had passed my test I hadn't driven a truck for a month. It happened on a couple more occasions which enabled me to learn a bit more about how things worked on the tanker.

In time the Gaffers realised I was going out with Joe on my own initiative and getting stuck into it without pay so they offered me a job on good money, more than I was getting at Huddersfield, which I was grateful for. The company was based near Chesterfield and I was introduced to a whole new world in which there was this huge field with loads of lorries parked up and rats running all over the place as you opened the doors. Talk about rough and ready, but I worked my tail off transporting industrial waste and then having to dig out the residue that had stuck in the baffles at the end of the day.

Make no mistake, it was genuine hard graft and there were several moments when I was forced to confront myself with how my relatively cushy life as a footballer had now turned, and the nature of the job ensured that I had plenty of time to consider that. One such occasion was the FA Cup semi final in 1993 when the two Sheffield clubs were destined to face each other at Wembley. As it happened I was driving the lorry on that morning in the traffic containing all the United and Wednesday fans on their way to London. I could see the streams of cars and coaches containing Blades supporters wearing the red and whites, and I was in the tanker thinking, I used to play for those people. But I pulled myself together because that was finished and I had to get on with what I had now. At least I was working and busy.

Our drivers were doing up to eighty hours a week and on one occasion when I was working a Saturday and the lorry broke down at Harworth pit, I was stuck there for about five hours after doing a long shift. It really got to me that I used to spend my Saturdays playing football for a living as I just sat there for hours, missing all the football and racing results. It was the day from hell and one of my worst ever. But Julie had wanted me to get a job and I had done, and she was delighted. When I came home, tired and stinking of chemicals, she ran a bath for me which she hadn't done when I had a comparatively easy life, so she felt for me. She had many qualities, including mental strength and although, Julie being Julie, we had massive fights, we would always make up and I wasn't concerned. But it wasn't enough to save us.

One day at home when I asked why she seemed a bit subdued, she showed me a piece of paper. It served notice of her petitioning for divorce. I could have knocked the house down because it was unexpected and I thought she would have stuck it out to see us through what, to my knowledge, was just a rough patch. The timing couldn't have been worse because not only was I knackered from work but, by getting back into work, I had done something positive for us. Nobody else was involved but I was staggered and wondered what the reason was, so it wasn't totally reassuring to be told the 'still love you but not in love with you' stuff, that I was a good Dad and so on. Even to this day I still love being a Dad, looking after their kids and taking the dogs for walks to give their parents a chance to go out. Julie is a fantastic grandmother, although probably a bit overbearing at times because she almost loves them too much, and I'm sure all parents will understand what I mean by that.

After a while I realised I couldn't change her mind because of the rowing and I was in the Granny flat at our house, almost living separate lives. Maybe I was not a good husband but I was a good father and Julie had put the children first all the time. Any woman reading this would probably say 'so she should' – but surely not all the time because there were occasions when I also needed a bit of help or attention. When I took those kids and their pals out to the park on Sundays to enjoy themselves, and I was copying my Dad as a father, I was almost inevitably the only Dad out there. Do I presume that all the other Mums and Dads were too busy to do that, although their kids were having a good time? It was right that the kids were given priority because they needed us, but when I needed a bit of support it wasn't there and I suppose it had gone from Julie by then.

Whatever I did never seemed enough although she had raised the subject of marriage guidance. That wasn't for me and my opinion is that she is a first class person, a first class mother but not a first class wife, while I probably wasn't a first class husband. Analysing a relationship that has run its course isn't easy when you have been part of it but I think that is a fair criticism of Julie and me.

Now I am a far more capable and independent person having learned through necessity how to cook, iron, clean and look after myself. What irked most was that after all the turmoil of being 'lost', then dealing with new work and long hours, I had just started to get over it all and was becoming stronger. I tried convincing her that I was changing as a person because I knew I was. My life ever since is proof of that because I have never lived with another woman yet learned so much on a practical level, and that is something I am quite proud of.

The immediate aftermath of the split meant I was only having the children at weekends to start with and I really didn't like the pain and loneliness of just being a Sunday Dad. It made absolute sense for her to have the house for the kids to grow up in and I moved out as the proceedings began. It wasn't in my mind to fight for much and when her solicitor asked me for the name of my solicitor I told him I wasn't having one because I had just stopped caring about haggling. Hiring a brief would only have cost money that I would rather have gone to the children, and my hands were tied anyway because she needed to raise them properly. I told Julie to get together with her solicitor and sort everything out and she did so very fairly, securing the income she needed to bring the children up but making sure that I also benefitted from some of the policies we had.

For me now life was just work, having a pint, seeing the kids when I could and doing my thing until Julie gave me an unexpected boost by suggesting I had Eddie, our youngest, stay with me occasionally. He had started work early within a routine that enabled him to stay with me for three or four days a week at the flat I had bought at Norton. It lifted my spirits immensely because living apart from my kids was heartbreaking.

Julie moved to Gleadless and in my early, dark days I would say to her, 'Why haven't I got the kids? You find a job, I'll have them and do a part time job.' Emma was fourteen, at that awkward stage, and wrote a piece at school about how hard the situation was for her. Although I had stopped longing for Julie I did long for my kids, but, in reality, my suggestion wasn't feasible and I knew that she would give them the best possible care. My time as a part-time Dad when I had the kids was the most precious, and emotionally difficult, part of my week. On most Sundays we went to the pictures, scrambling on the rocks at Padley Gorge in Derbyshire, to Fox House for a nice lunch or to KFC. I was on good money and made a point of ensuring that they had a great time.

However, one incident had a moving effect on me because it captured how sad I felt at not being with them as a reliable father all the time. Edward was about eight years old when he unexpectedly fell on the rocks at Padley but I was just in the right place to catch him. It hit me immediately how he needed me and I unashamedly bawled my eyes out in front of them for about five minutes. My lad cried, wondering what was wrong with his Dad, until I regained some composure, wiped my face and suggested we all went off for a lemonade. Those weekend arrangements can't have made things altogether fine for Julie either because sometimes the girls would go home and let their Mum know, in no uncertain terms, that they felt for their Dad as they had just left him in an empty flat. It was tough, as any divorce is.

Julie was definitely stronger than me and was living with more normality with the house and family around her. In one instance I had the kids because she was going out and we agreed I would return them at 8pm, but when we got there she wasn't, and neither did she land for another couple of hours. I had been driving round with our kids wondering what had happened, and when she admitted she had been with a bloke, and she had every right to, I was absolutely livid and the two older kids didn't talk to her for ages.

Admittedly we had split and she had her own house but the situation got to me and when I started questioning her about him she was reluctant to talk, but I obtained a few bits of information. Apparently he chopped down trees down for a living, owned a red car and lived in Beighton so I was able to track him down. For what, I wasn't quite sure but my mind was all over the place and I ended up making an embarrassing fool of myself.

When I found his house I thought I'll sort this bloke out, and banged on his door, then kicked it in frustration which only increased the likelihood of things getting out of hand, something that would have been all my fault. He apparently loved his shiny red car so, heckles rising, I thought I would get to him by standing next to it thinking, I'm gonna twat somebody in a minute. As I started to calm down and mull it over because he wasn't coming down I started to reconsider. Bloody 'ell, if he chops down trees he might be about six foot three! It suddenly dawned on me that I had asked so many questions but not how big he was. What happens if he comes down now and he IS massive?

Before I had time to change my mind he did appear and confounded my anger by being very calm and trying to be reasonable, but it didn't stop me from instigating a bit of a scuffle which he didn't deserve. Fortunately, I was perceptive enough to quickly draw two important conclusions. One, he didn't want to fight and, two, I couldn't fight, and within about ten minutes I was buying him a drink in the pub. He was a very likeable person and I realised that the situation had got to me because I was in emotional turmoil about her going out with someone, but it was for all the wrong reasons. I'm glad I resolved it with him and look back now at what I think was a humorous episode. It was saved from going really wrong when more rational thought processes clicked into gear and I wondered what the hell I was doing. Incidentally, his relationship with Julie didn't last but if he reads this I sincerely hope he recognises why I was so wound up and such a prat that night.

Happily, and many years later, Julie and I get on absolutely great and I can still give her a cuddle when we meet up on family occasions. When Dad died she drove the younger kids up to the north-east for the funeral and as usual, was there for me when I needed her strength and support. It was lovely of her to do that and as far as I am concerned there is still a bond there. We had met and fallen in love when we were so young and there was no question in my mind that we would grow old together, and I wanted that to happen. It would have been awfully difficult because of how we both developed, but we produced four lovely children and have much to be thankful for.

17

Crashing to Earth

My time on the tankers was coming to an end. But my love life was set to take off again.

Driving for Kennel services had been a part of my life that I probably needed for a number of reasons. There was good guidance from Joe who was excellent at his job, and I straightened myself out as a normal working bloke. I made friends at the firm and even played football for them on Sunday mornings which was a good laugh for Joe and me, especially on those dodgy pitches. I'm not saying it was all plain sailing because we took our share of stick. Sometimes I would be nutmegging and chipping people but then, if we made mistakes, we'd be ribbed mercilessly as we weren't expected to make any. It created a lot of fun.

One guy called Cozzi (sic), father of current Sheffield United prospect Diego De Girolamo, didn't work for them but played with us and when I knocked a ball to him slightly off target he looked at me and mocked, 'I thought you used to play fuckin' football?' It was good to work with blokes who were, in a nice way, rough and ready and I handled it but ended up leaving after three years. The job had given me purpose and structure, and plenty of cash to keep giving the kids a treat at weekends after I had pounded the hours in during the week.

Eddie was staying with me regularly and although I was

without a partner I could afford to take my time a bit as regards finding new work, having sold a few bonds. Julie had made sure some of them had stayed in my name and never rubbed my nose in it when we divided up our assets. There was plenty of opportunity to play golf regularly and make friends, some of whom are with me to this day, including Paul Dial who owned two or three hairdressers called Scissors. But I suppose I should have taken more notice of something that had happened many years earlier in my playing days which would have pre-warned me about how my hair might end up.

At Sheffield United Chico Hamilton asked me at one social occasion if I wasn't talking to Len after I had unknowingly ignored someone. I looked round and then recognised Len Badger which was a shock because when I had first known him he had hair, and now he had virtually none. I jokingly said, 'Bloody 'ell, Len, where do you get your hair cut?' to which he gruffly answered, 'Scissors.' So I told him I played golf with the shop owner so I'd better put a stop to that. Len, of course, took that with all the humour I had intended but he had the last laugh because Mr Dial has been subsequently solely responsible for the hole appearing in the back of my own hairline.

Golf also directly provided me with the chance to meet the lady who became my next love. Zoe was a businesswoman with two children and she played a bit of golf at the club. Our paths eventually crossed there but I am fascinated by the fact that ages before, at one match in which I played for Sheffield United against Stockport at the Lane, Zoe was watching with her husband David, so was her future husband Ted, and I, her future boyfriend, was on the pitch.

She divorced David, met Ted who was a member at Lees Hall and married but he sadly died of cancer and, in time, I plucked up enough courage to ask her for a date, at a barbecue in Ecclesall. If I'm being honest, Zoe is the one who got away because although I might have lost the battle with Julie, I felt as if I might win the war with someone I had clicked with almost instantly. Added to that, I got on really well with her mother, Audrey, who was a regular and keen Radio Sheffield listener. I have not enjoyed too many successes with women but the first couple of years with Zoe were my best courting days because Julie and I had been so young when we were getting to know each other. Zoe and I often drank on the Ecclesall Road stretch, met lots of folks and it was great to feel love again in a good relationship. It was really my first as a mature bloke with a grown woman and that is very different to the ones you have as a teenager. It is easier to talk, have a drink and relax. But to carry on with that I needed to get a job.

There was a short lived attempt to set myself up as a self employed gardener but then I had a job offer from Cancer Research UK. I wasn't proud and would have done anything and this was basically van driving but I didn't know at the time what it entailed. Although it was for a very worthwhile cause I look back now and regard it as nine years wasted because it was poorly paid and it drained my confidence through a lack of self esteem. One upside was that the job didn't take up the whole day which meant I could get on the golf course, but I take my hat off to those people who do the job all day, every day. If I take time to wonder whether my divorce was the hardest thing, or the three years at Kennel Services, or that charity job, I would have to plump for the latter because it was mundane work which left me feeling lifeless and unfulfilled. My work became secondary to other things rather than getting stuck into it because it was rewarding in some way, but something else of much more importance put all that into perspective.

Close to the end of my relationship with Zoe I suffered the second massive loss in my life when Dad passed away. He was taken ill after a bit of a stroke and one of the worst things about living so much of my life in Sheffield was that I was invariably 106 miles from Stockton when anything went wrong up there. That made things difficult for my brothers as well because they had to weigh up whether or when to ring me up, as had happened when Mam started being poorly. In this case though, Steve rang to tell me to take a bit of time off and go to the hospital to see Dad which obviously I did immediately.

We had a bit of a laugh as I sat on his bed and, when I had

to go and reached the door of his room, he did something that typified everything I had thought about Dad and the calibre of the man. He knew how ill he was, although it was never said by him or us, and none of us felt he would survive much longer, but he smiled at me, put his thumb up and nodded. It was the last time I ever saw him and it was as if he knew and had made it so easy for me which I think was wonderfully unselfish. It eliminated any awkward dwelling on his condition and tearful goodbyes, and I believe that right to the end by doing that he was still looking out for me.

Within days of that visit my close family in Sheffield were in St Lucia in the Caribbean for my daughter Emma's wedding. Zoe was with me, along with Julie and her partner, and two days before the ceremony Steve rang to say Dad had died, news which was devastating despite not being entirely unexpected. Although I told Julie and Zoe what had happened I felt I had to stay cheerful and say nothing to anyone else for two days before and two days after the wedding, purely for Emma's sake. Dad, seventy-nine, had never left the hospital and it made me illogically wonder once again why I was never on the Stockton doorstep whenever there was a crisis. This time I was on the other side of the world in a fabulous place, and my brothers again had to make all the calls and necessary arrangements.

I managed to keep a happy face for everyone and even though it did get to me a bit on the day of the wedding I knew Dad would have wanted me to carry that off and not spoil things. Eventually I told the kids which was upsetting, but throughout the whole episode both Julie and Zoe were absolutely fantastically supportive. Throughout this book I have joked about not getting it totally right with women throughout my life so far, but those two could not have done more for me in that situation and I will always be grateful. Then Julie played a big part in making some of the funeral arrangements whilst Zoe was invaluable in being by my side helping me get me through it all.

There is not a shred of doubt in my mind that I would not have become a professional footballer if it hadn't been for

Dad. Yes, I had the natural ability, but it was his guidance and encouragement which took me through the early stages of life, and then his support and interest I turned to first afterwards.

Zoe and I never did get engaged or married and during that time if anybody questioned it she used to say, 'Well, Keith's, Keith,' leaving the questioner to work out whether that was a reason in itself! She probably pondered whether she could ever move me in or not, even though we were very comfortable with each other. The nearest to the truth I suspect is that she just wasn't sure, but we never fell out about it and after nine years we sort of drifted apart. To give you a small example, I would come back after a Radio Sheffield game, having not seen her during the week, and ring her suggesting I came round for a drink. The problem was that if I had been somewhere like Bournemouth I would have slept all the way back and now be wide awake, but Zoe, understandably, would have been thinking it was getting close to turning in for the night, so things didn't quite fit.

You get awkward timing like that in most relationships but as somebody once said after I had announced that we were splitting up after so long, 'Well, what did you expect, you've been together for nine years and you don't even live together,' so I suppose it was inevitable. It was nobody's fault and maybe if we had both been more committed we would still be together, but we had some wonderful times in those early days. There were fantastic holidays during the first adult and relatively sophisticated relationship I had ever had because Julie and I never had the chance or the maturity to do that when we met. Would you believe that going to Tenerife with Zoe was the first time I had ever been away with a woman on her own?

She introduced me to the theatre which I thoroughly enjoyed and as her daughter was into dance, we also went along to that type of show. It was a whole new world to me and I racked up a whole set of 'firsts' by going out for a meal together, getting drunk together, going on holiday and spending time together. In some ways it felt wrong not to have the children around whilst I was doing those things, but I had been pushed down this avenue of life so I just got on with it. My kids were fine with it and they were always my priority, whatever Zoe and I were doing.

Things were changing in my life again and during one period of unemployment I did a couple of odd jobs, including a few weeks delivering special display units to shops and supermarkets who were going to use them for displaying fireworks. Doing that led to an episode that I wouldn't blame you for not believing as it sounds so far-fetched but I promise you that the following did happen to me. I remember the timing because it was about then that Kevin Keegan had left Newcastle and had gone missing, at least as far as the media was concerned.

Returning to Sheffield from a drop in Newcastle I called at Steve's for a bit of a giggle before tootling off southwards again after an early start. A red Ford Sierra overtook me with three youths in it but the real reason I noticed it was that there was a greyhound in the back. Just a few miles down the road I was conscious of the fact that there was no other traffic on the road but the red car still in front. I was still trying to fathom out why when a 4x4 police vehicle overtook me very quickly, closely followed by others with one of them pulling across the front of me so that I had no choice but to slow and stop.

Before I could even turn the engine off I now had an animated policeman, crouching outside the driver's door, with a gun pointing straight at my head, screaming at me to put my hands up where he could see them. I can't honestly say I felt frightened with it happening so quickly but then he was screaming at me to get out. It got rather more unnerving when I went to do just that but he repeated the order to keep my hands up which was difficult to do if I was to open the flippin' door!

When I managed it I was made to spread flat out and face down on the A1 with arms and legs spread-eagled in an X shape, but I could just see that the red Sierra and its occupants were getting the same treatment with coppers swarming all round us. The dog had panicked and shot off running across the field next to us, and I was lying there wondering what was going on, whether I was on a film set or something. It was unreal. I gingerly lifted my head to look in the other direction to see the whole of the other side of the A1 absolutely crammed with cars and lorries, and people rubbernecking at a snail's pace. I was centre-stage, lying there in the middle of the A1 thinking, I hope that poor greyhound's alright!

The police were largely focussing on the red car but one of them dragged me round to the back of my van, asking me what I was carrying. I told him display units but when he demanded that I open the doors up I swear on my children's life that I said, 'You're not fuckin' looking for Kevin Keegan are you?' He started chuckling away and more than probably realised that my throwaway comment indicated I had nothing to do with what they were looking for. On phoning my brother he told me that he had heard on the news about the police investigating something to do with the IRA, and that they were looking for a red Sierra and a white van travelling south. It went on to say that two such vehicles were stopped but found not to be involved, and Steve was astonished to hear about my experience.

When the fuss was over I was sitting at the side of the road chatting to the police armed response unit who were great, but I just wish that later somebody had got in touch to apologise for the trauma and inconvenience. It wasn't that I was brave or anything, and when you are innocent you don't worry so much, but it was still a bit of a shock – and I am still wondering if that greyhound was found and looked after.

Ironically, my son-in-law is in the armed response unit so I know a bit about how it operates and I am full of admiration for the professional way in which they shifted on the traffic ahead first to create the space to box us in before stopping the two vehicles. The three lads were also innocent and I suppose, if anything, the incident taught me not to do fiddle jobs, but it was a hard lesson to learn. After all, just for carrying a few cabinets I didn't think I deserved a gun putting to my head which was a bit extreme. And I have heard all the jokes about me giving the police a rocket ...

*****

My work with the BBC was going great and the Howard Kendall era brought a Wembley Play-off Final which was a particularly great experience to be involved with as I was learning my radio trade. But the last thing I expected from it all was meeting the third love of my life.

At a Radio Sheffield social gathering one night I got chatting to this little blonde lady who actually played football herself, in fact she was passionate about the game. Hayley Roach, as she was called, also had an involvement with the Sheffield Steelers and strangely enough had arranged that charity football match I mentioned earlier. I thought she was a really nice person, a football fanatic who loved involvement with radio which is why she had been invited on the night.

She was then working for the Sheffield & Hallamshire County FA and, although we had chatted, I hadn't given it much thought until a trip down to Millwall with Sports Editor Paul Walker who took a phone call from Hayley, asking if I was mobile friendly. We duly exchanged numbers which was a complete and pleasant surprise, especially as she was about seventeen years younger than me.

Another unexpected by-product of us starting to get together was that I had to quickly learn how to text for the first time really and I was thankful that Eddie was able to teach me. Finding Hayley, I suppose, helped me get over the split with Zoe but if it sounds as if I was a Jack the Lad with women I can confidently refute that because my kids can go down town and won't find anybody who would say to them that they knew their Dad was a right womaniser. That is because I have only really had three relationships, all at different times, and I didn't mess any of the ladies about.

Hayley is a Rotherham girl, her Dad is a Millers' season ticket holder, and she was a load of fun. She loved the Steelers which was something else I knew nothing about so my life was being enriched again with new experiences. I watched her play football a few times at Sheffield FC and eventually was asked to do a bit of coaching with the girls which was really enjoyable and enabled me to pick up a bit of fitness. The type of relationship with her was very new to me because of the age difference – she was early thirties to my late forties – and I loved her to bits. It tickled me that when I went to her house at Wickersley I would be trying to flick the TV on to golf, but she would be flicking it back to football. It was a comical argument about her devotion to footy that we had regularly, but that caught me out on one occasion, much to my disappointment.

She came downstairs and I got just a glimpse of thigh, something red at the bottom of her leg and inevitably I thought, this is handy, it looks as if my luck's changed here, we're having a night of passion. How wrong could I be? She leapt out of her robe wearing a full football kit and with a football under her arm, and asked me if I fancied a game of footy on the field so I could show her how to bend the ball like I did in training.

'I'm fifty years old with a bad 'ip ,' I said. 'And if somebody sees me on the football field now I'm going to look a right dickhead.'

Anyway, because it was Wickersley and I reckoned that nobody there would recognise me, I put my trainers on and off we went. There were only a few kids on there and as we were bending the ball backwards and forwards I loved her enthusiasm for playing sport. It was overwhelming, as was the thirst to learn that she and her team mates exuded in our coaching sessions, and I must say that ladies football has grown in quality tremendously in recent years. When I was a nipper it wasn't much at all but having watched Arsenal Ladies and the England women's team I found it a real eye opener.

As for my anticipated night of passion well, we played until it got dark before going back and then I had a shower and sat down in front of the telly again. When Hayley went for a bath I thought, that's good, I can get the golf on again now. But she soon reappeared with a naughty night on her mind and this time I could only gasp, 'My 'ip's killing me. You must be joking. Let's watch the golf.'

After a while, when I had also got to know her sister and parents, Maurice and Wendy, really well, I was beginning to think that Hayley was the one and, after speaking to my children about it, I asked her to marry me. She said yes but maybe it scared us both a little bit. About six months and one or two little arguments later she had the opportunity to further her career by doing some football work in South Africa, both before and during the World Cup there. It was something she really wanted to do and I wished her well because I always had, at the back of my mind, concerns about the age gap. For example, would there be children involved, and if there were, I would need a reversal operation.

We parted on very friendly terms and I was 100 per cent fine with that outcome. The proposal hadn't been flippant, it had seemed a great idea because we were having a laugh and getting on so well, plus she was offering something that I possibly had not had with Zoe in that I could pop round there at any time. We were together an awful lot, much of it almost like co-existing as a couple, and I think we were both of a mind to keep things moving forward but who knows, within a few months she might have started having the same kind of concerns that I had. Hayley was at a career crossroad in her life and we both understood that so we parted, but how many times in this book am I going to be rejected by women?

I make light of it and, although sometimes I miss the tender moments of being attached, there are peaks and troughs in every relationship and I am not bitter about not being in one. My relationships with Julie, Zoe and Hayley didn't last the course so clearly there is something in me that is not quite right because I am still on my own. But that's the way it is, I am dealing with it without bitterness and I am proud of the fact that I can still be friends with all three of those ladies.

Brother Len wasn't so fortunate because he tragically died at only fifty-seven years old through illness. Firstly, he developed stomach cancer and although he had treatment he kept it to himself for a while, presumably in his way, to protect his family, but then he had a brain tumour. It was distressing in hospital to see him asking questions about how old he was and so on, and really sad for a grafter who had worked tirelessly as a welder in South Africa, Aberdeen and Germany. Len had just started a wonderful relationship with his three year-old granddaughter that he was unable to build on, and throughout his working life he had always said that he wanted a Mercedes one day. I am glad to say that at least he had achieved that special purchase before he passed on. He died on 10 July, also my daughter Gina's birthday, so I go up there every year on that day for a three way golf match in his memory with Steve and Len's son, Lee.

*****

In April, 2008, within a matter of weeks of my leaving Cancer UK, the golf course played yet another part in my story, this time leading to my current job. I was sharing a round with Andrew Haigh, lifelong Blades fan and MD at Sheffield Insulations, and teeing off on the 11th when I casually asked the rest of the foursome if they knew where there was any work.

'There's a couple of jobs going at our place,' said Andrew straight away.

'Doing?'

'Warehouse work, driving.'

'Hmm, good.'

'What do you drive?'

'I'm Class 1.'

'Brill. You can have a job tomorrow if you want.'

I was as nervous as I had ever been in my life when I started, initially in the warehouse for a couple of weeks to familiarise myself with the hundreds of materials I would be delivering. I had to take a few more specific driving and refresher courses to drive the big articulated truck and learn about new machinery, but I picked them up and now I have to say it is the best job I have ever had outside football. It involves delivering insulation to building contractors all over Yorkshire and North Lincolnshire and I am indebted to Adrian Siddall, mentioned in an earlier chapter, for familiarising me with everything I needed to know. He's still a pal there now and I couldn't be happier. There are some very early starts but that isn't difficult for me now and I love being out on the open road, sharing banter at work and with the people I deliver to.

My forty-four foot long articulated lorry can carry over twenty tons and I had to obtain the qualifications to use the machinery to load and unload the vehicle. It is not unknown for me to mention what I do on air because I am quite often recognised by Blades fans and enjoy having a chinwag with them. But I didn't derive the slightest bit of pleasure from an accident in my lorry in September 2010 because it was the most frightening experience of my life.

It was raining heavily when I headed off to deliver in Hull, down the M18, up to Junction 2. As I moved across into the second lane the truck went over a bubble of standing water which lifted the cab up, but not the trailer, and I felt the cab start to aquaplane. Fortunately, there was nobody overtaking and, because I am quite safety conscious and never drive close behind anyone else, there was no immediate danger of hitting another vehicle, but I had no chance of keeping control.

For what seemed like around forty seconds I was in sheer terror, scared to death, especially when having thought I had regained control, I soon realised I hadn't. The cab completely turned round on itself and the whole lot jackknifed into the central barriers before everything came to a halt. The noise was incredible, absolutely deafening with the cab rearing up and finishing suspended in the air at an angle with the driver's side nearest the ground.

For a few seconds I froze waiting for another impact and when it didn't happen, asked myself if I really was alive and unscathed. Then there was pure relief that nothing else on the road seemed to have been involved. The satnav and my lunchbox had flown past my head because everything in the cab had moved. And believe me as this is true, I looked down at my elbow and saw it covered in what I thought was blood. My initial reaction was to worry about my golf but, a fraction of a second later, I realised the 'blood' was tomato from my lunchbox!

The lorry driving fraternity is a friendly bunch with a shared camaraderie and a lorry immediately pulled up on the hard shoulder. The driver came across the motorway to help, looked up at the cab in the air and shouted ... 'You alright, lad?'

'Yeah, I think so. Is anyone else involved?'

'No, only you. Don't worry, they're on their way, just sit tight.'

Fire engines were quickly on the scene although I couldn't really see because I was so high up and at the bottom of the cab. All of a sudden a ladder was raised to rest on the cab and a fireman looked down at me and said 'Alright, Keith?'!

He knew me and I was flabbergasted but so scared about crawling across, getting through the window and going down the ladder because I'm not that good with heights. Alright, it was wobbling a bit but it should have been nothing compared to what I had just gone through, which seemed to amuse him. That manoeuvre must have been why in the ambulance my blood pressure was sky high, even though I was unhurt. Although I was to some degree in shock I phoned work to let them know, and then contacted Emma to confirm that I was okay. She and her partner, Jason, are both Police Officers and the value of those contacts was evident a few minutes later when I got out of the ambulance and the first copper on the scene was Mick Henderson, my former Blades team mate.

'What a fuckin' mess you've made,' was his greeting. 'What are you doing, Edwards? Come on, I've come to take you home.'

I thought, tops, this is good, but there was a police dog in the back barking like crazy, non stop, which was just what I needed and reminded me of when Porterfield had loud music on in his car when he had taken me to hospital at Bolton. Does nobody have any sympathy! Apparently the news of my crash had gone like wildfire round the Police and Mick who, incidentally had thought I had crashed my car, wanted to come out to me. It was really good of him as I hadn't seen him for years but he was out there like a shot. Say what you like about footballers but that touched me and always will do.

The truck was written off, cost a fortune to move and Sheffield Insulations were fined very heavily for shutting the motorway for about five hours. After taking a day off and being checked out medically I reported to work where I was advised to jump back on the horse as quickly as I could, which I did with no ill effects on body or my mental state. Mind you, I still drive extra slowly past that little spot on the M18.

18

New Life for Old

Around thirty five years after I had left Stockton I found out that I was a father of five and not four. The news was as unexpected in its delivery as it was mind blowing to hear the consequences of my actions as a youth obsessed with playing football for a living

A young lady from up there gave her number to a group of Sheffield lads who were working in the north-east. One of them, a great lad and, believe it or not, an Owls fan called Terry Hogg, told her that they would pass it on to me but it would be up to me as to whether or not I acted on it. It took me several months before I did because I regard the way I handled it at the time as the worst thing I have ever done. I should have gone looking for her but I wasn't sure that Pamela was pregnant and we were basically still bairns ourselves at the time. My mind was saying, what the hell do I do?

It played on my mind, particularly when I started having children with Julie, and to be fair to Pamela, when I started hitting the headlines at United she could have got in touch with me and been a bit more demanding if she had wanted any help, but she didn't.

The daughter I had never known is called Kendra and when we first met I was extremely nervous, and she possibly more so, which was all perfectly understandable. I still hadn't been sure she was mine but as soon as she walked through the door I knew for certain that she was. Kendra was the absolute spit of me. We got on, had a three hour chat that night, and now every time I go home I take her out for a meal, accompanied by talk about the situation in those days and why her parents reacted as we did. Today's supertech world of easy and instant communication for the masses makes it relatively easier to establish contact with almost anyone, totally different to forty years ago, although I accept that being a professional footballer even then, would have made me easier to find if her mother had wanted to.

I was eighteen when Kendra was born and I didn't meet her until she was thirty-five. Having got to know her I quickly realised how both brave and beautiful it was that she made the effort to get in touch with me. And I am so impressed by the immensely adult and sensitive way she let me know she was around but left to me the choice of whether to meet her or not. Pamela and the man my daughter regarded as her father brought her up extremely well and she is a person I am very proud of. That is not down to me in the slightest but I'm glad we have a lot of similarities which makes our personal situation easier to cope with.

Not to have taken responsibility and owning up to it was the worst thing I have ever done in my life, especially as when Julie and I had our children I took things very seriously. That I didn't come clean about it I can only put down to trying to protect my own family in Sheffield, so it became something I just put in a compartment in my life called 'private' and left it there. When I have explained my feelings about that to Kendra she has been so chilled about it it's unreal, and she dismisses it by saying, 'Dad, get over yourself.' The fact that she calls me Dad is something to treasure in itself.

Sadly I haven't met Pamela again although I would like to and don't see why we couldn't, although I respect that things happen, we all move on and the decision can't rest just with me. At least my name has been mentioned occasionally which is a start because the whole episode of Kendra's biological father apparently wasn't an area of discussion in her household. But I have met one of my grandchildren, Louie, who was three at the time, and Kendra also has a son who is nine years older. He is aware of what has happened and is fine with it. Again, being in football can be an advantage because if he wants to know if his Grandad was a footballer, Kendra can just tell him to go upstairs and Google him. I am not sure if that sits well with me but I am old-fashioned. Every time I see her we always end with warm words for each other which is nice, but I am additionally pleased at how things have worked because I absolutely adore my four children with Julie. They were always my life and I wouldn't change anything.

Kendra and I are in phone contact but I am not the sort of person to keep in touch on too regular a basis if they live a distance away. I love my brothers but we don't have to live in each other's pockets, and Kendra feels a bit the same which makes it comfortable for both of us. I hadn't spoken to her for about a month recently but then she texted to say, 'Hi Dad, hope you are well, weather is getting nicer so I bet you are getting into your golf again.' We are relaxed with how we regard each other and connect when we feel the need to.

She has accepted what I did in a very gracious manner and made it very easy for me to come to terms with. Thankfully, she was most intrigued to find out what her father was like and now she has I think she is pleased with what she sees because I have made her smile a bit, we've shared photos and had a bit of a laugh. In a way, now the dust has settled, we think it's a bit of a giggle being how we are. Kendra now socialises with Steve's daughter Helen, and as they all live fairly close to each other, they always get together for family functions. How nice is that?

A positive aspect I hadn't considered is to do with health and genetics, something that is even more crucial for Kendra and she explained why to me. When she went for medicals and was asked if there were any heart defects in the family she couldn't say for certain as she didn't know about me, and I hadn't thought of that. Fortunately for her I say that I am always in fantastic condition.

*****

I really would not have considered the writing of this book if I had not gone on to work for BBC Radio Sheffield. There were several offers over the years from people willing to help me put it together, but having been retired for so long I really didn't believe that sufficient people would be interested enough in reading it to make a publication worthwhile. That might still be the case, of course, but I changed my mind when Andy Pack approached me, not just because of our long standing friendship, but also because we agreed that my public profile had been resurrected through my regular broadcasting stints.

There are probably thousands of listeners who never knew me as a player but listen to my comments on air, whether they agree with them or not, so that became a big factor in my decision. It is fascinating that the demographic of people who hear me on air – and hopefully read this book – must by definition be extremely diverse. They knew me as a player, or didn't, they liked me as a player, or didn't, agree with much of my radio comment, or don't. Mix all those up and it is an interesting thought.

Joining the station gave me a new lease of life, a voice in the Sheffield football region and a vehicle through which I can interact with Sheffield United supporters years after I might well have been forgotten by the majority. Now I am a fan like they are, working matches or just going down to watch and it is a real privilege to be recognised and to chat to them, especially on road trips when we amble down the road eating fish and chips beforehand. When Simon Clarke gave me my chance the first game I covered was a goal frenzy, a 4-4 draw with Birmingham City at Bramall Lane on 24 August 1996, and I have no idea how I came across because there was no definitive blueprint to follow in terms of hearing how anyone else might do it.

It is probable that my character comes through on air because I have been critical if I felt it necessary. I don't see anything wrong with that because I also had criticism to shoulder when I played and no doubt frustrated people. I didn't do an awful lot of research for the early part of my radio career but just went and did it to the best of my ability. That style has got me into trouble sometimes, as when current Sports Editor Paul Walker and I were summoned to Neil Warnock's house because he considered that I had been a bit harsh about Peter Ndlovu.

We went into his conservatory and he said, 'Sit down, lads, just want to have a little chat,' in the way that he did, and the ironic thing was that for the next hour and a half of conversation he agreed with everything I said. He went on to explain to me that he hadn't got a Colin Morris or a Keith Edwards or a Kevin Arnott, so he had to do what he could with what he had.

I learned that when he had a good relationship with his players he wanted them to be defended and I could understand that which was beneficial to us both. The pair of us left on much better terms but, as is often the case with Neil, it didn't always last too long because he is his own man, as I am. We once agreed at Radio Sheffield that I wouldn't be so harsh on Neil, but then we went to watch United and after twenty minutes he was sent off, so my reaction was sod that, I'll give him a bit of stick as I didn't like that polite route anyway. Whichever way you looked at it, he showed a lack of discipline and I had never been sent off so why should a manager? For twenty minutes I had been pussyfooting around but when that happened I thought, well, may as well go back to being what I'm normally like now!

Whilst talking about his reign I should mention that when United were in the Premiership I genuinely wondered whether Neil, and possibly the public, had had enough of listening to me, so I left and did a bit of broadcasting elsewhere. But, happily, within nine months I was welcomed back which meant a lot and provided a nice bit of symmetry between Radio Sheffield and Sheffield United because it meant that I had enjoyed two spells at each.

My radio career had started off on the basis that I had strong views on how to play, that I could see slight changes in tactics and so on, and I believe that I know the game. A lot of ex-footballers don't really give a monkey's about it and although I don't watch all the time at home, especially if golf is on, when I am doing the job I like to study games and players. My opinion is based on experience of playing the game, and on specifically watching both for faults and good elements at the same time. None of us can be right on every occasion but I bet all of us pride ourselves on spotting who will turn out to be a top player before many others do.

In my case it was Sheffield United's Greek God, Traianos Dellas, who eventually became a £10 million player. I banged on about what a great talent he was, nice and comfortable on the ball, could ping it around and although pace was a bit of a problem, he had a great shot – and I liked him. I got it right with him but I think my best 'spot' was Gary Hooper during a crappy game at Scunthorpe and I commented on what a player the lad was, before looking him up in the programme. A £175 grand signing from Southend, he had movement, ability, was good on the ball and I am glad I urged on the radio for Sheffield United to go out and buy him, but a year or so later he went for £2.4 million to Celtic.

On the other hand my opinion on Paul Devlin wasn't so positive at first. I used to look at him and think, he's not a midfielder, most definitely not an inside forward, not really a winger, he seems like one of those in between players who fits into a team somehow but I don't know where he plays. Then he hit the ground running as a winger and was outstanding. I hadn't seen that coming from him for a long time and I got it wrong, but eventually I was full of praise because he was excellent when he found his best role.

Summarising with a commentator is not an exact science because the two should dovetail together whilst delivering different inputs. The problem is that there can't be a set time pattern as to who will be speaking and when because of having to respond to the ever changing action, and every game is different. While the commentator has to describe what is happening and instantly identify every player where he can, the summariser has to spot more subtle changes and talk about why something is happening, to bring in more considered insight. You learn through experience when the commentator is suddenly going to bring you in, and when to stop because something important is happening and he needs to take over again.

Having a regular pairing definitely helps things flow because you develop both a rhythm and an understanding of how the other operates. A shared sense of humour is often a great tool to give the coverage variety, and also to pass the time when the match is particularly unmemorable. As I grew more used to my task I picked up all these nuances and techniques quite quickly. When a colleague needs a bit of help or a breather I can do that by, for example, talking about a player, or by filling in if the commentator is tackling some radio technical issue. Doing that for three or four minutes might not sound long but it flippin' is if you are doing it, trying to come up with unscripted and original observations.

There have been some wonderful days out covering matches and it goes without saying that the big games tend to stick in the memory more than most. It is all the more memorable when the trip involves staying over in decent hotels for Play-off Finals and spending time with the likes of Sean Bean and Joe Elliott of rock band Def Leppard, talking about old times at the Lane. I was a bit star struck so imagine my feelings when they came over and wanted to talk about my own playing days.

But don't you go getting the idea that this stuff is all champagne and luxury. Even now at the Golf Club I come across people who still like to label me with the 'lazy' tag I sometimes had as a player. I am doing ten hour shifts all week in the lorry and sometimes a fourteen hour one on Saturday if we play at somewhere like Bournemouth. There is a cost in time as we need to ensure we are in position at the grounds in good time so we do set off pretty early, arriving back late because of doing post match interviews and packing away the equipment afterwards. But the fact that many fans regard it as a dream job is fine by me.

In recent years Sheffield United Club employees Andy Pack and Kevin Cookson often travelled with us, guaranteeing that the banter and company has been thoroughly enjoyable and undoubtedly helping to make journeys seem quicker. In that company no-one's ego is safe and it isn't a place for shrinking violets, but it really is all in good fun, usually at the radio lads' expense. If we can batter them and get a rise out of them then the day is complete so, what they are wearing, their hairstyles, the time they set off, their tendency to wear too many clothes in the car and their driving, are all regular targets. Naturally, they all have their ways of dealing with it and it has rarely caused anything like the upset as when my humour upset former local presenter Steve Houghton when he was at the wheel on a trip to London.

As I said, the lads' driving skills, or lack of them, is a popular source of criticism and wind up and on this occasion, driving through Croydon, I asked Steve if he was going to take off his diver's boots because he was always hard and sharp on braking, causing me no end of rocking backwards and forwards in the back. I kept dishing it out until he just lost it, stopped at the traffic lights, got out, slammed the door and shouted, 'You fuckin' drive then,' and walked off.

The rest of us were laughing but in slight shock until Steve got back in and tried to drive off again, but really fast just to prove how good he was, only to stall the car. I was absolutely dying to laugh again but realised that I had maybe taken the little joke a bit too far so instead elected to apologise even though they're still all rubbish drivers.

*****

It seems now an awful long time ago that I started, and after Simon Clarke left, his replacement David Burns was great fun and someone I really enjoyed travelling with. Burnsy and I shared a sense of humour which we often exploited on air during commentary by competing to get out the most jokes and references to something irrelevant such as ... chiropody.

He was succeeded by Paul Walker who I had heard on Radio Hallam when he was younger and I recall being impressed by how well he projected his voice which gave interest and authority to his work. In his tenure as Sports Editor he has been a great Gaffer for me and is extremely good at what he does, and that has been rightly rewarded by his call-up to do national stuff as well. A few years ago I shared many a long trip with Seth Bennett, perhaps the most relaxed of all of them, although he could also pin people down with some straight questions. I always felt that I could get my humour over with him alongside me and Seth has also 'gone national'. These days I tend to be on air most with Andy Giddins who is very professional and far too nice a bloke to deserve all the banter we throw at him.

On a serious note I have a genuine admiration for these lads which I don't always show, and they aren't always appreciated by the listeners for their reliability and expertise. They have excellent knowledge and recognition of players across the divisions which is absolutely essential for commentary. They speak for an hour and a half, virtually nonstop with barely a pause or a mistake, often in cold, cramped conditions with all sorts going through their earphones, and it definitely isn't as easy as people think. I suppose it comes more easily if you do it on a full-time basis but it isn't for me and I am glad I am employed to add context and opinion instead.

There is no reason for you to give it a thought but the quality of the broadcasting facilities in our game these days stretches from the sublime to the ridiculous, and they undoubtedly have a bearing on how much we enjoy our day because they form our working environment. As the media in general plays such a significant part in everything today there has been a welcome move to accept that those involved are professionals doing a job of work, and as such they should be treated accordingly. Journalists of all kinds have to be officially licensed to gain access and that must be applied for and granted several days in advance. Media facilities are also subject to certain standards but largely remain the responsibility of each club so, with money tight, most find it difficult to go beyond offering the basics. How much those 'basics' are developed and exceeded varies hugely throughout the divisions, as you might expect.

Many smaller clubs still do not have a Press Room or even a cup of tea and a biscuit which makes it pretty miserable when you are waiting over a couple of hours before the game starts on a cold, wet day. I will always remember going to a game once at

Blackpool when I dared to ask a steward where the Press went for something to eat and he said, 'There's a burger van over in the far corner behind the corner flag.'

'Is that it?'

'Yeah, this is not flippin' Anfield, son!'

Seats can be cramped, uncomfortable and difficult to get in and out of if they are set in rows without sensible access, and views can sometimes be obstructed. These days everyone has laptops and cables everywhere which provide obstacles and a real potential for disaster when you try and slide past someone. One false step can whip out a wire and put a station off air, or slice a couple of hundred words off a written report if the journo hasn't saved his work as he writes his piece.

That's what makes visiting the big clubs, primarily in the top couple of divisions, such a treat and I make no apology for that because it is only human nature to enjoy the other side of the coin. A comfortable, warm and spacious press room with hot food and drinks, plus a couple of plasmas with the football on which you can also make use of at half-time and full-time. Then there are the well-designed press seats, easily accessed, and in the top Premier League, small televisions showing the game you are at which helps enormously with identification or analysis of the action. When new grounds are designed these days the needs of the media are factored in and going to The Emirates, for example, as a member of the media, borders on a luxurious experience – just fantastic in every way.

Fans, as is usually their lot, suffer the most hardship though and I welcome any initiative that makes the matchday experience more comfortable for them, whether that means bright and cheery concourses with a decent range of refreshments, cheaper prices, or protection from the elements. Compared to standing shivering on an open terrace, we media bods often get a better deal.

Covering United with Radio Sheffield has given me much to be grateful for, not least a host of memories and experiences, and the opportunity to meet and mingle with all sorts of new people. I never played at Wembley so to actually be interviewed there at pitchside was a real thrill, especially the Play-off Final, against Crystal Palace at the old Wembley in 1997, as I was also on air with my old mate, Colin Morris. While nothing beats being a player, radio work gave me the chance to come away from United's thrilling Play-off semi-final against Forest and think, wow, how good was that, just as the supporters had done.

There is no doubt in my mind that the involvement has helped me maintain an interest in football that wouldn't have been the case otherwise. I walked away from the game and thought that was that, but now I think about matches and tactics in a way I never have, even when I was playing. I think I have earned the right to comment on air by having played and I use that experience when I make judgements. That said, what I do is a very long way from managing a club and I say to fans who ask why I haven't gone for a manager's job that you don't go from radio summarising to managing Sheffield United, you have to be realistic, but I have often felt that I have something to offer in some way. Who knows what fate might have had in store if Eddie Gray hadn't been sacked when I was coaching the kids.

I never set out to be the best summariser in the world but it has become natural to me to watch and think, maybe the manager should switch those two round or, he should go three up front in this half, and that is how I watch all games now whether for work or pleasure. If I had been given an opportunity to stay in the game, under the right person like Eddie, I think I would have taken it because I believe I would have picked it up. I reckon I could have put things over well,and being used to having a laugh with the lads, I would bring humour to training as an essential element.

Even when Danny Bergara was coaching us I thought that what he lacked was someone else with him to provide balance to his serious coaching. In my world the good cop, bad cop scenario inevitably worked in a group of young men in a football environment. It isn't undermining the manager, it is about cajoling the ones who get bored or moody and keeping them onside for the greater good of the group. That brings me back to a dour manager like Colin Appleton who surely would have benefitted from someone of opposite personality to provide a more inclusive, friendly and productive training ground.

It's not uncommon in our game for a player to finish a training session thinking, I hate that so and so, about the manager. That's when a number two, with a bit of personality, can put things in perspective with a friendly word or little joke that can change a bloke's opinion and put the number one back in a better light. It happens. I have seen it. Even Porterfield didn't have that sort of lieutenant and we as a group of players used to bring ourselves round when he pissed us off. On the other hand, Bremner didn't need one even though he could scream and shout at you with the best of them. When we went in for a cuppa and something to eat minutes later, he would be sitting there having a laugh and a giggle with us, and I loved him for that. He would just be there and players would think, yeah, he's alright.

*****

I still love my golf as much as ever and look forward to seeing the back of the winter months so I can finish work for the day and go off and practise in the evenings as well. The end of my BBC work for the season coincides nicely with golf starting up again so I can then throw myself into it. A couple of years ago I succeeded in whittling my golf handicap down to nine, although I am now off ten, largely thanks to the pro at Lees Hall, Andrew Rossington, who is very good and has people coming from all over the place for lessons from him. I use him frequently to try and iron out faults in my own game and confess to being obsessed with the nuances of the game and the mechanics of how to use a club consistently to maximum effect. What appeals to me is the notion that I spend time on radio pointing out what is right and wrong on the football field, but give myself totally to him with full trust that as an expert in his field he can improve my game.

A perk of being a golf mad ex-footballer is the fairly frequent chance of being invited to play in charity events that often include brilliant players, celebrities and sporting legends from other sports. I usually accept these invitations, often with TC, Len Badger and Ted Hemsley, and they are great fun because we catch up on old times and meet many ex-players which is always a pleasure.

I will never forget one wonderful day at such an event at a course in Stockport when I played with Emlyn Hughes, Danny Bergara, and ex-Blades' favourite, Dane Whitehouse. In the presence of former Manchester United players, old and new, like Bobby Charlton, Alex Stepney, Dwight Yorke and Mark Hughes, I felt very much like a B-lister. It was a shotgun event with crowds at each of the main tees and I had never played golf in front of a crowd before.

We shuffled round and eventually reached the eighteenth where Emlyn, a lovely bloke but to be fair not a great golfer, had taken about six shots to get near the green. He smashed the ball through the green and then, with the waiting crowd unaware that he was taking about his eighth shot on a par five, chipped quite close. Everybody applauded but I couldn't resist shouting to him that he wanted that for a nine, which I thought was really funny though Emlyn didn't, but he had milked the applause of a crowd who thought he had played a good hole!

A couple of ex boxers were also involved that year. I shook hands with the delightful Henry Cooper who was playing behind me but 'Enery didn't take the golf too seriously because he was very popular and busy chatting to everybody. I didn't know Dave 'Boy' Green who was playing in a group ahead of us, and, when I was remarking how slow those in front were, somebody told me who it was and said that they weren't bloody tellin' 'im to hurry up. Later on we were introduced and 'Boy' said to me, 'You were behind us weren't you, Keith?'

'Yeah. How's it going?'

'Not bad at all, wife and kids are okay. You got any kids then?'

'Yes, three girls and a boy,' I said.

'Does your lad play football then?'

'He does a bit. What about yours, does he box?'

'No, 'e's a bleedin' 'airdresser!'

I was gobsmacked by his reaction and the way he said it was so funny because it seemed that he just couldn't understand how a lion-hearted, World Championship boxing contender could possibly spawn ... a hairdresser, but he was a lovely guy.

As a self confessed B-lister I sat back and watched how the genuine A-listers went about things, celebrities like Peter Alliss who turned up in his big Rolls Royce, and Eric Bristow and Willie Thorne. We were all raising funds to provide wheelchairs for the handicapped and all these well known stars were so friendly and chatty with everybody, which I interpreted as a sign of the confidence they gained from being at the top of their respective sports.

My own thrill in golf is winning something with a partner, not as an individual, and I have two regulars really. Holly Morgan is a young lady I have played golf with since she was about twelve through knowing her parents, Steve and Barbara, and she will more than likely go on to better things in America because she is down to a handicap of only two and plays for Yorkshire and England.

We don't talk about technical aspects of the game, instead we discuss the mental side such as dealing with pressure situations in sport and I hope that I helped with that – but it certainly isn't down to me that she is so damned good. I have, however, helped her become a better player by introducing her to parts of the course she had never seen, trying to find my ball when it has flown miles off line. Holly and I team up in an annual mixed competition and have won it twice in the last four years so you can make your own mind up as to which one of us is mainly responsible for that.

John 'Swordy' Wilkinson has the same handicap as me but although he is most likely two shots better, I always insist on being captain whenever we play because 'I'm the decision maker.' Fortunately, as a good pal should, he humours me. John, who travels up from Fulham almost every weekend just to see his pals and play golf with them, is probably the most popular guy in the club and everybody wants to partner him. Everyone's ambition at our club is to see their names entered on the winners board in gold letters and John and I eventually managed that which was special to John as he therefore emulated his father, John Wilkinson Snr.

Swordy is so laid back and as far as I can see he has only two disadvantages. Without question he is the smartest lad in the golf club and I get a bollocking every Saturday from him because I don't measure up in that respect, and secondly – and this is a pretty shocking deficiency – he is a Wednesdayite.

That is good, for when I reflect on my life, and I have plenty of time to do that given my job and personal circumstances, I recognise that humour is so important to me and I hope that you have found that as you have read this account. My intention hasn't been to offend even though football humour can appear cruel to those not used to boys' banter, for that is all it is. It may be juvenile at times, but it has worked for me and has shaped my character and informed how I have dealt with many people who I thought could handle it in the way it was meant.

I trust myself to be able to judge my audience though, and would be annoyed if I was stupid enough to be thought of as merely arrogant because of it. Believe me, my way is usually a front, a way of getting on and, although some of the times in my life have been difficult, I like to think I have learned from them and become a better individual. Marrying a Yorkshire lass probably made me a little bit lazy because, dare I say it, they traditionally do everything for their husbands, and I never did much at home as the youngest of four either because I didn't have to. Now I do everything for myself and having developed all these domestic skills, I can now even question what it is that these women moan about. It's flippin' easy, all this washing, ironing, cooking and cleaning. Oops! Messed it up with women again.

You may not believe this but my efforts to keep on developing as an individual have lately led me into a world that people from the north-east don't easily enter in to, and that is to fulfil an ambition to learn to dance. Through some organisation by Emma who works at Lees Hall, I started weekly lessons and am thoroughly enjoying doing it as well as making new friends.

Some of you might find it easy to suggest that by becoming a bit of a twinkle toes I am trying to get in touch with my feminine side. Well, funny that, seeing as I started this book talking about how different Mam's life would have been if I had been born a girl ...

Appendix

Career Statistics

Playing Record

		League			FA Cup		League Cup	
	Club	**Div**	**Apps**	**Gls**	**Apps**	**Gls**	**Apps**	**Gls**
1975-76	Sheffield Utd	1	2(1)	-	1	-	-	-
1976-77	Sheffield Utd	2	30(1)	18	1	-	1	-
1977-78	Sheffield Utd	2	32(4)	11	1	-	1	-
1978-79	Sheffield Utd	-	-	-	-	-	-	-
1978-79	Hull City	3	46	24	2	1	3	-
1979-80	Hull City	3	41	19	2	-	2	1
1980-81	Hull City	3	38(2)	13	6	4	2	-
1981-82	Hull City	4	5	1	-	-	2	-
1981-82	Sheffield Utd	4	41	35	2	1	-	-
1982-83	Sheffield Utd	3	37(5)	13	6	5	4	5
1983-84	Sheffield Utd	3	44	33	5	4	4	2
1984-85	Sheffield Utd	2	29	13	1	-	4	2
1985-86	Sheffield Utd	2	32(3)	20	2	-	3	1
1986-87	Sheffield Utd	-	-	-	-	-	-	-
1986-87	Leeds Utd	2	24(6)	6	2(3)	1	2	-
1987-88	Leeds Utd	2	4(4)	-	-	-	-	-
1987-88	Aberdeen	SP	6(3)	2	1*	1	-	-

1987-88	Hull City	2	9	3	-	-	-	-
1988-89	Hull City	2	44	26	3	3	2	1
1989-90	Stockport	4	26(1)	10	2	1	-	-
1989-90	Hudds T (L)	3	6(4)	4	-	-	-	-
1990-91	Hudds T (L)	3	10(8)	4	1	-	1(1)	-
1990-91	Plymouth A (L)	2	3	1	-	-	-	-
	Totals		**509(42)**	**256**	**38(3)**	**21**	**31(1)**	**12**

* *Scottish Cup*

The table above refers to English and Scottish League and major cup competitions only. Keith also scored two goals for Leeds United in the 1986-87 play-offs, plus numerous more in minor competitions and friendlies.

Hat-Tricks

Club	**Opposition**	**Competition**	**Date**	**Goals**
Hull City	Chester	Division 3	02-09-78	3
Sheffield United	Grimsby Town	League Cup	26-10-82	3
Sheffield United	Gillingham	Division 3	27-08-83	4
Sheffield United	Wrexham	FA Cup 1	19-11-83	4
Sheffield United	Southend	Division 3	26-11-83	3
Sheffield United	Orient	Division 3	03-03-84	3
Sheffield United	Hull City	Division 2	02-11-85	3
Hull City	Bournemouth	Division 2	14-01-89	3
Huddersfield T	Bolton Wands	Division 3	08-09-90	3

Golden Boot Awards (League Goals)

Sheffield United	36	Division 4	1981-82 (inc one for Hull City)
Sheffield United	33	Division 3	1983-84
Hull City	24	Division 2	1988-89